Praise for *Extreme Winning* . . .

"*Extreme Winning* is a winner! Its powerful examples and anecdotes on what it takes to succeed are what make this book special. Pat Williams always gets it right. I love the book and recommend it to everyone."

—**Larry Brown**
NCAA National Championship and NBA Champion Head Coach

"This superbly written book is packed with gems, one after another, each one seemingly brighter than the one before. I know it's a cliché to say I couldn't put it down, but I couldn't. Invest five minutes in it and before you know it an hour will have gone by. And when you finish the book, you'll find yourself wishing there were 14, 15, or 16 keys to winning, instead of 12."

—**Urban Meyer**
The Ohio State University Head Football Coach
2014 National Champions

"*Extreme Winning* provides the reader with a comprehensive road map on how to come out on top. In bringing together the absolute elements of a winner, this book will intrigue you through its showcasing of top performer traits, while staying grounded in the basic human desire to persevere. No matter what line of work you're in, do yourself a favor and read this book cover to cover."

—**John Harbaugh**
Baltimore Ravens Super Bowl winning Head Coach

"Pat's been a winner all his life. Everywhere this game has taken him, he has left each organization better than when he arrived. Pat has been around winning and he knows what it takes and how it feels—this book is a great example of that."

—**Doc Rivers**
Los Angeles Clippers Head Coach

"Just when you thought that nothing new could be said about a topic as universal as winning, along comes this excellently written book that will inspire and invigorate you. It did with me. *Extreme Winning* reinforced my beliefs and introduced me to and inspired me with ideas I hadn't yet considered—but do now."

—**Rick Pitino**
University of Louisville Head Men's Basketball Coach

"Pat Williams has an incredible feel for winning and now shares with us a blueprint to help us maximize our chances to become an extreme winner."

—**Paul Molitor**
Baseball Hall of Famer
Minnesota Twins Manager

"Pat Williams has written possibly the best book about *winning* that I've ever read. This book explains in great detail what qualities the extreme winners in sports, business, and life possess."

—**Steve Spurrier**
University of South Carolina Head Football Coach

"If there is anyone who has the edge on winning in life, it is Pat Williams and his extreme approach to everything he does, whether fighting cancer or running an NBA franchise. Sharing the lessons he's learned in *Extreme Winning* is the latest *win* for Pat, and a blessing for the rest of us."

—**Billy Donovan**
Oklahoma City Thunder Head Coach and two-time NCAA National Champion

"I don't usually buy into motivational-type books, for I believe each team and each individual needs separate motivation, and it is my job to figure out what that is. However, by about page three of *Extreme Winning*, I had my highlighter out and was taking notes. This book will help me today, tomorrow, and the rest of my career."

—**Jay Gruden**
Washington Redskins Head Coach

"*Extreme Winning* is brimming with wisdom. Pat Williams has hit a lot of home runs with his books. This one is a grand slam."

—**Fredi Gonzalez**
Atlanta Braves Manager

"*Extreme Winning* captures everything—and more—that I've always believed and taught; it has given me concrete reasons to back up those beliefs. You won't just find yourself reading it, you'll soon find yourself rereading it . . . again and again."

—**Art Briles**
Baylor University Head Football Coach

"Every so often a book captures the essence of its topic in ways that no other book before it has done. *Extreme Winning* is that book. It'll change the way you think, act, and perform."

—**Mark Richt**
University of Georgia Head Football Coach

"After you finish reading *Extreme Winning*, you'll find yourself, like me, wondering how you ever managed without it. The book is that good."

—**Lionel Hollins**
Brooklyn Nets Head Coach

"Everyone wants to win, but is everyone willing to go to the extreme to make winning a reality? In *Extreme Winning*—his 100th book—sports executive Pat Williams shows you the 12 extreme elements, from dreaming to attitude to teamwork, that lead to winning in sports and winning in life. His lessons are educational, motivational, and personal, and the book's pages are full of great quotes from sports' biggest winners."

—**Robin Ventura**
Chicago White Sox Manager

"If there is a better book on winning, I haven't read it. You should read *Extreme Winning*. It's the best there is on the subject."

—**Terry Stotts**
Portland Trail Blazers Head Coach

"I admire Pat Williams, his books, and his commitment to excellence. In *Extreme Winning*, he gives all of us striving to win valuable insights from the extreme winners in history. This book has inspired our program!"

—**Jay Wright**
Villanova University Head Men's Basketball Coach

"I love the 12 qualities Pat Williams writes about in his book, *Extreme Winning*. I believe that every day is a jump ball never to be wasted. Improve some way every day and strive to be the best in whatever you do."

—**Larry Krystkowiak**
University of Utah Head Men's Basketball Coach

"When I heard that Pat Williams and Peter Kerasotis were writing a book together, my expectations were very high. They didn't meet them. They exceeded them."

—**Fran McCaffery**
University of Iowa Head Men's Basketball Coach

"Pat Williams is an accomplished professional who I have followed and admired throughout my entire playing and coaching career. From authoring numerous books on leadership to spending 50-plus years working in professional athletics to helping to inspire and motivate professionals in all walks of life, he does it again with the thought-provoking book *Extreme Winning*. A man of high character, self-control, responsibility, faith, courage, perseverance, and love, Pat shares all of those things in *Extreme Winning*. The examples he gives in *Extreme Winning* are not only thought-provoking but an inspiration for everyone who wants to *win* in the game of life."

—**Danny Manning**
Wake Forest Head Men's Basketball Coach

EXTREME WINNING

To JOHN HARBAUGH — THANKS SO MUCH FOR YOUR HELP.
2015

12
Keys to Unlocking the Winner Within You

PAT WILLIAMS
With
PETER KERASOTIS

Health Communications, Inc.
Deerfield Beach, Florida

www.hcibooks.com

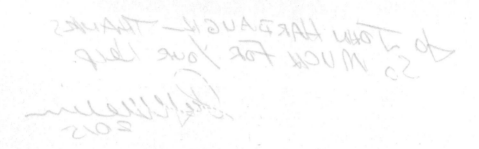

**Library of Congress Cataloging-in-Publication Data
is available through the Library of Congress**

© 2015 Pat Williams and Peter Kerasotis

ISBN-13: 978-07573-1780-4 (Paperback)
ISBN-10: 07573-1780-4 (Paperback)
ISBN-13: 978-07573-1781-1 (ePub)
ISBN-10: 07573-1781-2 (ePub)

Publisher: Health Communications, Inc.
      3201 S.W. 15th Street
      Deerfield Beach, FL 33442–8190

Cover design by Larissa Hise Henoch
Interior design and formatting by Lawna Patterson Oldfield

"Winning is a serious matter."

—Willie McCovey

Contents

Acknowledgments

With deep appreciation we acknowledge the support and guidance of the following people who helped make this book possible:

Special thanks to Alex Martins, Dan DeVos, and Rich DeVos of the Orlando Magic.

Thanks also to my writing partner Peter Kerasotis for his superb contributions in shaping this manuscript.

Hats off to three dependable associates—my trusted and valuable colleague Andrew Herdliska, my creative consultant Ken Hussar, and my ace typist Fran Thomas.

Hearty thanks also go to my friends at HCI Books. Thank you all for believing that we had something important to share and for providing the support and the forum to say it. Special thanks to founder Peter Vegso and my editor, Allison Janse, for their tireless effort in making this book a reality.

And finally, special thanks and appreciation go to my wife, Ruth, and my supportive children and grandchildren. They are truly the backbone of my life.

—Pat Williams

A special thank you to my wife, Shelley, for her feedback, her front-end editing, and especially, for her unwavering love and support.

Much gratitude to Bruce Bochy for his friendship, for writing the foreword, and for proving that good guys can finish first.

And, finally, deep appreciation to Pat Williams for entrusting me with this project and for being a pleasure to collaborate with.

—*Peter Kerasotis*

Foreword by Bruce Bochy

*World Series–Winning Manager of the
San Francisco Giants in 2010, 2012, and 2014*

I live in a bottom-line business. Always have. The 2014 season marked my 40th year in professional baseball, and if I've learned anything it's that of all the statistics for which baseball is known, there is one statistic that separates itself from all others; and that's the number that appears below the column that says W on it.

In the end, that's all that matters.

Win.

Win, or else.

So when I heard that my good friend Peter Kerasotis was writing a book with Pat Williams, and that it would be called *Extreme Winning*, I was excited. I knew it would have insights and wisdom I could take from its pages and apply to the clubhouse as a major league manager. More than that, I knew it would have insights and wisdom I could apply to life. There couldn't be two better guys to have partnered together for a book on this topic than Peter Kerasotis and Pat Williams.

Peter has written about me and my career from the beginning, back in the 1970s, when I was a minor league catcher in the Houston Astros' organization. He knows me well, and I know his work well. In fact, when

he asked me a few years ago for a testimonial for his website, www.Hey
PeterK.com, I wrote this: "I've known Peter personally and professionally for most of my career. Dealing with the media daily, I've never met
a writer more prepared or thorough. He makes sure readers get the complete story. His passion for the story and writing are unparalleled."

As for Pat Williams, I've long admired him and his work. In fact, dur-
ing spring training before my 2014 season managing the San Francisco
Giants, I quoted and used portions of Pat's book on John Wooden:
*Coach Wooden's Greatest Secret: The Power of Doing a Lot of Little
Things Well.* I had once met Coach Wooden, so this book had a special
impact on me.

Early during that 2014 season, Peter asked me if I would write the
foreword to this book. Who knew then that the season would end with
another World Series victory? It was my third over a five-year span with
the Giants and it was my fifth time in a World Series as either a player or
manager—once as a player and four times as a manager. Doing the math,
it means I get to the World Series once every eight years; and although
that might seem like a low figure, it isn't, and I'm extremely grateful to
have made it even once, much less five times. There have been many great
players and managers who never made it to the World Series. Believe me,
I know how hard it is to get there, much less win one.

It takes a lot of elements, and Pat and Peter have captured them so well
in this book on *Extreme Winning.* I've seen these 12 attributes that make
up the 12 chapters in this book over and over again throughout my career
as a player, coach, and manager, and I believe in them.

They start this book with a chapter on having an extreme dream. I live
that every year. Major League Baseball has 30 teams. All enter the season
with that extreme dream of being the last team standing. Only one will.
What will get them there? Pat and Peter nailed it with the other chapters
in this book; chapters on preparation, focus, passion, work, responsibility,
positive attitude, goals, perseverance, competition, desire, and teamwork.
It's funny, but as I write this, I can't help but think about preparation. I
talked, texted, and e-mailed back and forth with Peter many times during

the off-season after we won the 2014 World Series, and he can attest to how those several months were nonstop in preparation for the 2015 season.

So, yes, I've seen these 12 characteristics and I've seen them at the extreme degree they write about.

I consistently saw these 12 attributes while managing the Giants during our 2014 championship season. I saw one of our players, Travis Ishikawa, almost quit the game during that summer. Ishi, as we call him, broke into the major leagues in 2006; but now, at 30, he had been designated for assignment by the Pittsburgh Pirates, and then found himself languishing at our Triple-A affiliate in Fresno, California. What stopped Ishi from giving up is that he didn't want his three children to think of him as a quitter. So he persevered, dedicating himself to finishing the season, and finishing it strong. Well, as it happened, we ran into a spate of injuries with our major league club, and we called up Ishi late in the season, where we saw him willingly play out of position for us in the outfield. In Game 5 of the NLCS, with Ishi playing in left field, I wanted to get one more at-bat out of him before sending in a defensive replacement. That at-bat came in the bottom of the ninth inning, with the game tied 3–3 and two runners on base. On a 2–0 pitch, a fastball low and inside, Ishi lined a game-winning, walk-off home run. That home run became the first to send a National League team to the World Series since another Giant, Bobby Thomson, hit his famous Shot Heard 'Round the World in 1951.

It was good to see, not just because it sent us back to the World Series, but because Ishi is such a well-liked player on a team that truly was an extreme team: a group of guys who represented everything Pat and Peter write about in the final chapter of this book.

But don't read ahead. Read this book from start to finish. What they've written in these 12 chapters I've witnessed in my 40 years in baseball. What I know about what it takes to win, and to be an extreme winner, they've captured.

You can, too.

Bruce Bochy
February 7, 2015

Introduction

"You were born to win."

I have been watching the winners for many years—53 years in professional athletics and before that for four years in college and before that as a high school athlete who was fascinated with sports and athletics. What I've discovered is that the extreme winners are not normal. They are not average. Everything they do is to an extreme level. That's what has allowed them to have such great success and great careers. It's far beyond talent. Many talented people fall by the wayside and don't live to their full potential because they are missing one or more of these 12 extreme elements I have discovered.

I have discovered something else, too, and that is this: winning doesn't mean you must log a number into a ledger. It doesn't even mean there has to be a loser. Winning is a way of approaching what you do, whether it's work, a hobby, or what we most often think of it in terms of—competition. Winning is a mindset; a way of life. That thought struck me years ago when I was speaking at a convention. A woman named Joy Millis was assigned to look after me during this event. She was a chatty type and had one story after the other. I didn't pay attention to most of them. However, at one point she said, "I was on a flight once, reading a book, and I looked up and saw on the other side of the plane the great Baltimore Colts quarterback, Johnny Unitas." After the plane landed, Joy told me she went up to Unitas in the terminal and said:

> "Johnny, would you please sign this book for me? And don't sign it like you'd sign for anybody else—like 'Good Luck' or 'Best Wishes.'"
>
> Johnny Unitas looked at her and said: "Ma'am, how would you like me to sign the book?"
>
> Joy said: "With the best piece of advice you've ever gotten from one of your coaches."
>
> So Johnny Unitas signed the book: "To Joy, Win! —Johnny Unitas"

That is great advice. The winners in life are saturated, absolutely absorbed with this topic of winning.

"Winning is like a drug," said the great Vince Lombardi. "It's a hard thing to kick."[2]

Not that you'd want to.

Not in sports, not in the classroom, not in the boardroom, not anywhere.

After all, this country was established after our founding fathers notched a mark in the win column in the Revolutionary War. And this nation was preserved with a few other key wins in the Civil War, World War I, and World War II. That's not to make light of those wars by using sports metaphors. And, to be sure, we do use war metaphors with our sports. It's simply to emphasize that in American culture winning is in our DNA. It's been there since the beginning, and it's been hugely important. America was built on great leaders who settled for nothing less than being the best; nothing less than victory. It doesn't get any more extreme than winning those four wars I just mentioned. The stakes were high.

So winning is now indelibly etched, not only in our history, but also in our mindset. The great ones think only in terms of winning.

That was the mindset of great presidents. Once, after listening to a long briefing on the overall strategy for dealing with communism, President Ronald Reagan interrupted to say this: "Here's my strategy on the Cold War—we win and they lose."[3]

And this was President John F. Kennedy's philosophy: "Once you say you're going to settle for second, that's what happens to you in life."[4]

Extreme winners don't settle. They are not content with being second best. To them, being second is equivalent to being the first loser. There are a slew of golfers on the PGA Tour who make seven figures but never win, and they're perfectly content with that. The great ones, though, aren't. "I'd rather win one tournament in my life," said the iconic Arnold Palmer, who is a fellow Wake Forest alumnus, "than make the cut every week."[5] And that, in a nutshell, is why he's Arnold Palmer—an extreme winner of seven major championships and 62 PGA Tour titles.

"When I was little," said Mia Hamm, long the face of U.S. women's soccer, "people always used to say, 'It doesn't matter if you win or lose.' Well to me it did."[6]

It does. To the extreme winners, it is everything.

"There is winning, and there is misery,"[7] said Pat Riley, winner of one NBA title as a player, one as an assistant coach, five as a head coach, and two as an executive. It's why he's in the Naismith Memorial Basketball Hall of Fame.

Steve Nash, a future Hall of Fame basketball player, put it this way: "Nothing is black-and-white except for winning and losing, and maybe that's why people gravitate to that so much."[8]

We do gravitate to it.

What especially makes our sports so enjoyable is watching intense competitors—the extreme winners—compete against each other. Great sports rivalries aren't about great athletes competing against each other. Rather, it's about extreme winners competing against each other. One of the all-time great NBA rivalries pitted Magic Johnson's Los Angeles Lakers against Larry Bird's Boston Celtics; and what made it great wasn't just that Magic and Bird were great athletes—they were extreme winners. Their extreme will to win made watching those historic NBA Finals so much fun to watch, and so memorable.

Magic Johnson cut straight to the chase when he summed himself up this way: "I'm about winning."

Larry Bird was even more succinct, simply saying, "I crave winning."

What a fascinating way to put it: I *crave* winning. *Merriam-Webster's* defines that word *crave* as "to have a very strong desire for (something); to want greatly; to yearn for." I am here to tell you that the extreme winners crave winning; they are absolutely consumed with winning. To call them *extreme* winners is not to inject hyperbole or introduce a catchy phrase. They are extreme.

Listen to what Pete Rose, Major League Baseball's all-time hits leader who won the National League Rookie of the Year award, three batting titles, one NL MVP award, and one World Series MVP award, had to say: "The Wright Brothers were obsessed with flying. Henry Ford was obsessed with cars. I was obsessed with winning."[9]

It's easy to talk about winning in sports, when there is an actual ledger to keep track of wins and losses. But extreme winners are in every walk of life, every occupation and vocation. I once heard Charles Schulz, who drew the most successful comic strip ever, the *Peanuts* strip, talk about how he was not just competing against other comic strip creators, but also against himself.

"I try never to have any letdowns," Schulz said. "I try never to send in anything that I am not totally satisfied with, which is almost impossible, and I rarely send in anything just to get by. I'd rather fall a day behind in the schedule than send in something that I don't think is pretty good. I think I'm competitive. I regard the comic strip like a golf course or a tennis court. I want to win that comic page every day."

You can imagine Schulz, picking up the comics page every day and comparing his work with the work of the other comic strip creators. Nobody was keeping track of that on a ledger. But you can be sure he was keeping track.

Mostly, though, when we think of winning we think of sports. That's because winning jumps out at us in sports. When he was asked at one of his press confabs during the 2015 Masters what his "greatest motivation" is, a 39-year-old Tiger Woods unflinchingly said, "My greatest motivation? Winning."

You may have noticed, as I did, that after announcing that he was retiring following the 2014 baseball season, New York Yankees shortstop Derek Jeter held a news conference in Tampa, Florida, and the last word he uttered, at the end of a 27-plus minute question-and-answer session, was the word "winning."

This occurred when Jeter was asked what career moment of his stands out the most for him. Jeter cut the questioner off in midsentence to say this: "Anytime we win. And I'm not just saying that. You play an entire year. You work out an entire year. And the ultimate goal is to win. When we win, those are the memories that are going to stand out the most for me. Yeah, I've had a lot of things that I've done personally in my career that I've appreciated, that mean a lot, but if you ask me what stands out the most, it's winning."

So let's talk about winning: about winning in life and at whatever your pursuits might be. Let's talk specifically about the 12 qualities I've observed in extreme winners—these men and women who are not normal, who are not average. The good news is that you can take these qualities and incorporate them immediately. Whether you are the president of a company, in sales, in sports, in essentially whatever you do, you can take these qualities and apply them to your life right away.

Here are the 12 qualities.

1. EXTREME DREAMS

Somewhere in their lives extreme winners have an extreme dream that captured them, took over their lives, engaged their every waking and sleeping moment. That dream drives them throughout their lives. It can, and should, drive you, too.

2. EXTREME PREPARATION

Extreme winners possess extreme preparation. Extreme winners understand that "failing to prepare is preparing to fail." I learned that quote from the late John Wooden, the longtime UCLA basketball coach. I'll share with you his wisdom and the wisdom of others so that you'll know how to apply extreme preparation to your dreams.

3. EXTREME FOCUS

Extreme winners have extreme focus. They have the ability to block out distractions. They have the ability to zero in on what is going on right now. You can have that ability, too. I'll show you how.

4. EXTREME PASSION

Extreme winners are passionate about what they do. They are excited. They have enormous energy. They have great enthusiasm. They have great zeal and great zest for what they're doing. I'll show you where that passion comes from, what triggers it, and how you can have it.

5. EXTREME WORK

Extreme winners understand that you can't drift on your oars. You have to put in an enormous amount of work or you're not going to be successful. And you have to be consistent. You have to put shoe leather to the ground every day, and above all you have got to stay away from that dangerous word—entitlement.

6. EXTREME RESPONSIBILITY

Extreme winners are extremely responsible. They understand that no finger pointing is allowed. Extreme winners own what they do—good or bad. But because of that mindset, it is often good, if not great. You'll learn how extreme responsibility will help lead you to greatness.

7. EXTREME POSITIVE ATTITUDE

I've never met a pessimistic winner. There is great power in being positive, and I've found that extreme winners are positive by design. They take having an extreme positive attitude seriously. You will, too.

8. EXTREME GOALS

Extreme winners understand that setting goals is vital. And they understand that they must be clear-cut, specific, and definite goals with a deadline attached to them. You'll learn why that's important and how to set the kind of goals that will make you an extreme winner in life.

9. EXTREME PERSEVERANCE

To achieve your goals, you must have extreme perseverance. Extreme winners refuse to quit. In studying the great people of history, it amazes me that we never should have heard of any of them. The only reason we have heard of them is because they battled through tough times and never gave up. It's an important component to becoming an extreme winner, and you'll understand why.

10. EXTREME COMPETITION

Extreme winners love to compete. They thrive on extreme competition. In fact, if the competition is not strong enough they'll manufacture things to intensify the competition. They'll create mini-competitions inside bigger ones. Michael Jordan, for one, was a master of that. You can be, too.

11. EXTREME DESIRE

Extreme winners simply care more. It's more important to them than it is to the next person. They're more self-motivated, more inspired, more resolute. They have inner fire. They're hungry. They have great energy. They hustle all the time. Call it drive, doggedness, determination. Call it whatever you want. It's all of those things, and more.

12. EXTREME TEAMWORK

If you take these 12 qualities of extreme winners and put them into practice—which you can do, and do right away—your success rate is going to be very good. But none of it counts unless you do it as a team. When teamwork kicks in, when a group of people really link together, there is no telling what can happen.

And there is no telling what you can accomplish.
So let's get started.

Chapter 1

EXTREME
DREAMS

"If you can dream it,
you can do it."

—*Walt Disney* [1]

very extreme winner I have ever met, every extreme winner I have ever read about or heard about or studied, started on that path with one universal quality—they had a dream. Somewhere in their life a light went on; a fire was lit. A dream hit them, captured them, taking over their every thought, consuming them day and night. Even if they tried, they could not escape the power of that dream.

For me, that fire lit when I was seven.

June 15, 1947, was a bright, beautiful summer day in my hometown of Wilmington, Delaware. That morning, my father drove my 10-year-old sister, Carol, and me to Philadelphia, which was about an hour's drive away, to see the Philadelphia A's baseball team play a Sunday doubleheader against the Cleveland Indians.

It was my first time at a Major League Baseball game, and from the moment we walked into Shibe Park, I was captivated, just riveted by the sights, sounds, and smells of baseball. And the color, too. Everything was green—green grass, green walls, green seats. The ballplayers, resplendent in their bright uniforms, seemed to shimmer in the afternoon sun. From our seats high above the third base line, I watched the grounds crew drag, prepare, and line the field, and I thought it was the most beautiful artwork I'd ever seen. We stayed for both games, watching the ballet of baseball, and I'm fairly certain that Carol and I ate my father's wallet empty, stuffing ourselves with hot dogs, ice cream, and drinks. I hated to leave.

The next morning, I awakened knowing exactly what I wanted to do with my life. I had a dream; an extreme dream. I wanted to be a ballplayer, just like those guys I saw the day before. From that point on, as a seven-year-old, every moment of my life was dedicated to being a ballplayer. All the other little-boy desires disappeared. Everything was baseball. Yes, I played all the different sports through my high school years, but baseball was always number one. Eventually, I went to Wake Forest University on a baseball scholarship. Then I signed with the Philadelphia Phillies out of college, where I spent two years in their organization as a minor league catcher.

I had fulfilled my extreme dream.

But there were going to be more dreams.

You see, after those two years of professional baseball, it became evident that I was in the twilight of a somewhat mediocre playing career. But the Phillies saw something in me and threw a coat and tie in my direction. Thus, a front-office career was launched when I was only 24, providing me with many more dreams to pursue. I spent five years operating minor league ball clubs for the Phillies before embarking on what has now been a 47-year career in the National Basketball Association (NBA), which includes being a cofounder of the Orlando Magic franchise. My front-office career, which continues today, is going on 55 years. I'm living proof that extreme dreams can become reality.

So I encourage you—dream big, dream often, dream in depth, dream in Technicolor, dream with all your senses and all your passion. Because without a dream nothing is going to happen in your life.

People throughout history, people like former first lady Eleanor Roosevelt and inventor Robert H. Goddard, and one of my all-time favorite extreme dreamers, Walt Disney, have all tapped into the power of dreams, and like me, they invite you to do so, too.

Listen to their voices:

> *"The future belongs to those who believe in the beauty of their dreams."*
>
> —Eleanor Roosevelt, diplomat and activist[2]

> *"It is difficult to say what is impossible, for the dream of yesterday is the hope of today, and the reality of tomorrow."*
>
> —Robert H. Goddard, professor, physicist, and inventor[3]

"If you can dream it, you can do it."

—Walt Disney, business magnate, cartoonist, and animator[4]

I was tickled to learn during Derek Jeter's final Major League Baseball season that he, too, had an extreme dream when he was a young boy. His dream, which he wrote in a school essay, was to one day be the starting shortstop for the New York Yankees. How specific is that? As the story goes, he went into his parents' bedroom one night to ask if they thought he should change his essay, given how ridiculous his dream sounded to some of his friends. This is how Jeter related the exchange with his parents in his book *The Contract*:[5]

"Derek," his mother Dorothy told him, "it's never a mistake to dream. Without dreams, none of us would ever amount to much." His father Charles chimed in, "I agree. It's up to you if you want to change your essay—but only if you're *really* going to change your *dream*." Derek Jeter didn't. He not only kept his dream alive, he went on to fulfill it in a big, big way.

I certainly didn't reach those same heights in my professional baseball career. As I mentioned earlier, my playing days came to an end when it was apparent after two years in the minor leagues that I was in the twilight of a mediocre career. Whenever I say that, and say it that way, it always gets a chuckle. But in all seriousness, what if I had not dreamed big when I was a little boy? Would I have even gotten that far? Would I have gotten to experience the thrill of being paid to do something I love, even for two years? Would I have gotten to meet and play baseball with guys like Ferguson Jenkins, the Hall of Fame pitcher? I was Fergie's first catcher during his first year in pro ball (it was my first year, too), in 1962, when we both played for the old Miami Marlins in the Class A Florida State League.

So, yes, my dream as a seven-year-old boy was an extreme dream. But had it not been, I never would have gotten as far as I did, doggedly persevering every step of the way. And it does take dogged perseverance. The radio talk show host Laura Schlessinger put it this way: "When you dare to dream, dare to follow that dream, dare to suffer through the pain, sacrifice, self-doubts and friction from the world—when you show such courage and tenacity—you will genuinely impress yourself."[6]

I mention that quote from the woman people have come to know as Dr. Laura because it feeds into an important step I believe extreme winners take regarding their extreme dreams, and it's the same step you and I need to take. At some point you have to take that dream and move it into action. I call it extreme action. You have to put shoe leather to it and get moving. You have to stop staring up the steps and at some point start stepping up the stairs. Otherwise, nothing is going to happen to that dream. Instead, you'll find yourself simply dreaming your life away.

"The secret of getting ahead is getting started," is a quote often attributed to the great American author Mark Twain.

Most people know of Cal Ripken Jr. as the Hall of Fame baseball player who broke the great Lou Gehrig's Iron Man record, playing in 2,632 consecutive games. But these days, he is the president and CEO of Ripken Baseball, Inc. You might say that the business world is a whole new ball game for Ripken, but there are some constants to his approach that he carried over from his baseball career, the key one being his ability to take action.

"Now that I'm running my own company," Ripken said, "I sometimes get frustrated with all the planning and meetings that take place. Strategy is important and I know we have to do it. But you can only plan so much. You can only prepare so much. At some point, you have to test your plans. I believe that many people are simply afraid to fail. So they don't even try. Perhaps I was conditioned by baseball, where, as a successful hitter, you fail seven out of 10 times. Or perhaps my inner determination to succeed just kept propelling me forward. I don't know for certain. But I do know that my desire to take action has been a big part of my success."[7]

Notice again those two important words in the last sentence of Ripken's quote— "take action."

The late humorist and columnist Erma Bombeck used to say that people put their dreams in a little box and then exclaim that of course they have dreams. They have lots of dreams. They're right there in the box. Every once in a while they even bring the box out, open it, and show them to you. Then they immediately store the box away for safekeeping.

I once heard motivational speaker Zig Ziglar say something that made so much sense. "If you wait until all the lights are green before you leave home," Ziglar said, "you'll never get started on your trip to the top."[8]

So get started. Take action.

But I have to warn you that the minute you move into action, there are three deadly killers of dreams just waiting to rear their ugly monster heads and do everything in their power to destroy your dream. The first deadly killer is called *risk* because any dream worth pursuing involves risk. A voice in your head is constantly reminding you of all the risks involved, and that voice begins getting louder the moment you move that dream into action. All of a sudden you begin thinking, "Boy, this is kind of risky. I could fall flat on my face, and that would be embarrassing." You might even start talking yourself into believing you're not a risk taker, that it's just not your nature. People who do that, who let their dream sit on the sideline, always wonder years later what would have happened if they had just taken a shot at it.

That's why I tell parents that one of the worst things they can do to a child is introduce that ugly monster of *risk* into their psyche.

There is a wonderful story—one that is also verifiable—about Brian Williams, who replaced Tom Brokaw in 2004 as the *NBC Nightly News* anchor. When Brian was a boy, his father never attempted to squelch his son's dreams, prompting Williams years later to say, "I grew up knowing that the biggest risk you have in life is not risking anything at all."

Williams' story occurred in 1966, when he was seven, the same age I was when I decided to become a baseball player. Williams had seen what is now a famous photo of President Lyndon B. Johnson slumped over the Cabinet room table, looking dejected. So young Brian decided he was going to write the president a letter to cheer him up, and his father, a hardworking man who wanted to instill in his son the desire for significance, did not try to dissuade him.

In a *Guideposts* magazine piece,[9] Williams wrote: "Dad smiled sagely as he watched me scrawl my note at the kitchen table, ornamenting it with a picture of the American flag. I sent it off, imagining President Johnson reading my letter in the Oval Office. Soon enough I got a letter back on official presidential stationery. 'See, my letter did cheer him up!' I exclaimed. 'He wrote right back.' Talk about feeling important.

"I'm sure Dad noticed what I didn't: the response was a form letter, the signature done by a machine. Johnson himself probably had never read my letter. Still, my parents knew I wanted to believe I was important enough for the president of the United States to read my very word."

Years later, Williams contacted the LBJ Presidential Library and asked if they, perchance, might have the letter he once sent to President Johnson. He learned that not only did they have the letter, but that it was on display in the library. Williams discovered, too, that in the corner of the letter is a red checkmark of sorts. When he asked what that meant, he was told the letter was once in LBJ's daily folder, signifying that it had been part of a small sample of letters the president read daily.

"To now know that the old man read my letter is a great thrill," Williams later said on C-SPAN.[10]

So I ask you: What if young Brian Williams' father had told him the usual things you would expect? What if he told him that he probably wouldn't get a reply, and if he did, it would just be a form letter, and that the president was never going to read his letter? Instead, as we know, his father encouraged and nurtured his dream, which is why Williams can now confidently utter that wonderful remark—that the biggest risk you can take is never risking anything.

Or as Theodore Roosevelt said, "It is impossible to win the great prizes in life without running risks."[11]

And again, you're never too young to learn this lesson. In fact, it's usually when we're young that we're most willing to take risks and experience great things. For some reason, we tend to lose that as we get older. But we shouldn't. The writer Pearl S. Buck, who won the Nobel Prize in Literature, once observed, "The young do not know enough to be prudent and therefore they attempt the impossible—and achieve it, generation after generation."[12]

Look at the enormous risks Steve Jobs consistently took. And it started when he was young, as well. When he was only 12, little Steve actually called Hewlett-Packard cofounder Bill Hewlett on the phone and asked for spare computer parts.

"He lived in Palo Alto, his number was still in the phone book, and he answered the phone himself," Jobs said. "I said, 'I'm Steve Jobs, I'm 12 years old, I'm a student in high school and I want to build a frequency counter, and I was wondering if you have any spare parts I could have.

"And he laughed, and he gave me the spare parts to build this frequency counter, and he gave me a job that summer at Hewlett-Packard . . . I was in heaven."

And here's the lesson that Jobs related from all this:

Most people never pick up the phone and call, most people never ask. And that's what separates, sometimes, the people that do things from the people that just dream about them. You've got to act. And you've got to be willing to fail, you've got to be willing to crash and burn with people on the phone, with starting a company, with whatever. If you're afraid of failing, you won't get very far.[13, 14]

You will rarely find an extreme winner, whether they are in the boardroom or the State House or the sports arena or in any avenue of life, who isn't willing to risk failure. Why? Because they have an extreme dream, and in their minds that dream is going to become reality, and they're willing to risk anything to see it through. If you have that extreme dream, you'll stop at nothing. That's the way filmmaker George Lucas views it. "You have to find something that you love enough to be able to take risks, jump over the hurdles and break through the brick walls that are always going to be placed in front of you," he said. "If you don't have that kind of feeling for what it is you are doing, you'll stop at the first giant hurdle."[15]

And, to be sure, there will be more than one hurdle.

No sooner will you get past that first ugly monster that is *risk*, when the second one rears its head—*fear*. Fear is the second deadly killer. You know the feeling. We've all experienced it. That nervous knot in your stomach. That pounding in your heart. You're just afraid. You tell yourself, *I could lose all my money on this. I'm afraid of what my family might say. I'm afraid what my friends might think. It's just too much for me. I'm too afraid. I know this dream is really special, and I really want it, but fear is just killing me.*

And yes, *fear* is a killer. There is an old Oriental legend that tells of a desert traveler who one night met Fear and Plague, who were on their way to Baghdad to kill 10,000 people. The traveler asked Plague if he would be the one doing the killing. "Oh no," Plague said. "I shall kill only a few hundred. My friend Fear will kill all the others."

Fear is that powerful, which is why you can't let it fester in you. You can't let it take root. You can't let it paralyze you. We've all heard the saying: He who hesitates is lost. Well, along those lines the novelist Jessamyn West correlated hesitating to fear, saying: "Delay breeds fear."[16] It's true; it does. Which is why I love this quote from William Burnham: "The most drastic and usually the most effective remedy for fear is direct action."[17] So, as we previously mentioned—take action. Take that first step, and when you do, make it a running step. Absorb yourself in your dream and let your dream propel you. If you do, nothing will stop you. Lady Bird Johnson advised, "Become so wrapped up in something that you forget to be afraid."[18] Motivational guru Tony Robbins put it this way: "Focus on where you want to go" and not on what you fear.[19]

My friend Brian Tracy also acknowledges that a major obstacle to success and achievement is fear. He notes:

> The most common fears that we experience, which often sabotage all hope for success, are the fears of failure, poverty, and loss of money. These fears cause people to avoid risk of any kind and to reject opportunity when it is presented to them. They are so afraid of failure that they are almost paralyzed when it comes to taking any chances at all.

There are many other fears that interfere with our happiness. People fear the loss of love or the loss of their jobs and their financial security. People fear embarrassment or ridicule. People fear rejection and criticism of any kind. People fear the loss of respect or esteem of others. These and many other fears hold us back throughout life.[20]

The dreamers, people like the industrialist Henry Ford and the great American philosopher Elbert Hubbard and the songstress Olivia Newton-John and tennis champion Billie Jean King all preached the power of overcoming fear.

Listen to their voices:

> *"One of the great discoveries a man makes, one of the great surprises, is to find he can do what he was afraid he couldn't do."*
> —Henry Ford, industrialist and founder of the Ford Motor Company[21]

> *"The greatest mistake you can make in life is to continually be afraid you will make one."*
> —Elbert Hubbard, American artist and philosopher[22]

> *"Once you face fear, nothing is ever as hard as you think."*
> —Olivia Newton-John, pop music singer[23]

> *"A champion is afraid of losing. Everyone else is afraid of winning."*
> —Billie Jean King, tennis champion[24]

Probably my favorite quote on fear is the well-known one from modern-day philosopher George Addair, who famously said, "Everything you ever wanted is on the other side of fear."[25]

In summing up that ugly monster that is fear, let me share with you Michael Jordan's thoughts. Widely regarded as the greatest basketball player who ever lived, and a consummate example of an extreme winner, Jordan said this about fear:

> Some people get frozen by that fear of failure. They get it from peers or from just thinking about the possibility of negative results. They might be

afraid of looking bad or being embarrassed. I realized that if I was going to achieve anything in life I had to be aggressive. I had to get out there and go for it. I don't believe you can achieve anything by being passive. I'm not thinking about anything except what I'm trying to accomplish. Any fear is an illusion. You think something is standing in your way, but nothing is really there. What is there is an opportunity to do your best and gain some success. If it turns out that my best isn't good enough, then at least I'll never be able to look back and say I was too afraid to try.[26]

I wish I could tell you that once you get past *risk* and *fear* it is smooth sailing ahead. But it isn't. There is one more ugly monster waiting, a third killer of dreams—*change*. Everybody loves change. Right? Wrong! And you know the things we all say. *We've always done it this way. Why can't we keep doing it the way we've always done it? No need to change a winning horse. We've got a good thing going here. If it ain't broke, don't fix it.* And on and on.

We all fight against change. We embrace it as if it were a cactus. That's why it's not uncommon for people to get past risk and fear and then find themselves stopping dead in their tracks at change. But generally it is change that produces all the good things we have today. Can you imagine that there were once people who said that the horse and buggy was just fine, and why do we need an automobile? But there were. I recall, back in the '90s, when mobile phones were first hitting the market. They were called car phones back then. Many people wondered why they would ever want, or need, a car phone. And now? The mobile phone has revolution-ized the way we communicate. Again and again, change was resisted. The pages of history are, in fact, replete with those who fought change. But the agents of change consistently won. And when they did, we won, too.

I know Tiger Woods has his detractors, given his moral deficiencies, but if there is one thing about him that we should admire as an extreme winner it's his willingness to change.

In 1997, Tiger won his first Masters, and did so by a staggering 12 strokes. He was only 21. The world was his. Since we're talking golf here, you might say that he just needed to stay the course with his game. But shortly afterward, Tiger held a meeting with a few of his closest advisors—foremost among them his father—and told them his swing was good, but not good enough.

Not good enough?

Remember, it was good enough to win the Masters by an overwhelming 12 strokes. And at such a young age, too: only 21. He already was being considered the best golfer on the planet.

Even still, Tiger employed his swing coach, Butch Harmon, to completely break down his swing and rebuild it from the ground up. The results weren't immediate. In fact, his game suffered for a spell. But in 1999, the changes produced results—the kind of results that made all the hard work and effort worthwhile, silencing his critics in the process. Tiger finished in the top ten in sixteen of twenty-one PGA Tour events that season, winning eight times, which started an unprecedented run of greatness.

Even later in his career, in 2005, Tiger changed his swing again, this time under the tutelage of instructor Hank Haney. And then again, in 2010, Tiger employed another coach, Sean Foley, to revamp his swing.

If there has been one constant throughout Tiger Woods' golf career, it's been his willingness—in fact, his eagerness—to seek change. And through it all, Tiger has had enormous success, becoming the greatest golfer of his generation during a long and celebrated career that is now pushing toward 20 years.

The great ones are not afraid of change. You shouldn't be either.

So please don't let change stop you, because I'm here to tell you that your extreme dream is going to force change—with your life and in the lives of the people around you, who, by the way, are going to do everything they can to fight change.

I once saw an advertisement from Cigna, the global health services company. It played off the phrase we so often hear uttered, and utter ourselves, too. Trust me, it's the same phrase you're probably going to hear from the people around you. It's the well-known phrase I mentioned earlier—*if it ain't broke, don't fix it*. That's why that Cigna ad really caught my attention. It said this: If it ain't broke, fix it. Take fast. Make it faster. Take smart. Make it brilliant. Take good. Make it great.

To accomplish that requires not only change, but a change in thinking.

Which, again, also reminds me of Tiger Woods' thought process.

Geraldine Ferraro, who was the first female vice presidential candidate, offered that we not only need to change, but also change the way we think, saying: "It was not so long ago that people thought that semiconductors were part-time orchestra leaders and microchips were very, very small snack foods."[27]

When you think of change, that catchy line from one of Bob Dylan's most famous songs probably creeps into your head: "The Times They Are a-Changin'." I think most everyone knows that line. But few people recall that Dylan lived by those words. By 1965, Dylan had become the leading voice in America's folk music revival, and he could have sat there comfortably on his lofty perch, revered by scores of fans. But in March of that year, Dylan released an album that featured him backed by an electric band. Later, on July 25, 1965, when he plugged in an electric guitar at the Newport Folk Festival, the crowd booed and angrily shouted at him.[28] Imagine that. Bob Dylan was booed and shouted at for daring to change the way his music sounded. That same year, he released a single with an electric rock 'n' roll sound that angered many of his fans. The song, "Like a Rolling Stone," went on to become one of his greatest hits and is listed by the Rock and Roll Hall of Fame in Cleveland, Ohio, as one of the 500 songs that shaped rock music. But all along the way Dylan ran into resistance to change, which he ignored.

As fate would have it, that song, "Like a Rolling Stone," changed a 15-year-old kid in New Jersey. Perhaps you've heard of him. His name is Bruce Springsteen. During his 1988 speech inducting Bob Dylan into the Rock and Roll Hall of Fame, Springsteen talked about the change that Dylan and that song brought about in him, and in the world, saying:

The first time that I heard Bob Dylan, I was in the car with my mother, and we were listening to, I think, WMCA, maybe, and on came that snare shot that sounded like somebody kicked open the door to your mind. . . . He was revolutionary, man, the way that Elvis freed your body, Bob freed your mind. And he showed us that just because the music was innately physical, it did not mean it was anti-intellect. He had the vision and talent to expand a pop song until it contained the whole world. He invented a new way a pop singer could sound. He broke through the limitations of what a recording artist could achieve, and he changed the face of rock and roll forever and ever.[29]

Again, notice that key word in the last line of Bruce Springsteen's quote— "changed."

Bob Dylan could have rested on his laurels. Like that 21-year-old Tiger Woods with that golf swing he had that was so successful for him, Dylan at 24 could've kept doing what had already brought him enormous success. But he was willing to take a risk and overcome fear to create change.

Tiger Woods and Bob Dylan and all the great ones don't allow those three deadly killers—risk, fear, and change—to slay their extreme dreams.

You shouldn't either.

But what are some of the tools you can use to overcome risk, fear, and change?

I'm convinced that the antidote, the way to overcome risk, fear, and change, is extreme courage and extreme boldness. It takes courage and it takes bold decisions to overcome those risks and those fears and those changes that will come along and try to destroy your dreams. With extreme courage and extreme boldness, you can overcome that.

I learned that lesson early on. When I became a professional baseball player, I struck out my first two times on six straight pitches. Was I scared? You betcha. Did I feel overmatched? Without a doubt. Did I wonder if I belonged? Absolutely. But I stepped to the plate again, and in my third at-bat I was down 0–and–2 in the count, one strike away from striking out again, when I lined a double into the alley between right and centerfield, up against the scoreboard. As I cruised into second base, I was sure that I was the happiest 22-year-old guy in history. Suddenly, I knew I could do this. I had faced fear with courage and boldness, and came through.

Derek Jeter did the same thing. Not that I had the same career as the great All Star shortstop, but Jeter had a similar experience when he was a minor leaguer in the New York Yankees' organization, just starting out.

Jeter's professional career began in Florida, just like mine did, only 30 years later. In 1992, he played for the Gulf Coast Yankees in Tampa. In his first seven at-bats, in a doubleheader in Sarasota, Florida, Jeter failed to get a hit, striking out five times. It didn't get much better from there. He hit .202 in his first 47 games.[30]

Playing shortstop in the field, Jeter's pro career wasn't any better. Later that same year, his first year in pro baseball, when he played for the Greensboro Hornets in the Class A South Atlantic League, Jeter made nine errors in 48 chances over 11 games.

He was, by any definition, awful.

Even Jeter admits this. In his book, *The Captain: The Journey of Derek Jeter,* Ian O'Connor quotes Jeter as saying: "It was the lowest level of baseball, and I was awful."[31]

Jeter had his doubts, his fears. He'd never been this far away from home, which was a huge change in his life. Homesick, he'd burn up the phone lines to the tune of $300 to $400 a month, talking to his parents, his sister, his girlfriend, wondering if he had made a mistake, wondering if he should have taken that scholarship offer to the University of Michigan.[32] Even worse, he wondered if the Yankees had made a mistake by drafting him in the first round and giving him $800,000 to sign. He had risked not going to college, banking on—literally—that he was ready for pro ball.

But was he?

Well, if you know Derek Jeter's story, you know that from the time he was a boy, he not only had the extreme dream of playing professional baseball, he had the truly extreme dream of specifically playing shortstop for the New York Yankees. When he was a boy, he adorned his bedroom with all things Yankee, even hanging a Yankees uniform and cap on his bedroom wall in Kalamazoo, Michigan, for inspiration.[33]

He had an extreme dream and nothing—not risk, not fear, not change—was going to stop him. When things are not going well, when you're striking out almost every time you step to the plate, when you're afraid of embarrassing yourself, it takes extreme courage to step up there again before everyone and take another hack at it. Believe me, I know.

And so does Derek Jeter.

But now look at the career he has had. And while you're at it, look for him in 2019, when Derek Jeter makes a trip to Cooperstown, New York, for his induction into the National Baseball Hall of Fame and Museum as one of the greatest shortstops to ever play the game.

So face fear head-on, with courage. If not, you'll never achieve your extreme dream. It reminds me of a great quote from John Wayne: "Courage is being scared to death, but saddling up anyway."[34]

I learned that lesson again when I moved to Orlando in June of 1986 to pursue a truly extreme dream. I'd been the general manager of the Philadelphia 76ers for 12 years, but I needed a new challenge. I needed a new adventure. I was invited by some Central Florida business leaders to come to Orlando in the summer of 1986 and attempt to convince the community there, as well as the NBA, that we were worthy of having an expansion team. I left everything behind, all my roots in my home area of Philadelphia, and moved my family, which at that time was six young children, and tackled that extreme dream.

Well, that dream became a reality. The NBA granted us a franchise, which we called the Magic, in April of 1987. I learned that the only way to deal with risk, fear, and change, which I was facing head-on, was to battle it with extreme courage and extreme boldness. I learned a tremendous lesson about those two important qualities as we made that NBA dream a reality.

That's why I've always appreciated this observation from the late surgeon Maxwell Maltz: "Often the difference between a successful person and a failure is not one's better ideas or abilities, but the courage one has to bet on one's ideas, to take a calculated risk—and to act."[35]

It's not enough just to act, and act with courage, though. You also have to act boldly. That's why I call it extreme boldness.

Boldness is a quality that great leaders possess. They're aggressive; they don't sit on the sidelines. Even if they're afraid, they do what they have to do.

I have to believe that the worst feeling in the world is that during your later years, you look back and say to yourself, *I was always tiptoeing around the edges. I didn't want to offend anybody.* I think that's got to be a brutal feeling. Just brutal. To think that if you had just shown some courage, some boldness, that if you had just stepped up, there's no telling what could've happened, no telling where it could've ended up, no telling what you could have accomplished and become. But you just couldn't do it. You were just too intimidated, too frightened, too scared. You just didn't think you could make it work. You weren't strong enough. Wow! I think that would be a terrible feeling to take to your grave.

One of the best examples of extreme boldness and extreme courage is one of my heroes—George Washington. His extreme dream was very simple—a nation independent of Great Britain's rule. That was his vision. That is what drove him. And the risk . . . well, we know what the risk was—execution. The same was true of all those founding fathers. They battled fear, enormous fear. Change, too. And when you think about those three ugly monsters—risk, fear, and change—you have to keep in mind that George Washington and the founding fathers were going up against the most dominant world power ever known in human history. But they had that extreme dream of being an independent nation. And George Washington was the main guy, riding point on that dream. He commanded great respect and had great presence. He was bigger than the normal man of that era, about 6-foot-2. It must have helped because the tough things he and his troops went through would have caused lesser men to abandon their dream. The deprivation of his soldiers and all they went through was staggering. But Washington never faltered, he never left his soldiers; he was with them nonstop for eight years.[36] He never wavered from his extreme dream, and today we're the benefactors of that.

When we think of that, why should we ever cower from pursuing our extreme dreams? By comparison, the bold move I made when I resigned from my position as general manager of the Philadelphia 76ers and moved to Orlando in 1986 to try and start a new NBA franchise pales. But believe me, at the time, and even now when I think back on it, it was huge. So why did I do that? Because a year earlier, in September of 1985, I was in Orlando for a speaking engagement, and when I finished, a man named Jimmy Hewitt came by to see me and offered to take me to the airport.

On the drive there, I asked him, "Would pro basketball ever make a go of it in Florida? And if so, where would you put the team—Miami or Tampa?"

Well, Jimmy got very agitated. He looked me in the eye and said, "Neither place! You'd put it right here in Orlando!"

"But you don't even have an arena," I said.

"We're building one," Jimmy said.

"When will it be done?" I asked.

"Sometime in '90 or '91," Jimmy replied.

"Too late," I said.

"Then we'll build it quicker," Jimmy retorted.

As I was processing all that, Jimmy Hewitt uttered six words with such emphatic conviction that I'll never forget it.

"Orlando is the place to be!"[37]

You see, Jimmy Hewitt had a dream, an extreme dream, and he instilled that in me. I'll admit, though, at first I thought he was out of his mind. That's why, when I flew back to Philadelphia, I thought nothing more of it.

A week later, the phone rang in my office. It was Jimmy.

"Bubba," he said. He called everyone Bubba. "We're going to New York. We've got an appointment with David Stern, the NBA commissioner. We're heading up there next week."

I thought to myself: *This guy is a mover. He knows how to put shoe leather to an extreme dream.*

I said, "Well, Jimmy, keep me posted."

And he did. I got regular phone calls from Jimmy. And then I got that one phone call in April of 1986, when Jimmy told me, "Listen, I've done all I can. We've got an ownership group in place. The mayor assures me that we'll have an arena ready. If you'll come down and head this whole thing up, we will go forward. If not, we'll just drop it."

In other words, he put the ball squarely in my court.

Was it a risk? I think that goes without saying. But what also goes without saying is that this was a once-in-a-career opportunity to have a part to start a major league sports franchise from scratch.

I took the challenge on, in spite of risk, fear, and change. Keep in mind that Orlando in 1986 was not much to look at. There was not much of a skyline. There was no place to even play pro basketball. There was no real history of major league sports. There was not much of an airport or a convention center. There was no Universal Studios or Animal Kingdom. But for 10 months we rallied the community and pestered the NBA and NBA owners to death, trying to convince them that Orlando's best years were ahead; that they needed to look at this community as it would be in 10 years, and in 20 years. Our message was that the future in Orlando was unlimited.

I believed it. Jimmy Hewitt's extreme dream had become my extreme dream. I found myself visualizing the reality of that dream, and I would convey that to people at the hundreds of speaking events I made, drumming up support. I was basically selling tickets, season tickets, asking for $100 deposits.

In my speech, I painted a picture for the audience, telling them:

It's opening night, folks, and the beautiful Orlando Arena has just opened and the Orlando Magic are running out in their pinstripe uniforms onto their beautiful new court, and the place is packed with people. And there I am, walking around the concourse, and I see you on the other side of the glass, and you're pounding on the window, and I can read your lips: "I need two tickets to the game tonight." And I say, "Remember that time I came to your Rotary Club, and I said that now is the time to put a deposit down on two season tickets, or maybe four? Obviously, you didn't do it. And it's too late now. I wish I could help you, but I can't." So now's the time, folks, to buy your Magic season tickets. When Larry Bird and the Boston Celtics come in, early in the season, wearing their Celtic green uniforms, you don't want to be on the outside, banging on the window, begging to get in.

Just like when I was a little boy watching my first Major League Baseball game, absorbing it through all of my senses, I would speak to audiences and involve all of their senses.

Apparently, it got through, because the NBA in April of 1987 invited Orlando, along with three other expansion cities, to become a new NBA franchise. In 1989, our arena was finished and we had 10,000 season-ticket holders. It was tremendously gratifying, especially considering that when I left Philadelphia there was no safety net, no Plan B.

My extreme dream became a reality.

Yours can, too.

Chapter 2

EXTREME PREPARATION

"A winning effort begins
with preparation."

—Joe Gibbs, three-time
Super Bowl–champion head coach [1]

ne of the immeasurable privileges of my life was being invited into the great John Wooden's life. It occurred after I had an idea of writing a book that I eventually titled *How to Be Like Coach Wooden: Life Lessons from Basketball's Greatest Leader.* Before I could get to that point, though, I wrote Coach Wooden a letter and asked for his blessing on the project. Shortly afterward, I got a phone call.

"Mr. Williams," the voice on the other end of the phone said, "this is John Wooden, the former basketball coach at UCLA."

He paused.

"I'm not worthy of such a project. But if you would like to do it, you go on ahead."

That opened the door to about a decadelong relationship with John Wooden before he passed away in 2010, at the age of 99. Because of all the time I spent with him, I ended up writing not one, but three books about him, and believe me, I felt extremely honored to have been a part of his life.

I always had such wonderful visits with Coach Wooden. I'd pick him up at five o'clock at his condominium in Encino, California. He'd be waiting for me on the balcony, where he'd wave me in. Then he'd come down on the elevator and, with his cane, ease his way into my car. From there we'd head off to his favorite eating establishment, the Valley Inn Restaurant, for the early bird special. His favorite meal was both forms of clam chowder—Manhattan and New England—mixed together. As you can tell, I got to know Coach Wooden well, and I always got such great insights from him.

I remember once at dinner, asking him, "Coach, could you share with me one secret of success, above all others, which you have observed and believe in?"

He thought for a minute and he said, "The closest I can come to one secret of success is this: a lot of little things done well."

I ended up writing a book about that called *Coach Wooden's Greatest Secret*.

Anybody who knew Coach Wooden knows he was always extremely prepared during his career and that he was a stickler for the little things. During our conversation, he explained to me that when you take care of the little things, you end up with a lot of confidence. When you're fully prepared, when you've touched every base and done your homework, you're going to play or perform or take a test or deliver that presentation with a lot of confidence. All of Coach Wooden's former players, as well as people who never knew him, can quote that famous saying of his that he borrowed from Benjamin Franklin and then made his signature statement: "Failing to prepare is preparing to fail."

You'd think I would have remembered all of that when I was contemplating this book on extreme winning. But Coach Wooden reminded me of it again one night, after we had finished dinner and adjourned back to his condominium. We were sitting in his den, where I would ask questions and listen to him, getting his reflections on life and basketball. I showed him my outline for this book and he looked it over, nodding knowingly several times. He liked it, and he thought I was tracking well on the topic. But then he said, "May I make a suggestion?"

That was John Wooden. Always gentlemanly. Never forceful, never pushy.

I was all ears.

"Somewhere in here," he said, pointing to my outline, "I think you should probably include preparation."

Again, that tidbit should have been so obvious to me. Not only had I heard—and written about—how Coach Wooden preached preparation, I actually saw the evidence. For years I had heard about his famous filing cabinet, and one day I was able to look through it. Inside, I found that every one of his basketball practices, going back through all the decades he coached, was neatly outlined on 3 x 5-inch index cards. He kept them on file, so if you said, "Coach, what was practice like on December 8, 1949?" he could go right to that filing cabinet, pull the card out for that date, and every minute of that two-hour practice was meticulously outlined.

The great Duke basketball coach Mike Krzyzewski, the all-time wins leader in Division I basketball, is the same way. I read a February 2, 2015, *Sports Illustrated* article in which former Blue Devil power forward Mark Alarie had this to say about Krzyzewski: "He had every drill written down to the minute, and on the practice plan he would write the reason why we were doing it. He would explain that this is what the other team was going to do and then prepare us for it. I'm telling you, I played basketball all my life, I spent five years in the NBA. I never had a coach put one-tenth of the elbow grease into constructing a single practice as Coach did every one of those practices."[2]

Not only was preparation a huge part of the success of Coach Wooden and now Coach Krzyzewski, but as I studied this topic more I found that it's also a huge part of the lives and successes of all extreme winners. Many of them echo Wooden's words. Listen to some of them:

"You hit home runs not by chance but by preparation."

—Roger Maris, baseball great[3]

"When you have completed your best preparations, you go into battle without hesitation. And I tell you that it was this that made us act with confidence."

—General William T. Sherman in a letter to General Ulysses S. Grant[4]

"It's better to look ahead and prepare, than to look back and regret."

—Jackie Joyner-Kersee, Olympic gold medal–winning track star[5]

"Spectacular achievements are always preceded by unspectacular preparation."

—Roger Staubach, Pro Football Hall of Famer[6]

"The way I've always dealt with the pressure of big games is by preparation."

—New York Yankees manager Joe Girardi[7]

"I believe in preparation. I believe in attention to detail. There is nothing magical about winning in this league. It's the same with every winning team—preparation and attention to detail."

—Super Bowl–winning NFL head coach Sean Payton[8]

As I studied preparation and read about the importance of it with extreme winners, it got me thinking about my days in college at dear old Wake Forest University. I remember that there were courses I would take, and from day one I was on it. I'd sit up front, where I'd take copious notes. In the evening, I'd go to the library to study those notes. Sometimes I'd gather with some classmates to do it collectively. Eventually, I'd have the material mastered so that when exam time came it was just a matter of how many of those old blue books for writing essays I could fill. I remember being so confident I felt like telling my professor, "Give me a couple more of those blue books, because it's just a matter of how much time I have to get everything I know down."

Oh, that's a good feeling! Just a great, great feeling!

I'd go into those exams with extraordinary confidence, and with no sense of pressure. And when I finished the exam, I couldn't wait for the grade to be posted, because I just knew it was going to be a good one. That's called ultra preparation—or as I like to call it now, extreme preparation.

But then there was the flip side. I remember in college there were a few other courses I didn't take quite as seriously. Maybe I didn't study as hard because of our football team's game that Saturday or a basketball game that night. I'd reason that if I cut a class here or there, it was not going to matter. It would also be one of those classes where I'd sit in the back of the room and sometimes read a newspaper, or maybe catch a nap. And then at the end of the semester, before the final exam, I'd go into one of those 48-hour, no-sleep situations. I'd take NoDoz and tank up on black coffee. Everything I should've been doing all semester, I'd try to cram into two days. There's a reason, after all, why we call it cramming.

Well, the obvious problem with that is your eyes get so dilated you can hardly close them, and your heart is beating at a rate it shouldn't be beating at, and you're not really able to think properly. Because my preparation was so poor, I'd be terrified. And the pressure—oh, the pressure!—would descend on me like a burlap bag filled with lead weights, just crushing me. Afterward, I couldn't sleep because I'd be so wired, not to mention also being scared to death that I had butchered the course.

All these years later, I still have nightmares that it is final exam time and I'm not prepared, either because I didn't study or I had cut too many classes. I'm told that this is a common nightmare for many adults.

The point is this: When you wait until the last minute, you're inviting enormous pressure. And the seduction, which is really a danger, is thinking you can get by on talent. So please, no matter how talented you are, don't allow your talent to seduce you into thinking you don't have to prepare. You do. In fact, you must. Bestselling author Malcolm Gladwell, an expert on practice, has consistently said that "talent is the desire to practice."

One of the most talented hitters of his generation was former New York Yankees first baseman Don Mattingly. In 1984, when he was only 23, Mattingly won the American League batting title. The following year, he was the American League's Most Valuable Player. Don Mattingly was an enormously talented player. But he never allowed himself to try to get by on his talent. "I cannot stand in the batter's box and think I have not outworked and out-prepared the guy I am facing," he said. "I get such a mental edge looking out there and knowing there is no way this guy prepared himself like I have for this moment."[9]

So thorough preparation, which thankfully was driven home to me by John Wooden, is mandatory if you are going to be an extreme winner.

But, again, it's not just Coach Wooden who preached this. Many in sports, and in life, know this principle. I've heard Hall of Fame manager

Tony La Russa sum it up succinctly by saying, "Pressure is lack of preparation."[10]

I was once sitting with the former NFL player and broadcaster Pat Summerall in Tuscaloosa, Alabama, before a speaking engagement for both of us, and I got to talking with him about another one of the all-time great coaches—Tom Landry. I love these fortuitous moments when I can get insights into the giants of various professions. This is what Summerall told me: "The lesson I took from Tom Landry is that we all need intense preparation."

Or as I call it, extreme preparation.

The Pro Football Hall of Fame quarterback Bart Starr, who played for another one of the all-time legendary coaches, Vince Lombardi, learned the same lesson. Starr said that everything started with preparation, and when you are uniquely well-prepared, you can further develop the commitment that is necessary to drive you toward winning.

And while we're bringing great coaches into this discussion on preparation, note what Paul "Bear" Bryant said: "It's not the will to win that matters. It's the will to prepare to win that matters."[11]

Are you willing to make that difference?

If so, then prepare. And when you think you're done preparing, prepare some more. And then some more. Sir Anthony Hopkins, one of the great actors of his generation, said he'll go over sections of a script upward of 250 times and that you have to "prepare and prepare and prepare." So put the time in; put in the effort. And trust me, it will take more time and effort than you might think. But the great ones do it. They put enormous amounts of time into preparation. As Abraham Lincoln once said, "If I had eight hours to chop down a tree, I'd spend six sharpening my axe."[12]

If you're a leader, whether it be in sports, politics, or the corporate world, you must take the lead in preparation. The extreme winners not only prepare themselves, they prepare their teams and the people around them down to the minutest of details. The people whom you're leading will not only see this, they'll likely follow your example. If they see that you're winging it, they'll see right through it. The scientist, inventor, and educator George Washington Carver preached this, saying, "There is no shortcut to achievement. Life requires thorough preparation—veneer isn't worth anything."[13]

I was at a dinner before the 2012 Boston Marathon, chatting with the former NFL quarterback Steve Grogan. He was telling me about Raymond Berry, who coached him with the New England Patriots. According to Grogan, Berry was the best coach for whom he ever played. "He had an extraordinary eye for every detail, and he left no stone unturned in getting us prepared for game days," Grogan told me about Berry. "We knew that on Sundays we always had a chance to win because we were as prepared as we could be."

Grogan related to me a story about how, one day after practice, Berry took the team to the end of the football field and had them pick up trash, even the little pieces. It was a small detail, Grogan recalled, but it was a lesson in paying attention to the little things, just like John Wooden had told me that night in his condominium. It was a lesson that not only did Grogan and other Patriots' players carry onto the football field and into their lives, but it's a lesson you can learn, too. Especially if you're a leader. You see, if you're a leader and you've prepared yourself and your people well, not only will you feel an enormous sense of calmness in the face of pressure, but that same calmness will extend to those whom you are leading. That's not to say there won't be pressure, but it won't be the wrong kind of pressure: the crushing pressure that can cripple your dreams.

I once heard Pearce Landry, who played basketball for Coach Dean Smith at the University of North Carolina, say this about that experience and what it taught him. "When you've done all you can," Landry said, "then you can sit back and await the results." Interestingly, it was not only what Landry saw Coach Smith do, but what he also saw other coaches *not* do. "I have this image of Coach Smith during a game," Landry added. "You'd look over and he would be sitting there, watching the game with such calmness, while the other coach was running around yelling at players, sweating up a storm. Coach Smith prepared so much that he knew he had done everything he could do before the game even started."

It takes the pressure off both you and the people you're leading.

My friend Ernie Accorsi, a longtime NFL general manager, once told me about all the exceptional coaches he worked with through the years, men like Joe Paterno, Jack Ramsay, Marty Schottenheimer, Ted Marchibroda, and others. Accorsi told me there are two qualities he noticed that all these coaches have in common. One of them ties in with the title of this book and the other with the title of this chapter.

"Number one," Accorsi said, "they have a complete inability to accept defeat. They can't deal with it. It devastates them. Winning is that important. Number two is their preparation. Every day their preparation is thorough and meticulous. They try to take care of every detail in advance, and they are ready for every possibility."

That brings me to what we've been touching on regarding preparation, which Coach Wooden told me was so important. It's paying attention to the details, to the little things.

Brian Tracy, one of the best life coaches around, tells me that whatever your goal is, you can achieve it by simply focusing on one step at a time—one *small* step. How small? Here is one of Tracy's favorite sayings: "By the yard, it's hard. But inch by inch, anything's a cinch."

His words are similar to what I've heard former MLB general manager Ed Wade say about the former general manager Paul Owens, whom I worked with in the Philadelphia Phillies' organization. "Paul was constantly reminding me that you get better an inch at a time," Wade said. "You come in every day and you get better a little at a time, and then one day you look back, surprised at how much progress you've made."

When I read Tom Peters' book *In Search of Excellence*, I found that his words resonated with those of Brian Tracy and Paul Owens. "Excellence," Peters wrote, "is a game of inches."[14]

Beverly Sills, who was called the "American Queen of Opera," knew how crucial it was to focus on the little things. Most people wouldn't know this, much less even imagine it, but it's something she learned by watching Ted Williams, who is widely regarded as the greatest hitter baseball has ever known. Before every performance, Sills would go through what she called her "Ted Williams Drill." Sills explained that she once observed Williams walking around the outfield at Cleveland's old Municipal Stadium hours before a game, checking the turf for divots and bumps—little things like that.

Ever since then, whenever she had a performance, she'd go through a checklist that included everything—costumes, music, props, the stage, the hallway . . . even the curtain.[15]

People who knew Ted Williams knew that what Beverly Sills saw was not unusual. Jack Fadden, the legendary Harvard University trainer who was the Boston Red Sox trainer from 1950 to 1965, observed this about Williams:

> Williams doesn't hit just because of what he does that day. It's his advance preparation. He makes sure nothing material hinders him. His sweatshirts have to fit just right. He breaks in shoes a year in advance. You've seen him tug and twist a cap. That's to make it fit just so. A poor fit might distract him. He'll rip out a worn shoe lacing. Right down to the smallest detail, everything has to be just right. Nothing must interfere. He makes sure of that.[16]

As I read and hear these examples regarding details, focusing on the little things, Coach Wooden's words of wisdom ring even louder in my ears: "It's the little details that are vital," he would tell me. "Little things make big things happen."

Here are two of my favorite John Wooden insights that he shared with me on the topic:

★ "Whether you're a coach or a middle manager in a large corporation, I'm convinced that a significant difference between your organization and your competitor's organization comes down to details. It's the difference between being competitive and having competitive greatness."

★ "In my profession, teaching fundamentals even included such seemingly trivial things as insisting on double-tying shoelaces, seeing that uniforms fit properly, and getting players in position to rebound every missed shot. It's the person who is the perfectionist with those little things, and who makes it a habit to do them right, who gets the job done right. It's not just true in basketball or sports, but for any organization."

If you're scratching your head, wondering what something as insignificant as shoelaces has to do with anything, since now you've read that both Ted Williams and John Wooden paid attention to such a small detail, listen to what Coach Wooden told *Newsweek* magazine in a story published back on November 25, 1999:

"I think it's the little things that really count," he said. "The first thing I would show our players, at our first meeting, was how to take a little extra time putting on their shoes and socks properly. The most important part of your equipment is your shoes and socks. You play on a hard floor, so you must have shoes that fit right. You must not permit your socks to have wrinkles around the little toe."

I love it. I love that Coach Wooden, in paying attention to the little things, was even concerned about the *little* toe. And why was he concerned about the little toe? Because he knew that on the little toe, and also on the heel, is where you generally get blisters. So if you're not paying attention to the little things, it could lead to a big problem.

"It took just a few minutes," Wooden added, "but I did show my players how I wanted them to do it. Hold up the sock and work it around the little toe area and the heel area, so that there are no wrinkles. Smooth it out good, then hold your sock up while you put the shoe on. And the shoe must be spread apart, not just pulled on by the top laces. You tighten it up snugly by each eyelet; then you tie it. Then you double-tie it, so it won't come undone, because I don't want shoes coming untied during practice or during the game. I don't want that to happen. I'm sure that once I started teaching that many years ago, it did cut down on blisters. It definitely helped. But that's just a little detail that coaches must take advantage of; because it's the little details that make the big things come about."

Let me pause here to remind you that John Wooden won a National Championship as a player at Purdue University, and then 10 National Championships in 12 years when he was UCLA's basketball coach. When he finished his 29-year college coaching career with a 664–162 record, he had a remarkable .804 winning percentage. The *Sporting News* named him "The Greatest Coach Ever," and ESPN said he was the "Coach of the Century."

Attention to detail.

Don't minimize the little things.

I had this reinforced to me by *Reader's Digest*, when they wanted to use a quote from me in an upcoming edition of their magazine. The quote was about a center at the time for the Orlando Magic—a guy by the name of Stanley Roberts. Stanley was a big, heavy guy; a real big eater. My joke was that "Stanley had been told to eat from the basic seven food groups, and there are now only five left."

Well, I got a phone call from a *Reader's Digest* editor who said to me, "I've checked with the Food and Drug Administration, and they informed me that there are only five food groups, not seven."

"That's fine," I said. "Use the joke and change the numbers to five and three. It'll still work that way."

But then it got me to thinking. This was just a throwaway line in a joke. Do they really fact-check something this seemingly insignificant? So I asked the editor.

"Yes, we do," he said. "We have a whole staff checking the accuracy of everything we print. Every detail."

That really impressed me.

I guess there is a reason why *Reader's Digest* has a circulation of 4.5 million and has published since 1922.

Ken Anderson, who for almost a half century was an art director, writer, and animator for Walt Disney Animation Studios, marveled constantly at Walt Disney's attention to the little things. He used to tell the story about how, when they built a new studio, Disney involved himself with all the intricate wiring for the phones, heating, and so forth, all the minutiae that a man of his stature shouldn't—and wouldn't—worry about. But there was Walt Disney, overseeing which phone cords were which color, where the heating ducts went . . . everything.[17]

Of course, Disney's attention to detail in all the things that you and I would never see translated into the things that we did see, which was even more important to him.

Another one of his animators, Wilfred Jackson, said this about Disney's involvement in the iconic film *Snow White*, which came out in 1937 and is still considered the most memorable full-length animated feature film Disney ever did:

> "There is more of Walt Disney himself in that particular picture than in any other picture he made after the very first Mickey Mouse films. There wasn't anything about that picture—any character, any background, any scene, anything in it—that Walt wasn't right in, right up to the hilt. Literally, he had his finger in every detail of that picture, including each line of dialogue, the appearance of each character, the animation that was in each scene. . . . Nothing was okayed except eventually through his having seen it."[18]

I love stories about Walt Disney, and I particularly like this insight from Charles Ridgway, who was a longtime publicist for Disney and wrote about how Disney would make decisions down to the last detail. "It was amazing and great fun for me to watch how it succeeded," Ridgway wrote. "On those regular walk-throughs, Walt noticed every detail and made decisions quickly. One time he spotted a light in Tomorrowland pointed in the wrong direction and told someone to fix it. When it was still there two weeks later, well, the air was blue. There's a legend that Howard Hughes once walked through a newly purchased aircraft plant. When he got through, he said only, 'Paint it.' If that had been Walt, he would have said, 'Paint it a soft and pleasing color, use a lighter color on the ceiling and do it at night when it won't interfere with operations.'" [19]

Centuries before Disney, there was another genius who didn't miss the smallest of details—Michelangelo. If you've ever seen Michelangelo's masterpiece statue of David in Florence, Italy, you'll agree with me that it's breathtaking. Describing it doesn't do it justice. But whether or not you've seen it, you'll appreciate this story that has been passed down through the years.

Evidently a visitor had come to see Michelangelo while he was working on one of his statues. As the legend goes, a conversation followed that highlights our topic here.

Visitor: "I can't see that you've made any progress since I was here last time."

Michelangelo: "Oh yes, I have made much progress. Look carefully and you will see. I have retouched this part and I have polished that part. See, I have worked on this part of the statue and have softened the lines here."

Visitor: "But those are all just trifles."

Michelangelo: "That may be, but trifles make perfection and perfection is no trifle."

It's so true. It's all in the details.

Jim Dent, the Texas-based writer who wrote that wonderful bestselling book about Bear Bryant's early Texas A&M team called *The Junction Boys,* once wrote this funny line about former Notre Dame head football coach Ara Parseghian: "He was thoroughly prepared every day. He was so organized, I think he counted his chews at breakfast."[20]

Of course, I'm not saying you need to do that, but you do need to pay attention to the basics, the building blocks of your craft or profession, no matter how insignificant they might seem. If you can instill that attention to detail to those whom you're leading—paying attention to all the little things—then you'll experience the wisdom of Helen Keller: "The world is moved along, not only by the mighty shoves of its heroes, but also by the aggregate of the tiny pushes of each honest worker."[21]

In sports, we like to call that attention to detail and to the little things the fundamentals. *Merriam-Webster's Collegiate Dictionary* gives this definition for the word "fundamental": One of the minimum constituents without which a thing or a system would not be what it is.

In other words, if you're not paying attention to the little things, big things are not going to happen.

But not everyone wants to do the little things. They want the big results without putting in the necessary hours of practice and preparation that nobody sees. Joe Paterno, the former Penn State football coach, once said something similar to Bear Bryant about *wanting* to prepare. Said Paterno: "The will to win is important, but the will to prepare is vital."[22]

Different people have different ways of approaching it. In fact, Bob Knight had an interesting way of looking at this. In his book *The Power of Negative Thinking: An Unconventional Approach to Achieving Positive Results*, the former Indiana University basketball coach wrote:

> Fundamentals eliminate ways to fail, ways to lose. The greatest fundamentalists—in coaching, in warfare, in technology, in business—were and always have been more concerned about losing than about winning. One of the often criticized coaching axioms is "playing not to lose, rather than to win." For me, playing not to lose is actually the best way to win. It's an ingrained instinct that a real winner believes to the core. Critics will say it means playing too conservatively. I understand that, but my rebuttal is if you genuinely eliminate all the ways you can lose, you're a whole lot closer to winning.
>
> Try putting together a game-winning touchdown drive if your linemen can't go with the snap count and jump offside, if your backs haven't mastered putting the ball away to avoid fumbling when hit, if your passer doesn't check where the defense is as well as where his receivers are going, if the receiver doesn't look the ball into his hands rather than glance upfield to see where he can go before he has made the catch.
>
> All of those teachings are steps toward playing not to lose. There's no chicken-and-the-egg question here. Fundamentals come first. When you get down to the basics of any operation, the simpler the better.[23]

Or, as Vince Lombardi so succinctly said, "The key to success in football is to become brilliant in the basics."[24]

Cal Ripken Jr. learned those fundamentals early on from his father, the senior Cal. "In baseball, you can't always get the game-winning hit or make the game-saving catch," Cal Jr. said. "Those big things only happen once in a while. It's the little things that tend to define your value to the team. 'If you take care of all the little things,' Dad once told me, 'you never have one big thing to worry about.' "[25]

Cal Ripken Sr. was a career manager in the minor and major leagues, and instilled that same attitude in his players. So did Whitey Herzog, who managed in the major leagues for four different organizations and in 1982 won the World Series with the St. Louis Cardinals:

"Baseball, when it's played right, is made up of a lot of smaller plays and each one gives you an edge if you work at it," Herzog said. "It's also a game of large samples. Over 154 or 162 games, the little things accumulate and pile up and turn into big ones. That's the game's most essential fact. It's a game of percentages, and any way you can tilt the wheel your way, you do. Casey Stengel tilted it one degree here, another one there, until the ball just seemed to roll the Yankees' way and you looked up in August and saw New York right where they always seemed to be—at the top of the standings looking down. Writers and fans hardly ever notice these little things, and you hardly ever hear anybody mention 'em, but they decide championships. No good club ever won a thing without 'em. Baseball, more than anything else, is a game of intelligence, craft, and doing the little things right."[26]

Jim Calhoun, the former University of Connecticut basketball coach who won three NCAA Championships, once asked, "What is a basketball game?"

Calhoun went on to answer his question this way:

It's really a long series of little battles played out over forty minutes, hundreds of momentary skirmishes—battles for loose balls and rebounds, one-on-one matchups between a guy who, with the shot clock running down, is going to shoot the ball and a defender who must keep him from putting it in the basket. Win enough of those little fights and you win the game. You've got a few more points on the scoreboard than your opponent when the final horn sounds. By doing lots of little things well, you've accomplished a very big goal.[27]

Before we move on to what all this will accomplish for you, I have one more quote about the importance of little things. It happens to come courtesy of Jesus, and it's found at Luke 16:10, which reads this way from the *New American Standard Bible*: "He who is faithful in a very little thing is faithful also in much; and he who is unrighteous in a very little thing is unrighteous also in much."

When you are prepared—thoroughly prepared—and you are paying attention to what even Jesus tells us to pay attention to—the very little things—it will take you by the hand to an important component that leads to extreme winning.

And that is extreme confidence.

Perhaps you've already gathered that thus far from this chapter.

Remember how I told you how confident I felt when that final exam came in college and I'd prepared and studied throughout the semester? And conversely, how absolutely terrified I was when I wasn't prepared?

Preparation breeds confidence. And confidence leads to winning.

The great tennis player Chris Evert, who tirelessly practiced and paid attention to the little things, knew that. "In a decisive set, confidence is the difference," she said.[28]

Once again, Cal Ripken Jr., whose father instilled in him that attention to detail, knew how important that was when he needed to summon confidence.

"I always felt that the best way to move forward was with a positive frame of mind," he said. "If I had a miserable day, rather than moping around, I tended to be honest with myself. I'd evaluate the situation and formulate a plan based on what I knew I *could* do. All my preparation, all my 'perfect' practices, all those grounders and throws, all those hours in the batting cages, gave me the confidence that I had skills I could count on. And once I focused on those skills, I was able to dig deep down to pull myself out of a batting slump or a mental rut."[29]

In the late 1950s, Pat Summerall was a player for the New York Giants when Vince Lombardi was the offensive coordinator and Tom Landry the defensive coordinator. He later said that both men taught him the value of preparation and confidence, linking the two together.

Successful athletes approach preparation as if it was a set of rituals. In repeating them time after time, it not only keeps them prepared, it feeds into confidence.

"The entire morning on race day is a ritual, solely designed to give me confidence," said the Olympic gold medal–winning Alpine skier Lindsey Vonn.[30]

In his book *Win Forever*, Pete Carroll, who is one of only three coaches to have won a Super Bowl and a college football National Championship, recounted something that struck him when he first started on his coaching journey. "Years ago in New England, as I searched for my personal truths, I remembered being a teenager reading a story in a magazine about future NBA Hall of Famer Rick Barry," Carroll wrote. "As I recall the story, the writer was interviewing him during a shoot-around before a game. Rick was shooting jump shots as they talked, moving from left to right twenty-five times and from right to left twenty-five times, draining almost every shot from the top of the key."

(Allow me to pause and point out here the preparation on the part of Barry, and how it was likely a ritual for him, and how that feeds into confidence.)

Carroll continued, "I have always remembered the question the reporter asked as well as the answer from Rick. 'Hey Rick,' the reporter asked. 'Do you have a philosophy of life or some principle that guides you?' Rick turned to him, with an arrogant look that was practically his trademark, and simply said, 'Yeah—I'm a 46 percent lifetime shooter. If I miss my first ten shots, look out!'"[31]

That, folks, is confidence.

And again, I love it that Rick Barry spoke those words regarding confidence while he was in the throes of preparation.

"Confidence," said NFL Hall of Fame quarterback Roger Staubach, "is the result of hours and days and weeks and years of constant work and dedication."[32]

No athlete who is confident is going to feel pressure. When I was the Philadelphia 76ers' general manager, I saw that with one of our players—Andrew Toney. We had a great team back then, one that won the 1983 NBA Championship, sweeping the Los Angeles Lakers in four games. Many say it was one of the greatest teams ever. We had Julius "Dr. J" Erving, Moses Malone, Bobby Jones, and Maurice Cheeks. But Andrew Toney, while not the most gifted or talented player on that team, was unique. I never saw anyone like him. He had no fear of anything. The word *pressure* meant nothing to him. He didn't feel it, didn't believe in it, didn't have any concept of it. He had extraordinary confidence that every time he shot that ball it was going in. And I'm sure that came from preparation. He had gotten himself so comfortable, shooting thousands of shots in practice, that there was no pressure. Larry Bird was the same way.

Billy Cunningham was the head coach of that '83 Philadelphia 76ers championship team. Billy had a long career as a player and coach, and he made an interesting observation to me that I never forgot. He told me that when it came down to the wire in a tight game, and there was a timeout, that you'd be amazed at how many great former All-Americans suddenly had to tie their shoes. They didn't want to look at the coach, and they didn't want the coach to look at them or obviously think of them. They didn't want the ball. Billy told me that there were very few players who wanted the ball when it really counted, in what we call pressure situations.

Why didn't those players want the ball? Likely it was because they lacked confidence due to a lack of preparation and thus they felt pressure. And I'm convinced that confidence is the antidote to pressure. When you have confidence, pressure doesn't really affect you, because you not only know that you're good, but that you're *ready*.

Coaches quickly learn who their go-to players are, and which players are not. It's in a player's body language, in how an athlete carries himself or herself. There are visible, tangible signs with those who want pressure, who feed and thrive off it, and those who allow pressure to turn into stress.

In her book *Sum It Up,* Pat Summitt, the legendary women's basketball coach at the University of Tennessee, observed this: "The thing you need to know about pressure is that it may be invisible, but it has physical properties. It constricts the blood flow to your smaller muscles, costing fine motor control; narrows your vision; and slows your reactions. It's real."[33]

But it doesn't have to be. Not for you.

The great Peyton Manning, who is known for his almost maniacal preparation and attention to detail, says that "pressure is something you feel when you don't know what the hell you're doing."[34]

So borrowing from Pat Summitt's book title, to sum it up: The extreme winner deals with pressure by being thoroughly prepared, paying attention to the little things. The fundamentals are in place and the building blocks are there, which builds confidence. When you have confidence, pressure doesn't affect you. In fact, you actually want to be in those pressure situations, which is just a great, great feeling.

When that happens, your viewpoint will be like that of the great Olympic discus thrower Al Oerter, who won a staggering four gold medals at four different Olympic Games. Said Oerter, "Pressure is opportunity."[35]

That's what it will be for you, too.

And I'm convinced that with the proper preparation, you'll make the most of that opportunity.

Chapter 3

EXTREME FOCUS

"No life ever grows great
until it is focused."

—*Harry Emerson Fosdick, pastor* [1]

I've always been fascinated with extreme winners, picking people's brains to see what makes these men and women tick. One of the all-time extreme winners is Michael Jordan, winner of six NBA titles and six NBA Finals MVP Awards with the Chicago Bulls. He isn't just one of the greatest basketball players of all time, he's one of the greatest winners of all time.

Years ago, I was writing a book about Jordan that I came to call *How to Be Like Mike: Life Lessons from Basketball's Best*. As I usually do when I'm researching, I talked to anybody who knew Michael, trying to get a take on him. Around that time, B.J. Armstrong joined the Orlando Magic. B.J. had been Michael's teammate with the Bulls when they won their first three championships in the early '90s, a fact not lost to me at that time. On one of our Magic road trips, I found myself sitting next to B.J. at 2 AM, going to our hotel in New York. I knew it was late, but I used that opportunity to show him the outline I had prepared for the Michael Jordan book.

B.J. studied my list and after several thoughtful moments said, "You've captured Michael very well, except for one thing. You're missing one thing."

"B.J., I am all ears," I said.

"It's his focus that sets him apart," he said.

He went on to explain to me that if the Bulls were in the third quarter in the game tonight in Miami, then Michael was in the third quarter in the game tonight in Miami. He was not in the fourth quarter during the third quarter, and he was not in last night's game back in Chicago. Michael was always totally locked in, totally focused. He was so focused that nothing could break his concentration. There was nothing that could go on in that building or courtside or in his private life that could affect his total concentration, his extreme focus.

"He has an almost superhuman ability to focus on *this* moment, *this* task, *this* goal," B.J. said. "I think that is his greatest strength."

On that topic, Michael Jordan's old coach, Phil Jackson, the most successful head coach in NBA history and owner of 11 NBA championship rings, has this to say: "It's no accident that things are more likely to go your way when you stop worrying about whether you're going to win or lose and focus your full attention on what's happening *right this moment*."[2]

Because of being involved in sports my entire career, I've seen this again and again with athletes. One particular time I saw it was when the Magic were playing the Boston Celtics. It was the 2008–2009 season, and the Celtics were coming off a world championship. Kevin Garnett, the All-Star power forward, was still in the prime of his career, and I wanted to give him an autographed copy of my most recent book and also get his autograph on a Wheaties cereal box that depicted him, so we could auction it off for charity.

If you've ever seen Kevin Garnett, you've seen that almost maniacal look in his eyes of extreme intensity. TV cameras often focus on that during games. We've come to expect Garnett to be like that in the heat of action in a game. What I didn't expect was to see that same look in his eyes inside the Celtics' locker room an hour and a half before the game. As a trainer taped his ankles, Garnett's gaze was intently focused straight ahead, no doubt seeing something only he could see. He was, frankly, intimidating, even to me, and I've been a general manager and around athletes all my life.

For a moment there, I thought about taking my book and my Wheaties box and quietly tiptoeing out of the locker room. But instead, I mustered the courage to approach him. Somehow, I managed the words:

"Kevin, I have a book for you, and a Wheaties box I'd like you to sign—"

He looked up, as if a spell had been broken.

"Mr. Williams," he said firmly though politely, "I don't *sign* anything, I don't *look* at anything, I don't *do* anything before a game."

And then at that point, Kevin Garnett said and did something I'll never forget. He raised his right hand to his face and held it in front of him as if it were a shark's fin cutting through turbulent seas. Then he made a chopping motion with that hand and said:

"Focus! Focus! Focus!"

Looking back at me, Garnett added: "I don't want any distractions. After the game I'll sign the box. But right now I'm focused on the game."

And just like that, his eyes glazed over into two laser beams of intense focus.

Kobe Bryant is like that. It's not uncommon to walk into the Los Angeles Lakers' locker room before a game and see players sitting around idly waiting for the game, listening to music on their headphones, or fidgeting with cell phones. But not Kobe. He'd be the one player you'd see with his face a foot away from a TV monitor, watching game film, oblivious to everything going on around him.

I'm sure you've heard the expression regarding putting blinders on. There's a good reason why that saying is so apt. My publisher with HCI Books, Peter Vegso, has a big horse farm in Ocala, Florida. Peter has told me many times that, without those blinders on, those horses would be all over the track. Horses are very social creatures, and without those blinders they would be out there mixing and mingling, having a wonderful time cavorting around the track. But the blinders keep them absolutely locked in on what is right in front of them—now.

Extreme winners live their life that way. Nothing knocks them off their balance. Their vision never gets distorted.

Ernie Accorsi told me about something Marty Schottenheimer would say when Ernie was the general manager and Schottenheimer the head coach for the Cleveland Browns:

"Marty used to say, 'Row your boat backwards.' In other words, you can't always see the finish line and you don't always know the outcome in advance. Therefore, just keep working your oars every day and keep stroking the boat. If you do, the outcome will take care of itself. That's really all you can do anyway."

I'm often surprised at how many people point to focus as such a key ingredient. I remember years ago, sitting with Philadelphia Phillies scout Art Parrack at one of my son David's high school baseball games. We got to talking, and I asked Art:

"What one quality allows certain equally talented players to rise above other ones?"

Art's answer was immediate.

"Their focus," he said. "It's their ability to concentrate on every pitch, every game, every year. They never lose their focus."

That's the way Tom Seaver was. A lot of people don't know it, but the Hall of Fame pitcher joined the Marine Corps Reserves after high school, and he learned an invaluable trait there that he carried through his baseball career.

"I hated boot camp," Seaver once wrote. "But I learned in the first couple of days the importance of discipline and focus. I took the traits the Marine Corps gave me right into the game I love. I learned that it didn't matter to me as a pitcher whether we were one game out or 40 games out. It didn't make any difference if it was April or September."[3]

The Hall of Fame strikeout pitcher Nolan Ryan, who was Seaver's former teammate with the New York Mets, said it this way: "Deal with one pitch at a time, and make every one count."[4]

When you make a habit of focusing, no matter what the situation, it'll be there when you really need it. Focus is not something you can flip on and off like a light switch; nor would you want to. That's what Tom Seaver was saying—focus whether you're a game out or 40 games out. Either way, it shouldn't make a difference in approaching what you do with laser focus.

As Cal Ripken Jr. said, "I can't go 4–for–5 all at once. I can only do it one at-bat at a time."[5]

As you can see, I'm using a lot of baseball examples here. It's a good platform to use to advance this topic because baseball is such a long, tedious season. Games can be long, too. It's so easy in baseball to lose focus. But the great ones don't.

One of the greatest, in fact, is Hank Aaron, who in my mind is still MLB's all-time home run king. Though Hammerin' Hank had that kind of focus, he also made sure to work on it, too. Whenever he stepped into the batter's box and peered at the pitcher, Aaron said, "I would take my baseball cap, pull it down over my face, and look through a little hole in my cap, and focus on nothing but him." Aaron added, "I'm not bragging, but I think I focus on things very well."[6]

The extreme winners do.

Listen to some of their quotes:

"A lot of players were faster and stronger, but I think being able to just zero in and focus was my strength."

—Chris Evert, tennis great[7]

"The glue that holds a team together is clear focus."

—Bill Koch, businessman[8]

"I've spent a lifetime trying to improve concentration and focus."

—Tom Coughlin, two-time Super Bowl–winning head coach[9]

"You always have to focus in life on what you want to achieve."

—Michael Jordan, basketball great[10]

"Maintaining focus is a key to success."

—Bill Gates, technology giant[11]

I had lunch once in Orlando with a friend named Buddy Smith, who used to live in Lexington, Kentucky. He told me about how one time he sat next to the legendary University of Kentucky head basketball coach

Adolph Rupp at an old ABA exhibition game between the Kentucky
Colonels and the Virginia Squires. I asked Buddy what he remembered
about Adolph.

"He wore a brown suit," Buddy said.

"What else?" I asked, pumping him for details. Rupp's wearing of
brown suits was well-known, steeped in his superstitious nature. He'd once
bought a new blue suit to replace a brown one, and wore it to a game. But
after his UK team lost badly, Rupp never wore anything but brown suits
again. So I didn't want to hear anything about brown suits; I wanted some
insights into the man.

"He sat there the whole game, totally concentrating on both teams
and what they were doing on the court," Buddy said. "He was completely
focused on the action. It was as if he were coaching both teams."

Did you notice what Buddy said in that penultimate sentence—that
Adolph Rupp was "completely focused"? And keep in mind that this was
for an ABA exhibition game. How do you think he was when he was sitting
courtside, coaching the Kentucky Wildcats?

The great ones, the extreme winners, have that extreme focus.

Richard Petty was certainly one of those extreme winners. Petty won
200 NASCAR races and the NASCAR Championship seven times. In
his book *How Champions Think: In Sports and in Life*, Dr. Bob Rotella
recounted something Petty had told him during a conversation. "Doc,"
Petty said, "you just reminded me of something about myself when I was
in my prime. My mind was so good. My attitude was so good. When I
got to that starting line, there was like a laser beam from the middle of
my forehead to the finish line. And all I cared about was getting to that
finish line first. I never got off that beam, that single-minded purpose of
getting there before anyone else. Most of the drivers wanted to win. Or
I should say they would have liked to win. But they also didn't want to
finish last, didn't want to blow a tire and wreck the car, didn't want to
look really bad. I didn't care about any of that stuff. I just wanted to get
to that finish line first. And I dominated. One of the reasons I found it

easy to win out there is that very few people have that laser beam, that single-minded purpose."

There are two things that are sure to sabotage focus—yesterday and tomorrow.

"To live in the past and future is easy," said Walker Percy, the author whose books are so rich in philosophy. "To live in the present is like threading a needle."[12]

In his wonderful book *American Triumvirate: Sam Snead, Byron Nelson, Ben Hogan, and the Modern Age of Golf*, author James Dodson recounts a telling story about Hogan and how he expressed his frustration to his wife, Valerie, about his "inability to close the deal coming down the stretch—admitting he still allowed his nerves or something in the gallery to distract him. She stared at him with her sweet brown eyes and said in an almost childlike manner, 'Well, Ben, maybe you just need to find a way to ignore the gallery completely and focus only on your next shot. Maybe you should concentrate harder and forget all of that.' A simple piece of advice. Yet years later Ben credited his wife with giving him the key that unlocked his greatness. 'Before she said it so plainly, I seemed to think about everything else out there except what I had to do at that very moment.'"

When B.J. Armstrong told me about Michael Jordan, it got me thinking—not just about Michael, but about people in general. So many people live in the woulda, coulda, shoulda world. The if-only world. *If I could only redo yesterday. Oh, if I had only gone to a different college. If I had only married somebody else. If I had only raised my children differently.* And on and on they go with this litany of all the things in the past that they can't do one thing about.

To those people, I say: Yesterday is gone. That page is written. And tomorrow has not yet arrived. It's coming, but it's not carved in granite yet. So that really leaves you with one choice, and that is to live today to the fullest. Focus on today. It's okay to think about the past, and you definitely want to plan for the future, but don't lose your focus on all that you have right now, which is today.

This is what Buddha preached: "The secret of health for both mind and body is not to mourn for the past, not to worry about the future, or not to anticipate troubles, but to live widely and earnestly for the present."[13]

I believe that. I believe that if you take care of today, tomorrow will take care of itself.

Paul "Bear" Bryant understood that. In fact, the iconic college football coach even kept a poem in a framed plaque on his desk[14] to remind him of that. It read:

What Have I Traded?

This is the beginning of a new day.
God has given me this today to use as I will.
I can waste it or I can use it for good.
What I do today is very important because
I'm exchanging a day of my life for it.
When tomorrow comes, this day will be gone forever,
leaving something in its place I have traded for it.
I want it to be gain, not loss; good, not evil;
success, not failure, in order that I shall not
forget the price I paid for it.

Comedy writer Robert Orben had some serious things to say about the topic:

"One of the problems of growing older," he said, "is that you begin to collect regrets as you did baseball cards when you were a child. Many of my regrets center on the mistake of deferment. For most of our lives we have the feeling there will always be tomorrow. We proceed, as we should, that everything is possible. Indeed, everything *is* possible. But this feeling also encourages and abets deferment. I'll write it tomorrow. I'll read it tomorrow. I'll learn it tomorrow. I'll do it tomorrow. Missed opportunities."[15]

Don't miss your opportunity to be an extreme winner.

Sometimes, as odd as it might sound, being extremely focused might mean suspending for a moment that ultimate goal of winning. I heard a professional golfer put it this way: "Don't think about winning. Don't think about losing. Think about how best to play that hole." It's similar to what I heard LPGA veteran Sandra Haynie say. She offered this pearl of wisdom: "While playing, never think of beating someone. Just think of the course."

When you're doing that, athletes call it getting into the zone or flow. They don't hear anything going on around them. Time seems to stand still. Some describe it as an out-of-body experience. They move into the realm of intense concentration, which is really sustained extreme focus. Here's a dictionary definition of "concentration": "The direction of all thought or effort toward one particular task, idea, or subject." When you're able to do that, you become totally absorbed in what you're doing. Nothing external can penetrate. You're in that zone. Things move in slow motion. A 110-mile-per-hour tennis serve seems like a lob; a 95-mile-per-hour fastball looks like an underhand softball pitch; you don't even feel the motion of your arm as you're throwing that 40-yard touchdown pass.

And it isn't just athletes who experience this. Writers, artists, musicians, public speakers, and generally people in any walk of life can, and do, experience it. When you're in it, it's a wonderful feeling.

The better prepared you are (see chapter 2), the better equipped you'll be to stay in the moment. It will help you to stay calm and in control under pressure and to stay focused.

Boomer Esiason, a great quarterback in his own right, said this about one of the greatest quarterbacks of all-time—Joe Montana: "The one with the coolest head survives. The one with the coolest head wins. Joe's cool-headed because he prepares."[16]

John Brodie, the former San Francisco 49ers quarterback way before Montana's era and a College Football Hall of Fame inductee, said that "a player's effectiveness is directly related to his ability to be right there, doing that thing, in the moment. All the preparation he may have put into the game—all the game plans, analysis of movies, and so forth—is no good if he can't put it into action when game time comes. He can't worry about the past or the future or the crowd or some other extraneous event. He must be able to respond in the here and now."[17]

That comes from extreme focus, that is, the sustained concentration that will lead you to the end result you desire.

"Skillful leaders have the ability to focus on the important factors in their life—both professionally and personally," said Brian Billick, who won Super Bowl XXXV with the Baltimore Ravens. "Not only do they know what's important and what they want, they also have an aptitude for keeping their eyes on the prize. As such, they do not allow themselves to be distracted or dissuaded from their proper role within the organization. In that regard, they are able to systematically expend their time and energy in a targeted manner. As a consequence, they are able to make the maximum use of their strengths while minimizing any weaknesses they might have. Of all the attributes of the many great coaches I have been fortunate enough to work with, one of the distinguishing characteristics that singled them out from others was their ability to focus."[18]

Sustaining that focus is what will lead you to success. We live in a world where there are so many distractions. Our attention spans are getting shorter and shorter. Our smartphones appear to be making us dumber. I see so many people unable to concentrate without almost habitually picking up their phone and fiddling with it. And even if we're determined to concentrate, we hear one little chirp from our phone, or the click of an e-mail message on our computer, and off we go, our concentration broken and an enormous amount of time eventually wasted.

Janet Evans, the multiple gold medal–winner who is generally considered to be the greatest women's long-distance swimmer, showed remarkable concentration early on in her life. An *Investor's Business Daily* article about her said this:

"Her secret: an extraordinary ability to focus, a trait that surfaced in her driver's education class."

The article pointed out that Evans' driver's education instructor had a unique way of measuring concentration. What he did was create deliberate distractions. "The driver and instructor would sit in the front seat, and three other teenagers would sit behind them," the article stated. "The back-seat drivers' job was to chatter nonstop and give the student driver confusing directions—at the same time the instructor was telling the student what to do. Most students couldn't execute half of the instructor's commands. Evans got a perfect score."

Evans explained, "I think that's what athletes do—focus. People ask me about Michael Phelps and what makes him so great. Obviously, he is very talented in the pool. But to show up in Beijing (and win eight gold medals in 2008) and not let all the outside criticism, excitement, hype, media, fans, and all of that affect him, well, I think that's what was extraordinary. I think athletes have an inherent, incredible ability to focus. They have to."[19]

Pete Carroll had an interesting take on concentration, which he wrote about in his book *Win Forever: Win, Work, and Play Like a Champion*:

Like any other sport, football presents physical and mental challenges. It is our job as coaches to prepare players in every regard possible. When players know they have mastered the rigors of training, whether on the football field or in the weight room or in the classroom, their confidence leads to an unusual focus, free from distractions, doubt or fear. This attentiveness, also known as a quieted mind, clears the way for athletes to perform to their highest potential.

Think of young children playing. They don't worry about being judged and they are only concerned with having fun. In those moments it's easy to observe true, uninhibited play. We witness a level of concentration where the children are totally immersed, unaware of the world around them. This fascination and ability to be focused are essential for their development, much like an athlete.

And here's where Carroll says that such focus and concentration can put an athlete, or anybody really, in the zone or flow:

> "An athlete's immersion in and focus on performance allows for a lost sense of time in much the same way," he said. "When we have confidence and allow ourselves to become fascinated, the world seems to move in slow motion. It is an altered state of consciousness that comes from an extreme level of focus. Some performers describe this as resembling an out-of-body experience."[20]

Again, this doesn't just apply to sports. Brian Tracy, an expert in motivation, has told me that the two most important qualities for achieving success and becoming a winner in whatever you do are focus and concentration. He said, "Your ability to focus clearly on your highest priorities and to concentrate single-mindedly on them until they are complete will determine how much you achieve, more than any other qualities you can develop."

It reminds me of something former Mexican president Vincente Fox once said, which I read in *Investor's Business Daily*: "Only when we are fully immersed in challenge," Fox said, "can we forget our weaknesses and our fears, and summon the courage, stamina and strength to overcome obstacles."

My co-writer for this project, Peter Kerasotis, tells writing students that one of the most important qualities for being a successful writer is keeping your fanny in your chair. It's so easy to get distracted, so easy to get up and get a cup of coffee, check your email, go off on an Internet surfing tangent that has nothing to do with what you're working on.

You know that saying about the NFL, that on any given Sunday any team can win? Tom Landry, the legendary Pro Football Hall of Fame coach for the Dallas Cowboys, attributed that to concentration. Said Landry:

> Concentration is when you're completely unaware of the crowd, the field, or the score—other than how it might affect strategy. You're concerned

only with your performance, playing well at your position. Golf is an excellent example of concentration. When you see a golfer blow a hole and then go bogey on the next two holes, you know that his concentration has been broken.

When my concentration isn't broken, I'm never on the defensive. When you start thinking defensively, you think such things as, "Gee, this field's bad and we're behind and we're not gonna be in the championship game." It's difficult to recover then. Most people don't realize it, but a great measure of a football player is his ability to concentrate. This is why any team in the NFL can win any game, if a better team isn't concentrating.

Landry pointed out that this is what made those Green Bay Packers teams of the '60s so exceptional.

"Vince Lombardi was a driver who kept his teams concentrating. I've trained myself to concentrate. I blank out everything else. If you do that, you don't show emotion. I trained myself by watching Ben Hogan, who had tremendous concentration. He never let anything break his concentration."[21]

There is a story about the great golfer Ben Hogan, winner of 64 PGA Tour titles and nine Majors. The greats in golf are great at focusing; great concentrators. And few, if any, were better at it than Ben Hogan. Here's the story that illustrates that so well with Hogan.

It was a big tournament and Clayton Haefner was winning and playing what he said was the best golf of his career. But Hogan came from behind to overtake him and win. Throughout the final round, Haefner was aware of Hogan and what he was doing, so it wasn't a surprise when he saw Hogan had passed him for the lead, though it was disappointing. Afterward, knowing how well Hogan had played, Haefner consoled himself with the thought that he hadn't lost the tournament; it was Hogan who had won it by, in his words, "shooting the lights out." In the clubhouse later, Haefner ran into Hogan, who was reading a telegram. When Hogan saw Haefner, he looked up and said with all sincerity, "Oh, hi Clayt. How'd it go today?"[22]

When you're obsessed with winning, you get so focused, so totally absorbed, that you hardly even notice who your competition is.

Pete Sampras, the tennis star who won 14 Grand Slam titles, was another athlete who was obsessed with winning. "I never wanted to be the great guy or the colorful guy or the interesting guy," he wrote in his autobiography. "I wanted to be the guy who won titles." Toward that end, Sampras, like Ben Hogan, rarely showed emotion when he was competing. In his book, *Pete Sampras: A Champion's Mind: Lessons from a Life in Tennis*, Sampras explained: "Distractions are another daily threat to winning matches. But nothing intruded on my mind when I was on the court, and it was as simple as that. Girlfriends, coaching problems, family issues—I was almost always able to block it all out."

Sampras added that one of the worst emotions you can let creep into you is anger. "Pundits and fans sometimes wondered why I didn't show more anger or emotion now and then, and the answer is simple; I didn't feel it—or if you prefer, I didn't *allow* myself to feel it. I internalized it instead. With rare exceptions, anger is an impediment to playing well and winning matches. I remember seeing Goran Ivanisevic lose it a few times in our many matches at Wimbledon. I would watch as he broke a few of his [racquets], and at that point I always felt that I had him. The meltdown told me that I had broken my opponent's composure and will. I now had him exactly where I wanted him."

And then Sampras invoked that word—focus:

"I also didn't want anyone to be able to read *me* like that," he wrote. "By being opaque, I have made some of my opponents a little more cautious and fearful. But that dynamic wasn't an orchestrated strategy. I never tried to intimidate anyone, and I never played mind games. My biggest weapon was being myself; I showed that I could meet and handle the most nerve-racking situations in a calm, focused way—my natural way."[23]

Again, it all comes back to being focused.

Unlike Pete Sampras, where it was his natural way, most of the rest of us will have to work at it and practice it. But it's worth it. When you can sustain that focus and concentration, you can accomplish some amazing

things. One of the most difficult times to maintain focus is when our emotions get involved. But listen to what Tommy Heinsohn, who won eight
NBA titles as a player and two as a head coach, said about some of the
great players he played with, against, and coached:

> The great ballplayers have always been the ones who could focus their
> emotions like a laser beam, burning away their opponents with intensity.
> Jerry West, Elgin Baylor, Magic Johnson, and John Havlicek were all like
> that. Havlicek was the most focused athlete I ever met. From the day he
> showed up as a rookie until he retired 16 years later, his approach and
> attitude never changed. Then again, you could not talk with John Havlicek
> about the war in Vietnam. It was as though the NBA was his world at that
> moment, and everything else was excluded. As long as he played, I never
> knew of John to be involved in anything but basketball.
>
> A real professional is someone who gives you the same effort, the same
> game, the same dedication, every night. That's my definition of a pro's pro.
> That was Havlicek. That was Baylor. That was West. Night after night the
> production never varied. The world could be blowing up and they'd still
> have their minds focused like laser beams on winning.[24]

It's easier to notice that, of course, in one-on-one sports, which is probably why Tom Landry pointed to golf as a great example of where you see
concentration, specifically singling out Ben Hogan. In one-on-one sports,
where you can only rely on yourself, concentration is vitally important.

Phil Mickelson learned this early in his PGA career, back in 1991,
when he was an amateur playing a practice round with Arnold Palmer at
Augusta National in Georgia, preparing for The Masters. When he and
Palmer reached the 18th tee, Mickelson noticed that Palmer was angry.

"I thought I had done something wrong," Mickelson said.

Then he noticed Palmer walk over to the side of the tee.

"Right there!" Palmer exclaimed. "That's where it happened!"

Palmer went on to explain to Mickelson that in 1961, a fan had con-
gratulated him on winning The Masters. Palmer shook the man's hand

and then made a double-bogey on the 18th hole and lost to Gary Player by a stroke. He had lost his focus, his concentration, and it cost him. Thirty years later, it still angered him.

For Mickelson, it was a lesson in staying focused; on not losing concentration.[25]

There are other dangers to having your concentration broken, or to simply having the inability to concentrate. It's not only ruined many a dream, it often also leads to an absolute killer for accomplishing those dreams—procrastination. When your concentration lapses, procrastination is waiting, lurking in the shadows, ready and willing to fill that void.

Wayne Gretzky, generally regarded as the greatest hockey player ever, knew the dangers of losing focus, losing concentration, and thus lapsing into procrastination. Said Gretzky, "Procrastination is one of the most common and deadliest of diseases, and its toll on success and happiness is heavy."[26]

The other danger to focus and concentration is the myth of multi-tasking. But I'm here to tell you that you can't do two things at once. The mind simply cannot do it. Don't believe me? Well, let me ask you this: Have you ever read a paragraph or maybe an entire page in a book, and then recalled nothing of what you just read because your mind was thinking about something else? We've all done that, and the reason why that happens is that the mind can only concentrate on one thing at a time. When you think you're multitasking, you're really ping-ponging your focus from one thing to another, back and forth, back and forth, thinking that it's a good thing—but it's not.

There's an old saying that if you chase two rabbits, both will escape. If you're trying to do two things at once, you'll end up doing neither.

It's important to remember that you can only focus on . . . one . . . thing . . . at . . . a . . . time.

Hall of Fame pitcher Charles Albert "Chief" Bender once said this: "All games were the same to me. I worried about each pitch and that was all."[27]

That's right. One pitch at a time, one golf swing at a time, one . . . thing . . . at . . . a . . . time.

To sum it up, what you need to do is what Kevin Garnett told me in that visitors' locker room five years ago.

"Focus! Focus! Focus!"

But on what?

Good question.

Once again, I'm going to come back to John Wooden. When he was a 12-year-old boy, little Johnny Wooden received a wonderful piece of advice from his father. His father encouraged him with this simple statement: "Make each day your masterpiece." For 99 years, Coach Wooden did that. And in doing that, he was ensuring himself great tomorrows. Making each day your masterpiece is an investment in tomorrow. You're going to have a wonderful future if you focus on today, and do that every day for the rest of your life.

When you make each day your masterpiece, it means that every day you're striving for perfection. Will you attain perfection? Probably not. But in the process you can attain and achieve excellence.

The extreme winners really do pay attention to this. They're constantly striving for perfection. They want to do everything they can at the highest level of excellence. I'm reminded of that living in Orlando, or what I like to call the excellence or the quality capital of the world, which I think all goes back to a man named Disney, one of my heroes. Walt Disney came to Orlando on November 22, 1963, with an idea, with a vision, with an extreme dream to build a huge celebration in Orlando and call it "The Magic Kingdom." And all of it, everything he dreamed, came to fruition.

One of the many facets of Walt Disney was that he was a fanatic about quality. Nothing would leave his film rooms, much less his studios, unless it was at the highest level of quality. And to this day, whenever you visit Disney World, it's always at the highest level of quality. As a result, every other theme park in Orlando, every other hotel, every other restaurant, has to be at this same highest level of quality. If they're not, they look so bad by comparison that they really can't compete. That's why I like to say that Orlando is the excellence or quality capital of the world that Walt Disney triggered.

David Stern, who was probably the greatest commissioner in the history of sports, said of his philosophy that it's "the relentless pursuit of perfection."[28]

You're not going to attain it, but you can have flashes of it.

"No player can perform perfectly all the time, and we certainly aren't perfect as people," said Donna Lopiano, founder and president of Sports Management Resources and a former collegiate national champion as both a player and coach. "But perfection is possible. Most players have experienced the perfect shot, the perfect swing, or the perfect fake at some moment in their careers. If you try to give your best effort every time you do something, and don't quite achieve it, the result will be twice that of the person who didn't give their best. Strive for perfection."[29]

Extreme winners focus on being perfect, even though they know that overall they won't be able to achieve it, but they'll have flashes of it, and in the process they achieve greatness.

It's another one of the things John Wooden preached.

"Perfection is a goal that can never be reached," he told me. "But it must be your objective. Work ceaselessly to improve. Remember, the uphill climb is slow; the downhill road is fast. The quality of your effort counts most."

That's what legendary New York Yankees first baseman Don Mattingly strived for in his career.

In his book on Mattingly, called *Donnie Baseball: The Definitive Biography of Don Mattingly*, author Mike Shalin got this wonderful observation from Butch Wynegar, a former Yankees catcher and teammate of Mattingly's.

"He was a perfectionist!" Wynegar said. "I remember a day, and I don't even remember what year it was, '84 or '85, and he had gotten three hits the night before off Bruce Hurst while playing Boston, and Bruce was a tough pitcher at the time. Three line-drive hits the night before and the next day I came out for batting practice and Donnie's over with a bucket of balls and a net, hitting one after another, all by himself.

"I walk over to him—this was in late August so it was pretty warm—and he's got sweat dripping off him. I think he was hitting something like .350 at the time. He was leading the league in hitting, and I said, 'Donnie, what are you doing? You just got three hits last night against Hurst.' He looked at me and said, 'I just . . . I just feel . . . I can't feel this . . . I'm trying to feel this one thing.'

"He couldn't really explain it to me, but it was a feel thing that he was trying to get. And that was Donnie. He was hitting like .340, .350, and he was trying to find something to hit .360. I know if he was hitting .360 he would have been doing something to hit .370."[30]

Keep in mind that perfection as a baseball hitter would be batting 1.000. Nobody is ever going to do that. But in focusing on perfection, Don Mattingly achieved greatness.

You can, too.

Just do the three things Kevin Garnett told me several years ago.

Focus! Focus! Focus!

Chapter 4

EXTREME PASSION

"Passion is energy. Feel the power that comes from focusing on what excites you."

—Oprah Winfrey, TV talk show host [1]

People who know me know that I'm the guy who represents the Orlando Magic whenever our franchise has a lottery pick to be determined in the NBA Draft. I enjoy those trips to New York City, where the draft is held, and where I hopefully can squeeze in a couple of hours at one of my favorite places in the world—the Mecca of bookstores that is the wonderfully cavernous Barnes & Noble on Fifth Avenue. I also enjoy taking in a dinner with good food, especially with a good friend and good conversation.

I had one of those dinners years ago with Jay Bilas, the college basketball analyst for ESPN. Jay played basketball for Mike Krzyzewski at Duke and was part of Coach K's first really great recruiting class back in 1982.

Being an eternally inquisitive sort about successful people, I asked Jay: "What is your most vivid memory playing for Coach Mike Krzyzewski?" Jay pushed the rewind button on his memory reel, contemplating the question for several seconds. As he was deliberating, I thought along with him, thinking for sure that Jay would recount a passionate timeout speech or a play Coach K had drawn courtside to set up a game-winning shot.

"It was my freshman year," Jay finally said. "We had just finished practice, preparing for a big game the next night. Coach K sat us down and addressed us about the game. He was wearing a pair of Duke coaching shorts and a golf shirt. As I looked at him as he was talking, explaining to us things about the game, I noticed goose bumps all over his legs. Then I looked and noticed he had goose bumps all over his arms, too. And all around his neck. In fact, anywhere there was skin showing, there were goose bumps."

Can you imagine? Some twenty years later, Jay Bilas's most vivid memory of college basketball's all-time winningest coach was goose bumps.

I'm no physiologist, but I think it's safe to say that those goose bumps emanated from passion—and in this case extreme passion.

What are you extremely passionate about? What gives you goose bumps?

What Jay Bilas told me about Mike Krzyzewski fascinated me, but after contemplating it, it didn't surprise me. I have found that to be the case with the extreme winners in life. They are ultra passionate and they don't hide it. They're passionate, and the whole world sees it. It might not necessarily show in the form of goose bumps. But it shows. It oozes from them like sweat from pores.

You can't fake that. At least not for very long. People do try; they try to wear passion like a mask. But you can tell soon enough that it's not who they really are. "The most beautiful makeup for a woman is passion," said Yves St. Laurent. "But cosmetics are easier to buy."[2]

I believe you can fake passion for, oh, maybe about 14 days. But after those two weeks, the gig is up and you're going to be exposed. If you don't love what you do, you're going to be absolutely out there—stark naked and without makeup.

"You've got to get obsessed and stay obsessed," said the bestselling novelist John Irving.[3]

I couldn't agree more.

By now, I'm sure most everyone is familiar with former North Carolina State head basketball coach Jim Valvano's impassioned "don't give up, don't ever give up" speech when he was dying of cancer. That was Jimmy V—not just that evening in 1993, at ESPN's ESPY Awards, but throughout his life, and even in his death. On his tombstone are the words: "Take time every day to laugh, to think, to cry." Jimmy V embodied passion.

"Jim is probably the only person I've ever met who lived each day to its fullest," said Nick Valvano, Jim's brother. "That goes back to his insatiable appetite to do everything. Life with Jim didn't have a slow lane. He had this insatiable desire to do everything and to know everything. If he hadn't had to sleep, he wouldn't have slept at night. For example, he read a lot, but he (rarely) read fiction. Fiction didn't teach him anything. He would read all these nonfiction books and remember a lot of what was in them."

I can relate because I'm the same way. When I'm in a Barnes & Noble, like the one I mentioned in New York City, I head straight for the nonfiction books. In fact, I only read nonfiction, and I keep every book I've ever read in a library I've fashioned in my home. I'm up to about 7,000 books now. All nonfiction. Whenever I see my wife, Ruth, reading a fiction novel, I tease her that she's reading a storybook. Not that I have anything against fiction. Anything that gets people reading I believe is good. I just feel you have to streamline your passions. You have to figure out what really excites you, what gets your juices flowing, what gets the goose bumps popping, and pursue that and not get distracted and waste time with other things. Time, as we know, is so precious.

By all means, though, try things. Explore. You'll be surprised at what might capture your imagination. Alex Martins, our CEO with the Orlando Magic, recently discovered that he loves fly fishing, and I think that's great. One of the wonders of life is that you never know what might grab you and where it might take you. If it does, go with it. If not, if you don't feel that passion, move on.

That's what happened with JoAnne Shaw. Back in the 1970s, she and her husband were selling specialty coffee to vendors when they decided to open their own coffee shop. One thing Shaw already had going for her was that she was passionate about her product and was determined to be successful with it.

"I never dreamt of owning my own business," she said. "But I do remember my high school graduation when we heard a motivational speaker who at the end of the speech said to the class, 'Everyone stand up.' I don't remember the speech but I do remember the entire class standing up. There were a few hundred of us, and he said, 'Look around you. Five of you will be successful and perhaps one will be very successful.' That made an impact. I knew I was going to be one of the five. I didn't think through how or why that would happen. As for coffee, I don't know what drew me to it, but I love the product. It's a warm, friendly beverage and it really fit me."

Again, notice how she said that she *loved* the product. In other words, she was passionate about it.

So instead of providing coffee to vendors and vending machines, she opened her first coffee shop and knew she'd have to operate it. "It was then when I realized what a passion I have for the business. I liked going to the store every day. It smelled wonderful. The customers were fun."

Shaw called that first store the Coffee Beanery, which now has more than 100 franchises throughout the United States and 25 and counting around the world.[4]

You'll never know when the passion will hit you, but when it does, pursue it. For the prolific and enduring rock 'n' roll singer-songwriter Bruce Springsteen, he discovered his passion when he was just a young boy and saw Elvis Presley on *The Ed Sullivan Show*. From that moment on he was hooked. He knew what he wanted in life.

In his biography, simply titled *Bruce*, author Peter Ames Carlin wrote that once Springsteen determined that he wanted to play music, he "threw himself into his guitar with a passion and determination far beyond anything he had ever experienced." Carlin quoted Springsteen as saying, "If I wasn't in school, I was either playing my guitar or listening to records." Mostly, though, it was playing the guitar, which the teenage Springsteen would do six, eight, and sometimes 10 hours a day.[5] Another iconic rocker, Eric Clapton, was the same way. Originally an art student, once Clapton discovered the guitar he pursued it with compulsive passion.

And as any rock 'n' roll enthusiast knows, some of the best guitars in the industry are the ones Les Paul designed and built. Paul was a leader in developing the solid-body electric guitar that is widely credited with producing that distinctive rock 'n' roll sound. It was a labor of love for Paul, who was an accomplished guitarist himself. "It's a privilege to be able to do what you love to do and be good at it," he said. "My hobby is my work and my work is my hobby. That's the secret. There's no distinction."[6]

Sadly, so many people have disconnected from the passion they once had. They have taken their foot off the gas pedal and decided to coast through life, just getting by. The passion is gone and the dreams they once harbored have left port. Afraid of being disappointed they settle for less than what they could be. Don't let that happen to you. Keep the passion burning, fueling it daily. You'll find that it will motor you through all the speed bumps and roadblocks that are sure to come, plowing through any and all obstacles. "Passion," said the motivational guru John C. Maxwell, "is putting everything you've got into everything you do."[7] And if I may add to that, it's doing it all the time, consistently, without letup. Tony Bennett (the basketball coach, not the crooner) has pointed out that everyone is passionate when they're winning, but the successful are passionate when it's hard.[8]

I love the way a pastor friend of mine, Johnny M. Hunt, described it. He contends that "almost nothing can stop passion. You can have all the talent, ability, and spiritual giftedness in the world. You can be a diesel engine with high capacity and tons of horsepower, but that big train will take you only so far unless there's fuel in the tank." And that fuel, Johnny says, is "high-octane, premium-strength passion."

Johnny went on to say that "passion sees no unstoppable barriers. It will plow through, jump across, or dig under any obstacles. Where some see a dead end, passion sees a possibility. Where some grow tired from the struggle, passion is energized to see it through. Where some are ready to quit, passion rocks on. Passion is only getting started when others are conceding to failure. Passion will separate you from the crowd. It will give you unquenchable desire, an all-consuming drive."[9]

I was reading a March 15, 2015, *USA TODAY* story on a flight and circled this comment from Ivanka Trump on her father, Donald Trump. "He has more energy in one pinkie than most people have in their entire body. Some people just move through the paces. They have no spirit or passion. My dad's energy is fueled by his passion. He loves to build."

Sam Walton was another guy who had that all-consuming drive, a man whose energy was fueled by his passion. Walton had an extreme dream of building a retail store empire, and he pursued it with extreme passion. Walton's rise to the top wasn't smoothly paved. There were setbacks, disappointments. But the one thing that helped him persevere as he built Wal-Mart and later Sam's Club into retail giants was this: "I think I overcame every single one of my personal shortcomings by the sheer passion I brought to my work. If you love your work, you'll be out there every day trying to do it the best you possibly can, and pretty soon everybody around will catch the passion from you—like a fever."[10]

There is no substitute for passion, and yes it is contagious.

People know all about future Hall of Fame quarterback Peyton Manning's work ethic and how prepared he is for every NFL game, and how his teammates feed off of him. But have you ever wondered what it is that drives Peyton Manning?

"I've always had a passion for the game, and the game has changed at every level from high school to college to the NFL," he said. "But I still have the same passion and I still get excited for games today just like I did when I was playing in junior high. There's something about when you wake up in the morning, knowing you have a game that day."[11]

Bobby Bowden felt the same way during all those years when he was Florida State's head football coach. "Some nights," Bowden said, "I go home and just can't wait for sleep to be over, just so I can go out and begin the next day."[12]

What is it that makes you eager for a night's sleep to be over? What makes you want to jump out of bed every morning? When you find whatever that is, it's electric. When you have that type of feeling about what you do, it's different than just being dedicated to your profession. At least that's the way the legendary opera singer Luciano Pavarotti saw it, and I agree with him. "People think I'm disciplined," Pavarotti said. "It is not discipline. It is devotion. There is a great difference."[13]

Devotion speaks to passion. It speaks to putting your heart and soul into something.

And when you find something that you love—really love—and it becomes your passion, then what you do never seems like work. Paul Allen's father instilled that mind-set in him early in his life. "He told me that you should love whatever work you do," Allen said. "You should try to find something you truly enjoy."[14] Paul Allen did. Today he is known as the cofounder, along with Bill Gates, of Microsoft Corporation, and also the owner of the 2014 Super Bowl–champion Seattle Seahawks.

"You have to love what you're doing," said the Hall of Fame basketball player John Stockton, in a January 28, 2015, *Investor's Business Daily* article written by Michael Mink. According to Stockton, this meant that during his teenage years, "you'd rather give up going out on a Friday night to go shoot the ball, even if it's by yourself at the gym or on the courts at the park. It's those kinds of traits that you can't teach. And really, that's the key, that you love it so much you just want to keep sticking with it."

I once heard the prolific author Ray Bradbury say, "I know you've heard it a thousand times before. But it's true—hard work pays off. If you want to be good, you have to practice, practice, practice. If you don't love something, then don't do it."

Of course, that philosophy of following your passion is not new. It goes back millennia and transcends all cultures. There is that well-known Chinese proverb from Confucius, who said: "Choose a job you love and you'll never have to work a day in your life." Or, as George Halas, the former player, owner, and NFL pioneer, said: "Nothing is work unless you'd rather be doing something else."[15]

That sure sounds like the advice Coach Dean Smith gave to Michael Jordan, when Jordan was one of Smith's basketball players at the University of North Carolina. "Treat basketball like something you really enjoy," Coach Smith told Jordan, "and don't treat it like it's a job." If you ever had the pleasure of seeing Michael Jordan play basketball, you'll know that he brought extreme passion to the game and to his craft. It never looked like a job when you watched him play. It looked more like a love affair.

It is said that the Hall of Fame baseball manager Connie Mack used to judge baseball players not so much on their ability and what they could do, but whether they loved doing it.

People like to say that if you do what you love—what you have a passion for—the money will follow. And that's usually true. But you have to determine whether it's the money you have a passion for, or your chosen profession. Would you do what you're doing even if the money wasn't there? If so, then you're on the right track.

The inspirational writer Veronica Hays says passion makes all the difference. She says it's the difference between:

★ A job and a career
★ An actor and a star
★ A song and a symphony
★ A painting and a work of art
★ Caring and intimacy
★ Romance and rapture
★ Intelligence and genius
★ Living and being alive

Lee Corso, a fellow Orlandoan who is known for the passionate way he brings his analysis and commentary to college football, lives by a simple credo, and it has served him well. "You take a job because you want to be happy in it," Corso said. "Never take a job for the money, because you'll never have enough."[16]

That important bit of advice struck one of my favorite sports columnists—Mike Bianchi of my hometown *Orlando Sentinel* newspaper. Years ago, Bianchi interviewed Fran Papasedero, who was the head coach of the Orlando Predators in the Arena Football League. When Coach Papasedero tragically died in a car crash in June of 2003, Bianchi remembered that conversation and wrote about it in a column he penned in memory of the energetic, fun-loving coach:

"I only interviewed him once," Bianchi wrote, "but during the interview he said something that always stuck with me. Being curious, I asked him if one could get rich as an Arena Football League coach. His response told me all I needed to know about the man. 'We don't do this to get rich. We do it because we love the game. Don't tell anybody, but even if they didn't pay me, I'd do this job for free. How many people in the world wake up in the morning and look forward to going to work? I'm one of the lucky few.'"[17]

You can be one of those few, as well, and you don't even have to rely on luck. All you have to do is find your passion, pursue it, and you'll then find the power of passion.

That power sustained Hall of Fame baseball player Lou Brock, who was one of the game's greatest base stealers. Back in 1990, a writer asked Brock what motivated him to surpass everyone who had preceded him as a base stealer. Brock answered: "Passion for the moment, a love affair with the act."[18]

He's not the only one who feels that way. Listen to what some others say about passion:

> *"One person with passion is better than forty people merely interested."*
>
> —E. M. Forster, novelist[19]

> *"Passion is another word for enthusiasm, which translates to energy, which in turn produces action."*
>
> —Jim Calhoun, basketball coach[20]

> *"Without passion you don't have energy; without energy you have nothing."*
>
> —Donald Trump, real estate mogul[21]

> *"Nothing great in the world has been accomplished without passion."*
>
> —Georg Wilhelm Friedrich Hegel, philosopher[22]

> *"I always believe that, if you want to excel at something, you must be genuinely interested in what you're doing. You must have passion for it; otherwise success will elude you."*
>
> —Andrew L. Tan, billionaire businessman[23]

> *"You can only become truly accomplished at something you love. Don't make money your goal. Instead, pursue the things you love doing, and then do them so well that people can't take their eyes off you."*
>
> —Maya Angelou, author and poet[24]

> *"Success is not the result of spontaneous combustion. You must first set yourself on fire."*
>
> —Fred Shero, hockey player, coach, and general manager[25]

> *"A man is only as good as what he loves."*
>
> —Saul Bellow, author[26]

> *"There is nothing more energetic and passionate than being productive in what you love to do."*
>
> —Jerry Lewis, comedian and actor[27]

You're probably noticing two important byproducts of passion from some of those quotes—enthusiasm and energy.

Both are vitally important.

How important? Well, notice what the great positive thinker Norman Vincent Peale had to say: "If you are not getting as much from life as you want to, then examine the state of your enthusiasm."[28]

Have you examined your enthusiasm lately?

People who knew Vince Lombardi say that enthusiasm just crackled off him like electricity. But I doubt that when people think about Vince Lombardi today they think about enthusiasm. Mostly, folks think about Lombardi's work ethic and the hard work he put his players through and the championships he won as the head coach of the Green Bay Packers. But please don't overlook the role that enthusiasm played in making Lombardi an extreme winner. After all, Lombardi never overlooked enthusiasm.

When he took over at Green Bay before the 1959 season, the Packers were not only woeful, they were in danger of going away as an NFL franchise. Coming off a 1-10-1 season in 1958, the organization was at a low point. Lombardi quickly changed things, and he did so by immediately infusing enthusiasm into the Packers' operation.

"Gentleman," he said when he first addressed his team, "we are going to win some games. Get that! You are going to learn how to block, run, and tackle. You are going to outplay all the teams that come up against you. You are going to have confidence in me and enthusiasm for my system. Hereafter, I want you to think of only three things: your home, your religion, and the Green Bay Packers! Let enthusiasm take a hold of you!"[29]

It did. That first season under Lombardi, the Packers went from a 1–10–1 team to a 7–5 record. In Lombardi's second season, the Packers won the NFL Western Conference for the first time in 16 years. The following year, they won the NFL Championship. Over the next six years, the Packers won four more Championships, including the first two that were called Super Bowls.

Jerry Kramer lived and experienced those years as an offensive lineman, and later with Dick Schaap wrote one of the most iconic sports books of all time, *Instant Replay*. It became one of several books he wrote about Lombardi and the Packers.

"Vince Lombardi was so full of energy and enthusiasm," Kramer said. "I can still hear his voice: 'We're going to have a great practice today! What a terrific game we have coming up this Sunday!'"[30]

Needless to say, the enthusiasm had returned to Green Bay.

Years later, Reggie White, who was one of the all-time great Packer players, exuded that type of enthusiasm. "I've never seen a guy enjoy it more," said Mike Holmgren, White's head coach at the time. "It was contagious. He set the tone for the whole team."[31]

Henry Ford was a firm believer in enthusiasm, and in instilling that in his employees. Ford had an unfailing enthusiasm for his vision, and he wasn't shy about showing it. "You can do anything if you have enthusiasm," he said. "Enthusiasm is the sparkle in your eyes, the swing in your gait, the grip of your hand, the irresistible surge in your will, and your energy to execute your ideas. Enthusiasm is at the bottom of all progress! Without it, there are only alibis."[32]

One of the most enthusiastic guys I've ever seen in sports was Tommy Lasorda. When he was the Los Angeles Dodgers manager, Lasorda radiated enthusiasm, and it rubbed off on his players. Lasorda's Dodger teams were always high-energy, and it was always apparent why. It started with their manager.

"Tommy was a great leader," said Steve Sax, his former second base-men. "When it comes to Xs and Os, strategy and chemistry, Tommy was one of the best. He knew which guys to have out there in every situation. He knew who to bring in to pinch hit and which relief pitcher to come in at which time. But what made Tommy so unique, in my opinion, was his contagious enthusiasm. His ability to galvanize so many people from all different walks of life and keep them up at a high level, even in the face of intense adversity, that's what made Tommy so unique."[33]

Sax and the rest of the Dodgers' players saw that in 1981, when Los Angeles was down 2–0 in the World Series against a very formidable New York Yankees team.

"Tommy never got down and was always encouraging us, telling us that he believed in us and that we could still win," Sax said. "That confidence he had in us was huge, and I'm convinced that it played a big part in us rallying back to win the title that year."[34]

Not only did the Dodgers come back to win, they took that 1981 World Series by winning four straight games from the Yankees, who didn't return to the World Series again for another fifteen years.

My friend Jack Canfield, the originator of the Chicken Soup for the Soul series, points out that the word for enthusiasm comes from the word *entheos*, which means to be inspired by God, or to be filled with God's spirit. Needless to say, it's an appropriate definition. When you are inspired in that way, you are passionate, and it shows in your enthusiasm. And with that enthusiasm, as the investor and businessman Charles Schwab has often said: "A man can succeed at almost anything for which he has unlimited enthusiasm."

Another byproduct of passion, especially when it is combined with enthusiasm, is energy. People who are passionate and enthusiastic with what they're doing seemingly have boundless energy. Fatigue and discouragement have no hold on them. They are indefatigable, and they are the type of people you want to be around, the ones whom you want on your side.

"The world belongs to the energetic,"[35] said Ralph Waldo Emerson, who was one of America's great poets, essayists, and lecturers.

"All men are not created equal," Vince Lombardi said. "The difference between success and failing is energy."[36]

Oh, how true that is.

Dr. Orison Swett Marden, who was one of America's early pioneers in inspirational writing, penned one of my favorite poetic passages on the importance of energy. Here's how it goes:

> A lobster, when left high and dry among the rocks, does not have the sense enough to work his way back to the sea, but waits for the sea to come to him. If it does not come, he remains where he is and dies, although the slightest effort would enable him to reach the waves, which are perhaps within a yard of him. The world is full of human lobsters; people stranded on the rocks of indecision and procrastination, who, instead of putting forth their own energies, are waiting for some grand billow of good fortune to set them afloat.[37]

Don't wait for something to set you afloat. Don't let procrastination and indecision leave you high and dry.

Find your passion, apply enthusiasm to it, and you'll find that you'll have no problem expending the needed energy—and more—to reach your goal of becoming an extreme winner.

David Cottrell, a real guru in leadership and life lessons, notes that "energy is not something you can see, touch or smell. You can only see its results. . . . Energy is essential to success. If there is no excitement, enthusiasm, or passion, there's no catalyst for achievement."[38]

Notice that word *passion* again. It all comes back to passion.

The great Russian writer Fyodor Dostoevsky saw that the difference between having passion for what you do, and not do, can mean the difference between life and death. Literally. Dostoevsky was once imprisoned for being a dissident. While incarcerated, he observed firsthand powerful insights into passion and the human condition.

Dostoevsky saw the misery of prisoners who were assigned to move sand from one end of the prison camp to the other, back and forth every day, every week, every month. Some of those prisoners lapsed into such despair that they literally flung themselves into the electrified barbed-wire fence that surrounded the prison—thus committing suicide.

But then Dostoevsky noticed at another prison camp that there were prisoners who were building a railway, and how different their attitude was. To and from work every day, those prisoners sang songs and were happy in spite of their situation, passionate with what they were doing although they were incarcerated. They didn't give up, not in their assignment and especially in their lives.

If you have passion, you won't give up. Thomas Alva Edison, perhaps the greatest of all inventors, taught us that. Edison lived a life passionate about inventing and devising new and better ways of doing things. His passionate curiosity overcame his lack of formal education and led him to invent the phonograph, the motion picture camera, and, of course, the lightbulb. But he did so much more. At the time of his death, Edison held a staggering 1,093 patents in his name.

Edison had such extreme passion that he barely slept.

Not to say that it was always easy. Hardly. In achieving all his inventions, Edison encountered countless setbacks and failures—except that he never saw them as such. "I have not failed," he would say. "I've just found 10,000 ways that do not work."[39] He added that every wrong attempt that he discarded brought him one step closer to success.

This reminds me of something that Helen Tworkov, the founding editor of *Tricycle: The Buddhist Review*, once said. "The most important ingredient for success is the willingness to fail, to be made a fool of, to fall on your face a hundred times a day, and to be dumb," she said. "What makes repeated failure endurable is being in love with the work you do, and being convinced of its value. The process then becomes self-rewarding."[40]

With Thomas Edison, it wasn't just self-rewarding. He rewarded the world with his wonderful inventions. Edison's legacy lives on, as does this quote from him about passion: "I never did a day's work in my life. It was all fun."[41]

I'm glad Edison mentioned fun, because I believe it's an important component of extreme passion. It's not only okay to have fun; I believe it's necessary. Fun is not illegal; fun is not illicit; fun is not immoral. I always encourage people to have all the fun they can. People like to hang with fun people. They like to do business with fun people. Extreme winners like to have fun people around them, who understand the importance of extreme fun. I live in the fun capital of the world in Orlando. In 2014, more than 62 million visitors saved their money and came to Orlando from all over the world. They had one goal in mind—to have all the fun they could have in a week or two. I think Walt Disney's great message to all of us is that fun is good. Fun works. When you have fun, you're going to be far more productive.

Anybody who ever watched Derek Jeter play baseball knew that he was not only committed to his craft, and that he had extreme passion for it, but he also had enormous fun playing.

Years ago, Jeter wrote a book with former *New York Times* sports writer Jack Curry titled *The Life You Imagine: Life Lessons for Achieving Your Dreams*. In that book, the Yankees' future Hall of Fame shortstop devoted an entire chapter to fun, titling it "Be Serious, but Have Fun."

"I love baseball, I love getting better, and I've never been averse to working hard at it while having fun," Jeter wrote. "That started from the first time I threw a ball to my father as a toddler. You've got to like what you're doing. One of the reasons I can work out so fervently in the off-season is because I like the process. I like getting myself in better shape and doing the things that are going to make me a better player. If I hated lifting weights and doing flexibility training, it wouldn't be so easy to do this. I admit that. That's why you have to find something you love doing and then be willing to devote yourself to it. If you really love it, it will really show in your effort. Someone who wants to be a chef should not have any trouble spending hours and hours cooking. You have to want to be better. I know I do."[42]

Sports Illustrated writer Tom Verducci once asked Jeter about something so imperceptible that few people picked up on it. It happened right before the first pitch of Game 7 of the 2001 World Series between the

Yankees and the Arizona Diamondbacks. Jeter and Diamondbacks' pitcher Curt Schilling looked at each other right before that first pitch and gave each other a slight, knowing smile.

"I remember it," Jeter told Verducci years later.

And why the smile? Jeter had a ready response.

"It was fun," he said. "Schilling was as big a big-game pitcher as there was. So Game 7 of the World Series and you're facing the best? That's fun."

Jeter went on to explain that "you're playing *a game*, whether it's Little League or Game 7 of the World Series. It's impossible to do well unless you're having a good time. People talk about pressure. Yeah, there's pressure. But I look at it as fun. If I stop having fun, then I'm not going to play."[43]

No wonder, then, that the great industrialist Andrew Carnegie opined, "People rarely succeed unless they have fun in what they are doing."[44]

During his rookie season in 2015 with the Chicago Cubs, Kris Bryant already displayed that he understood that concept. When asked about the pressure of playing in his first major league game, Bryant told *New York Times* writer Ben Strauss: "There's no pressure in this game. You let pressure creep in, you're not having fun." Bryant's approach was the same as one of his manager Joe Maddon's Maddonisms—don't let the pressure of the moment exceed its pleasure.

One of the great things about approaching what you do with great passion and great fun is that it alleviates pressure. That's another thing Jeter believes, and I do, too.

One of the closest beaches to where I live in Orlando is Cocoa Beach, home of Kelly Slater, who is generally regarded as the Babe Ruth of surfing. Slater has won the Association of Surfing Professionals (ASP) World Tour title an unprecedented 11 times, but not always easily.

Back when he was poised to win his seventh world title, Slater got beat in the first heat of the final round. With only two more heats to go, the pressure was really on. Here is how Slater chose to meet that pressure: rather than pushing himself to try harder, which would likely add more pressure and possibly lead to making a critical mistake, Slater said he made a conscious decision to just let go, to relax, and to have as much fun as possible. The result is that he notched two perfect 10 scores in his next two heats en route to another world title.

So whenever you feel pressure, remind yourself that you're doing what you love, and just how much fun that is. That's what extreme winners do, no matter how big the stage or how bright the spotlight.

That same imperceptible smile that Tom Verducci noticed on the faces of Derek Jeter and Curt Schilling was also there on Janet Evans' face when she was about to dive into a swimming pool at her first Olympic Games. Regarding that, I once heard an interview where Evans, who was one of the great swimmers of all time, said this: "On the starting block before my first Olympic race I was smiling because I was having fun. That's what it's all about . . . to have fun."

So don't be afraid to have fun, to smile and laugh. Passion is like fire. And like a literal fire, it needs fuel. One of the best ways to fuel the flames of passion is by doing exactly what golfer Peter Jacobsen says: "Above all, you have to go out there and have fun. If you don't build in that component, it gets very stale and you can burn out."

Angelo Dundee, best known for being the man who trained Muhammad Ali, was an acute observer of athletes, and he saw something similar in two of the all-time great extreme winners in boxing and golf. "There is one parallel between Ali and Tiger Woods," Dundee said. "Muhammad always had fun in what he was doing, and I see that in Tiger. He has the wonderful smile after he swings. It makes you feel good to watch him."

People might not automatically assume that Tiger Woods is having fun, but those who have been close to him know better. One of his former coaches, Butch Harmon, told the writer Charles P. Pierce that one of Tiger's three greatest attributes was simply having fun. In a pressure-packed individual sport like golf, having fun can go a tremendously long way toward breaking tension and relieving pressure. The legendary sportswriter Dan Jenkins once noticed Tiger and his then-caddy Steve Williams high-fiving before Tiger hit a shot on the 17th hole during the second round of the 2000 British Open. Obviously, Jenkins was curious as to what the high-five was all about, so later he asked Tiger:

"Were you celebrating the discovery of a decent lie?"

"No," Tiger replied. "We were just telling jokes."[45]

Tiger Woods went on to win that British Open, all while having fun.

And really, why not have fun?

Andy Van Slyke, a former baseball player and now a coach with the Seattle Mariners, once observed, "The problem with a lot of players is that they don't have enough fun."

Thankfully, a lot of athletes do have fun. Listen to what some of them have had to say on the topic:

"I play baseball for fun. I love to play."

—Don Mattingly, baseball player

"There's nothing like getting out there in the outfield, running after a ball and throwing somebody out who is trying to take that extra base. That's real fun."

—Willie Mays, baseball player[46]

"Baseball is about having fun."

—Ken Griffey Jr., baseball player

"When you have confidence you can have a lot of fun. When you have fun, you can do amazing things."

—Joe Namath, football quarterback[47]

"The drive is always to get better. You can always get better. You never get there. It's a never-ending struggle. That's the fun of it."

—Tiger Woods, golfer[48]

"I see players in their 40s, grinding away, and they don't seem to be having a lot of fun. I want to have fun."

—Dottie Pepper, golfer

"I love this game. There's not a morning I wake up that I don't want to run to the ballpark to play. There's not a day I don't go out there that I'm not having fun."

—Rickey Henderson, baseball player[49]

"Fun? The most fun in baseball is hitting the ball. My whole life was hitting. Hitting, nobody ever had more fun."

—Ted Williams, baseball player[50]

"Even old pros can't win unless they're having a little fun."

—Bill Russell, basketball player

"The game is serious, but you need to have some fun. When the fun is all out, you don't need to play the game anymore. I want to have fun while working hard."

—LeBron James, basketball player

"When I talk to kids about football, I talk to them about having fun."

—Archie Manning, football quarterback

"Nobody ever said, 'Work ball!' They say, 'Play ball!' To me, that means having fun."

—Willie Stargell, baseball player[51]

Of course, having fun doesn't just apply to sports. It should apply to whatever your passion is.

Business? "Business ought to be fun," says bestselling author Tom Peters.

Politics? "Have fun. Be yourself and have fun," John McCain said to Sarah Palin just before she walked on stage to debate Joe Biden on October 8, 2008.[52]

Inventing? "I have no paying job. I always make my work my play," said Orville Wright.

Entertainment? "My guideline is to have as much fun as you can," said Dolly Parton.

Yes, have fun. Have as much fun as you can. Be enthusiastic. Be energetic. It's easy to do when you're extremely passionate about what you're doing.

Chapter 5

EXTREME WORK

"You can't have a million-dollar dream and a minimum-wage work ethic."

—*Anonymous* [1]

Let me tell you a Michael Jordan story.

Years ago I wrote a book called *How to Be Like Mike: Life Lessons About Basketball's Best*. I did over a thousand interviews with people who knew him, played with him, played against him, worked with him . . . essentially anybody and everybody who could offer me some insight. One of those people I tracked down was his personal fitness trainer, Tim Grover, and he gave me a wonderful perspective into what made Jordan such an extreme winner.

Back in 1990, the Bulls had just lost in the playoffs for the third straight year to the Detroit Pistons—twice in the Eastern Conference Finals and once in the Semifinals. Chuck Daly was the Pistons' head coach, and he employed a defensive strategy he called the Jordan Rules, designed to limit Jordan's offensive effectiveness. There were various nuances to the Jordan Rules that involved mixing and shifting defenses to keep him off-balance. But the basic premise was for the Pistons to use players like Bill Laimbeer, Rick Mahorn, Dennis Rodman and James Edwards to just physically beat Michael into submission: to just attack him and destroy him physically.

What people tend to forget about Michael in those days is that he was kind of willowy. He was lean and lithe. But after that third devastating loss to the Pistons—a 93–74 setback in Game 7 at Auburn Hills, Michigan—Michael was sitting in the back of the team bus getting ready to go to the airport to fly back to Chicago. And he was crying. The loss, which prevented the Bulls from going to the NBA Finals, hurt him that much. From the airport, he called Tim Grover and told him, "Okay, that's it. I'm going to put myself in your hands." And from that point on, Michael got in the weight room.

When I talked to Grover, he told me that Michael never—and I mean never—missed a day of work. "If it was the seventh game of the Finals and it was Michael's day to lift heavy, then he was lifting heavy," Grover said. "For the rest of his career, he was under my supervision, and he never let up. For example, if the Bulls were out on the West Coast on a five-game road trip, I would go and follow the team at Michael's expense. If the Bulls had just played a game in Portland and the next stop was in Phoenix, I would fly ahead and I would be waiting in the lobby of the hotel for the Bulls to arrive. It might be two or three in the morning, but I always had a gym ready somewhere, because many times Michael would want to lift weights before he went to bed to make sure he got his work in."

And that, needless to say, was just Jordan's work ethic in the weight room. On the practice court, he was working equally as hard.

The following season, the Bulls won their first NBA Finals, advancing to the championships by beating—who else?—the Detroit Pistons in the Eastern Conference Finals. It began an incredible run in the decade of the '90s that saw the Bulls win three straight championships, and then three more after Jordan returned from his brief hiatus to play baseball.

Michael Jordan's Chicago Bulls teams became unstoppable, although there were a good handful of excellent teams that tried. But after talking to Tim Grover, it got me thinking about how back then it really was a joke that the rest of us in the NBA were trying to catch the Bulls. In retrospect, we didn't have a chance because Michael, who was now into his 30s, was so far ahead of everybody simply because he was outworking everybody. Think about it: if you're Michael Jordan and you're in the weight room at 2:30 in the morning in Phoenix *before* you go to bed . . . well, it's going to take an awful lot of extreme work to catch up with a guy like that.

Again, a lot of teams certainly tried. Back in the mid-'90s, with my team, the Orlando Magic, we thought we were making ground. We had a great squad with Shaquille O'Neal and Penny Hardaway, and we even beat the Bulls when Jordan returned from baseball in 1995. We sincerely thought we were ready to take over the league. But Michael and the Bulls came back the next year, with Michael more determined than ever, and they just destroyed us four games to none. Jordan would not be denied, and he was en route to taking the Bulls to another run of three consecutive NBA titles.

So if you really want to know how Michael Jordan became perhaps the greatest player in NBA history, that's it. Yes, he had talent. Yes, he had skills. Yes, he had drive. Yes, he had incredible focus. Yes, he was flamboyant. But at the core is that Michael Jordan outworked everybody in professional basketball, and he never let up. And because of that, he not only got bigger and stronger, but he was also always getting better with the skill side of his game. Every summer, he'd pick up something new—another move, another shot, another way to better defend you. He was always coming back in the fall having added something, and coming into camp in such great shape.

Google pictures of Michael early in his career in the '80s, and then later in the '90s, and you'll see how he really filled out, adding noticeable muscle. He worked at that, and he worked extremely hard. We call that extreme work.

Years later, when I heard Michael Jordan say that "championships are won while the stands are empty," his comment just jumped out at me. I think many of us look at the great athletes, the great achievers, the great success stories and the great winners, and we think they got to where they're at because of skill or talent or some divine blessing. But the truth is they got there when the stands were empty, when the office building was empty, when others were sleeping, when nobody was watching. How many of us have ever seen Michael Jordan lift one single barbell, do one squat, or pedal one stationary bike? Yet, I'm here to tell you he spent literally thousands of hours doing those things. On top of that, ask any of his former teammates, and they'll tell you that Jordan was almost always early to practice and usually the last to leave.

In his book *Masters of the Game: Essays and Stories on Sport*, author Joseph Epstein writes about Jordan:

If Michael was a natural, he was a natural who worked hard to improve his game, and who possessed, along with great court savvy, an indomitable, a really quite fanatical, will to win. He began as a slashing, driving player, able to elude defenses and then arrange to score in some inventive way. Later in his career he developed one of the game's great jump shots, which he released high in the air and fading away—a thing of beauty and a joy, if not forever then till the next time he did it.

Michael Jordan epitomized the famous quote from Robert Half, an employment specialist who often said: "Hard work without talent is a shame, but talent without hard work is a tragedy."

That's why, because of his extreme work ethic, Michael Jordan's career was triumph instead of tragedy.

We started this book with a chapter on extreme dreams, which makes this quote from life coach Joyce Chapman so appropriate: "If your dream is a big dream, and if you want your life to work on the high level that you say you do, there's no way around doing the work it takes to get you there."[2]

The late boxing champion Joe Frazier often said that if you cheated on your roadwork in that premorning darkness, it was going to be exposed under the bright lights when you stepped into the middle of the ring. I believe that. But I guess the real reason why I so firmly believe in the foundation of a work ethic, and why I believe it is essential to success and to extreme winning, is because I know what it has done for me.

I realized early in life that I had tremendous goals, tremendous desires, tremendous ambition . . . but I had mediocre talent. So as a baseball player throughout my high school and college days, just to hold in with the other players and accomplish what I wanted to do as an athlete, I had to outwork people. There was no other way I could've played at the different levels that I did, all the way to the minor leagues in professional baseball, if not for the work I put into it. If I had been an average worker, I'd have never succeeded, and I never would've reached the levels that I did.

And as far as my administrative career, particularly when I got into basketball, I did not have a coaching, front office or even a personnel background in basketball. I was a minor league baseball player, and then a young executive in that sport. But then suddenly, after working most of the decade of my 20s in baseball, I was a 29-year-old general manager of the Chicago Bulls. I hardly had the experience that the other NBA general managers had. But I knew, once again, that the only way I could succeed was to outwork people.

Then there has been my career as a writer. I'm not the most gifted writer. But what I am is relentless in gathering information and pursuing ideas. I really work at it. In fact, this book that you are reading is my 100th published book.

Needless to say, everything I've accomplished in my life is through sheer effort and hard work, and it remains that way today, proving that you don't have to be the most gifted or most talented person. In fact, I'll always take a person with average gifts and talents who is a relentless worker over a supremely gifted and talented person who just mails it in.

John Wooden was a big believer in effort. Gail Goodrich was a star guard on Wooden's first two UCLA National Championship basketball teams, and he said Wooden always told his players: "You've got to look yourself in the mirror and be able to ask yourself, 'Did I play the very best I could? Did I give that 100 percent effort that was necessary for me to be successful?'" I received that same message from Wooden when we used to visit. "When you put forth your best effort," he'd tell me, "you can hold your head high regardless of the byproduct called the final score. That's why I've always taken greater pride in the effort than in the score."

It struck me when New York Yankees shortstop Derek Jeter, in his final news conference after his last game at Yankee Stadium, responded to a question about what was his way of doing things by saying this: "I know that there are a lot of people that have much more talent than I do—throughout the course of my career, and not just now. I can honestly say that I don't think anybody played harder. I don't. Maybe just as hard, but I don't think anybody had more of an effort. Every single day I went out there I tried to have respect for the game and play it as hard as I possibly could. And I did it here in New York, which I think is much more difficult to do. And I'm happy for that."

He should be.

Another guy who never had that mail-it-in attitude, who always gave his best effort, is Heisman Trophy winner Tim Tebow. When he was a little boy, Tebow understood the power of extreme work. He read a quote that he put on his bedroom door. It said: *Hard work beats talent, when talent doesn't work hard.* The Hall of Fame quarterback Bart Starr thought along the same line. "If you work harder than somebody else," Starr said, "chances are you'll beat them even though he has more talent than you."[3] And once again, listen to Michael Jordan, who opined, "Everybody has talent, but ability takes hard work."[4]

My fellow Orlandoan Davey Johnson learned that lesson early in his baseball career. A former player and manager, Johnson once told me on my radio show about his rookie season with the Baltimore Orioles in 1965, and how he saw the great third baseman Brooks Robinson's work ethic. Brooks had already won five Gold Glove awards for his outstanding defensive play. Even still, Davey saw the future Hall of Famer tirelessly working on his infield drills, taking 100 ground balls every day.

"So I went up to him and said, 'Brooks, you've already got these five Gold Gloves. Why are you taking 100 grounders a day?'"

"How do you think I got 'em?" Brooks asked.

After that, Davey told me that he started taking 100 ground balls every day; four years later he won the first of three Gold Gloves for his play at second base.

There is a similar story involving Ben Hogan, which James Dodson chronicles in his book, *American Triumvirate: Sam Snead, Byron Nelson, Ben Hogan, and the Modern Age of Golf.* Wrote Dodson:

The sight of a solitary Ben Hogan on the practice range at Colonial was becoming familiar to members. Tex Moncrief remembered asking him once why he spent an entire morning hitting nothing but wedges.

Ben looked at him and tersely replied, "Because a good short pitch can almost always make up for a mistake." But his calculations didn't cease there. A year later, Moncrief spotted him hitting nothing but four-woods for an entire afternoon, pausing only for an occasional cigarette, Coke, or Hershey bar.

"Why four-woods, Ben?" the oil man asked him later in the bar. "You hit four-woods better than anyone in golf."

He told him, "I lost a tournament last summer up in Chicago due to a poor four-wood shot. I don't want that happening again."

"The message I took away from that was that he intended to leave no margin for failure of any kind," Moncrief said. "Ben didn't practice swings. He practiced shots. He wanted no shot to surprise him. He wanted them all, by God, to be perfect."

All of it reminds me of something another golfing great, Sam Snead, used to say. "Practice," Snead would intone, "puts brains in your muscles."

But no matter how many times we hear stories like Ben Hogan's, many people still believe that extreme winners were simply born that way. They buy into the myth that people become overnight success stories. Well, don't believe it. It's just not the way success happens. When I was a young man, a band from Britain exploded onto the pop music scene, seemingly arriving from nowhere to sudden stardom. That band was the Beatles. And, yes, it might've seemed as if they were an overnight sensation. But now we know that the Beatles routinely played marathon eight-hour sets at, of all places, strip clubs, honing their craft. It's also been estimated that the Beatles performed more than 1,200 times before they became that so-called overnight sensation in 1964.

But again, we don't often see it that way. People often look at extreme winners and marvel at their talent and wish they had been endowed with the same abilities. But trust me on this: the talent you see wasn't magically bestowed on them. Author Malcolm Gladwell has forged a career studying top performers, and he has discovered that it isn't innate talent or intelligence that is the key to success. Instead, it's practice and experience.

Gladwell writes that it takes about 10,000 hours of practice to climb the ladder to the highest level of your ability—no matter what the profession. It's the people who do that, who are willing to put the time into practice and work, who are the ones who will stand out. "Practice," Gladwell said, "isn't the thing you do once you're good. It's the thing you do that makes you good."[5]

Some people are afraid to put in the work, because they are afraid of failure. Author and philosopher Alain de Botton has the antidote to that. "Work," he said, "begins when the fear of doing nothing at all finally trumps the terror of doing it badly."[6]

In his book *Talent Is Overrated: What Separates World-Class Performers from Everybody Else*, author Geoff Colvin writes that "there is absolutely no evidence of a 'fast track' for high achievers." He noted that there have been studies done on people we would assume were born talented, but Colvin writes that "researchers found few signs of precocious achievement before the individuals started intensive training. Such signs did occur occasionally, but in the large majority of cases they didn't. We can all think of examples of people who seemed to be highly talented, but when researchers have looked at large numbers of high achievers . . . most people did not show early evidence of gifts."[7]

What did they show, then?

Answer: A willingness to work.

I love this quote from Freeman Hrabowski, an educator, advocate, and mathematician. Hrabowski said, "It's hard work that makes a difference. I don't care how smart you are or how smart you think you are. Smart simply means you're ready to learn."[8]

The so-called child prodigies that became immortal in their field didn't just happen; they weren't born that way. Wolfgang Mozart's father, Leopold Mozart, was an accomplished composer and performer and a teacher of music. He began intensively instructing young Amadeus in music at three years old. Same with Tiger Woods. His father Earl had Tiger gripping a golf club while in his bassinet. And I'm sure we've all seen that video clip of Tiger at the age of two on the *Mike Douglas Show* with Bob

Hope, showing his young skills at golf. Early in their lives, and throughout their youth, both Mozart and Tiger put a tremendous amount of hours into working their craft, and they continued that into their adulthood.

Colvin writes that after much research he believes in what he calls a 10-year rule. He contends that no matter the field, no one became great without at least 10 years of very hard work—that is, extreme work. And he says that "top performers repeat their practice activities to a stultifying extent."[9]

I agree with that, but I don't necessarily agree that it has to be stultifying, which is to say dull. That's because another thing I've learned is that you need to know what you're passionate about and leave the rest of it alone. I am not passionate about golf. I am not passionate about fishing. I am not passionate about antiquing. My passions are pretty narrow in scope—helping run a basketball team, writing books, reading books, delivering speeches, and looking after children and grandchildren. And that's it. Thus, I stay closely focused on those areas and don't dabble with other things.

That's not to say you shouldn't try things, because you never know when the passion bug is going to bite you.

And here's the beauty of it all. In the previous chapter we talked about passion. In this chapter we're talking about work. If you're passionate about something, then it's not work. I doubt Michael Jordan ever moaned and said, *Oh, I've got to go shoot 200 jump shots.* Or that Tiger Woods sighed and said, *I've got to hit another 10 buckets of balls.* Or that Charles Schulz groaned and said, *I've got to go draw another comic strip panel.* Or that Mozart complained, *Do I have to write another classical masterpiece?*

Extreme winners are passionate about what they are doing; thus, when it comes time for extreme work, it isn't work to them.

"The only way to do great work is to love what you do,"[10] said Steve Jobs, founder of Apple and Pixar. And speaking of love, I love how Jim Henson, the creator of the Muppets, once put it. He said, "The only way the magic works is by hard work, but hard work can be fun."[11]

That's not to say that at times it won't feel like work. "You can't get much done in life if you only work on the days you feel good,"[12] said Jerry West, the great Hall of Fame basketball player. I would imagine that there were times, when his plane got in at two in the morning in an NBA city, that Michael Jordan really didn't feel like lifting weights. But he pushed himself through those times. And you will have to, also. Which brings me to another maxim from Michael: "We have become a shortcut culture."[13]

It's true, we have. So get that shortcut mentality out of your mind. Remove it from your psyche. There are no shortcuts to becoming an extreme winner. There are no shortcuts to becoming a great athlete, a great artist, a great businessperson, a great company. It's work—hard work. So embrace work. Love work. Look for work, and when you're done, look for more work to do.

The inventor Thomas Edison aptly said: "Opportunity is missed by most people because it is dressed in overalls and looks like work."[14]

This leads me to two very important words in the English language that I want to share with you.

What else?

Why *what else?* Because *what else?* is the mind-set of extreme workers. They're always thinking: *What else* can I bring, *what else* can I contribute, *what else* can I offer, *what else* can I do? That's always going through their minds. So when you get a whole organization of *what-elsers?* then that team, that company, that organization is going to be extremely successful.

Christianity was founded by a man who preached a *what else?* philosophy. Just read Matthew 5:41 to see for yourself. It's where Jesus implores us to go the second mile, or the extra mile. And, as self-help guru Wayne Dyer says, "It's never crowded along the extra mile."[15]

Paul "Bear" Bryant saw the power of that *what else?* philosophy early in his legendary career coaching college football. "Work hard," he said. "There is no substitute for hard work. None. If you work hard, the folks around you are going to work harder. If you drag into work late, what kind of impression is that going to leave? Don't tolerate lazy people. They are losers. People who come to work and watch clocks and pass off their responsibilities will only drag your organization down. I despise clock-watchers. They don't want to be part of a winning situation. They won't roll up their sleeves when you need them to."[16]

In other words, what Bear Bryant wanted was that *what else?* type of worker instead of that *how can I get out of this?* person.

The great American poet Robert Frost observed that "the difference between a job and a career is the difference between 40 and 60 hours per week."[17]

I love how Albert Einstein approached things. Yes, Einstein was a genius and one of the greatest figures of the 20th century. But he was also a *what else?* type of person. He was once asked to explain the difference between himself and the average person. You'd probably think that Einstein would comment on intellect, but he didn't. Instead, he said that when directed to find a needle in a haystack, the average person will stop looking when he or she finds one. He, on the other hand, would keep looking until he found all the possible needles.

So, really, how is it that Einstein's name is synonymous with genius? Perhaps Thomas Edison has the answer. "Genius," Edison said, "is 1 percent inspiration and 99 percent perspiration."[18] In connection with that, I love this quote that's been attributed to a number of people. It simply states: "No one ever drowned in sweat."[19]

The late Hall of Fame baseball player Tony Gwynn was another one of those *what else?* type of people. I've heard former San Francisco Giants third-base coach Tim Flannery, who was Tony Gwynn's teammate with the San Diego Padres, talk about Gwynn on several occasions.

"People always ask me, 'Is there one moment that you remember about Tony Gwynn?'" Flannery said. "And I always say, yeah, one moment that happens every single day at 3:30. Everybody else comes out at 4:20. Tony Gwynn is out every day at 3:30 to take extra batting practice. His work habits are beyond anybody I've ever seen."

Flannery recalled how Gwynn was that way even down to the final few weeks of his iconic career.

In our last home stand, he was retiring in 18 more games, and he was still hitting extra every single day. He was totally committed to his craft. That's why he's who he is. Tony was committed to being the most prepared player on the field. Perfect example: Two years ago we're in Cincinnati. There were runners on first and second and it started raining, so the game was suspended. The next day it picks up exactly where it left off—same pitcher, same everything. That night, Tony told me, "This guy's going to throw me a first-pitch slider and I'm going to hit it in the left-centerfield gap." First pitch the next day was the slider. He hit it in the left-centerfield gap. Tie score. I really believe at that moment he knew what that pitcher was going to throw before the pitcher did, because he'd studied the tendencies and studied the history of that pitcher.

Tony Gwynn was always working hard—an extreme worker—and he was always looking for that *what else?* to make himself better.

You might think that Gwynn was just incredibly talented, given his .338 career batting average and the 3,141 hits he amassed. But he wasn't a naturally talented player, and Gwynn knew that early in his professional career when he was still a minor leaguer. "I didn't run well," he once said. "I was an average outfielder and I didn't throw well. I went to the minor leagues with the mentality that I was really going to have to work hard to get to the big leagues. I think those who are successful are those who put a lot of time and effort into it, and a lot of thinking into it, before they actually go out and do what they do."[20, 21]

After Gwynn died, *New York Times* sportswriter Tyler Kepner wrote that back in 1994, when Gwynn was en route to the fifth of his eight National League batting titles, he spoke about his disappointment regarding modern players.

"They just feel like stuff is supposed to happen to them," he said. "They're not going to have to work for it. And that bugs me because I know how hard I had to work to get where I got. Sometimes they sit there in amazement at why I come out here every day. But I cannot let their way of thinking in my head."[22]

One of the all-time winners in college basketball, and a man with a *what else?* philosophy, is Coach Roy Williams, who has won two National Championships at the University of North Carolina—one in 2005 and the other in 2009.

Williams didn't have an easy upbringing. When he was a young boy growing up in the mountains of North Carolina, his alcoholic father abandoned him, his sister, and his mother. It might've been just as well that he did, given how abusive his father was. Home during those years was a series of motels, trailers, and occasional accommodations with relatives. His mother often worked two jobs—one in a factory and the other washing and ironing rich people's clothes. Young Roy learned early on that if he wanted anything in life he'd have to work for it, which he started doing as a child, taking on various jobs.

Williams worked at another thing, too—basketball. He wasn't the most athletic kid—not particularly tall or fast. But he spent hours honing his game, and especially his shot, always looking for *what else* to do to make himself better. Early on, however, he knew his future didn't rest on being a player. Somewhat like me, he was an average athlete. But what Roy Williams really wanted to do was coach. And he wanted to learn coaching from the great Dean Smith at the University of North Carolina. He walked on as a freshman, but his playing career didn't last long, which he'd already accepted. He worked various part-time jobs to pay for his tuition and studied hard enough to earn two degrees, which again is another example of that *what else?* attitude. In addition to two degrees, Williams also earned something else. During his time as a student there, Williams earned a way onto the team as a volunteer statistician. It gave him an entrée into North Carolina's basketball practices, where he'd sit in the bleachers absorbing everything while taking copious notes. Soon, he was also working Dean Smith's summer basketball camps.

It provided a good foundation for him, and by the mid-1970s, Williams had forged a career as a successful high school basketball coach. Then, in 1978, Dean Smith offered him a job as an assistant coach. It wasn't for much money—only $2,700. But Williams made do by supplementing his income working part-time jobs. If there was one thing he knew how to do, it was work.

Williams worked for 10 seasons under Smith and was on the staff when the Tar Heels won the National Championship in 1982. That team featured a rather famous North Carolina player whom Williams had recruited to the school. I'm sure you've heard of him. His name is Michael Jordan.

Eventually, Williams became a college head coach and had a great run at the University of Kansas, coaching there from 1988 until 2003, before returning to coach his alma mater, where he still is. It's an inspiring story of hard work. In fact, when Roy Williams wrote his autobiography several years ago, he appropriately titled the book *Hard Work*.

Williams' winning percentage as a college head coach is near 80 percent, which tells you that not only is he an extreme winner, he stays consistent. That's important to note, because the danger is that after success arrives you can become complacent instead of staying consistent. But extreme winners understand that you can't drift on your oars. You've got to continue to put in an enormous amount of work or you're not going to be successful. Interestingly, hard work and consistency were the first two of the three keys of success that the inventor Thomas Edison once laid out. Said Edison, "The three great essentials to achieve anything worthwhile are, first, hard work; second, stick-to-itiveness; third, common sense."[23]

Jim Plunkett had that type of attitude. Plunkett, the 1970 Heisman Trophy winner, took a lot of knocks during his pro career as a quarterback, mostly from those who believed that his college successes didn't translate into anything more than an average pro career. Plunkett never allowed the naysayers to distract or discourage him. He just kept working. "I worked very hard to achieve what I wanted to achieve," I once heard him say. "You just have to hang in there, put your head down, and walk against the wind. Just keep plugging away." Plunkett did, and before his pro career was over he was a two-time Super Bowl champion.

Though Plunkett had success in college, he never allowed it to give him a sense of entitlement as a pro. Feeling entitled will kill your dreams, yet

I see that sense of entitlement so often these days. Sadly, where I see it most is in young people, and even in some of my children. The attitude is: I'm due it, Dad, or I'm entitled to this, or I'm owed. And I have to point out: People, people, please listen to me. You're not due anything. You're not entitled to anything. The only thing you're going to get in life is that which you work for, and work consistently at so that it would take two people to replace you should you ever leave. A great mentor of mine, Bill Veeck, often said: "There is nothing owed to you."

And that's true even after you've had success, and perhaps even if you've had the type of enormous success that an extreme winner like Michael Jordan had. Jordan, as we know, never got complacent. "I never believed all the press clippings and I never found comfort in the spotlight," Jordan said. "I don't know how you can, and not lose your work ethic. I listened. I was aware of my success. But I never stopped trying to get better."[24]

My introduction to this book starts with an anecdote about Johnny Unitas, the great Hall of Fame quarterback. Raymond Berry, who was a teammate on the Baltimore Colts and another Hall of Fame player, remembers Unitas this way: "John had a tremendous work ethic. That was one thing that led to success. John wanted to throw after practice, and I stayed there to run pass routes with him because I wanted to work after practice, too. The significance of this can't be underestimated. We went to work timing every pass route in our playbook."[25]

On the field, all that hard work between Unitas and Berry made the game look easy, fluid, almost effortless. Of course, it isn't. Said the great sculptor and artist Michelangelo: "If people only knew how hard I work to gain my mastery, it wouldn't seem so wonderful at all."[26]

Of course, it was—and is—wonderful; made all the more wonderful *because* of the hard work.

Brian Tracy, who is an entrepreneur and a leader in personal and professional development, often says that in working his way up from poor beginnings, all he had going for him was the ability to work hard and to continue to work hard. In researching and studying the topic, Tracy found, as did I, that every successful person will invariably tell you that the secret to their success isn't really a secret at all—it's simply hard work. And hard work requires sacrifice. To be an extreme winner in the future, you must be willing to make sacrifices in the present. Get up earlier, stay later, and when it is time to work, then do just that—work. Don't waste time. Whatever time you have allotted for work or practice, use up every second of that time. Make the most of it. Push yourself.

Jack Nicklaus, in his autobiography *My Story*, said that "achievement is largely the product of steadily raising one's levels of aspiration and expectation."[27] That's just another way of saying that we all need to consistently work at our craft.

One of my heroes, Abraham Lincoln, put it in this poetic way: "I do the very best I know how, the very best I can, and I mean to keep on doing so until the end."[28]

Listen to what other extreme winners have had to say about extreme work and the importance of consistency:

> *"I was determined I was going to outwork everybody, and I worked day and night."*
>
> —Paul "Bear" Bryant, college football coach[29]

> *"I'm working hard because I want to be perfect. I know I'm never going to be perfect, but that helps me work hard every day."*
>
> —Alfonso Soriano, Major League Baseball player[30]

> *"The onliest way I was going to improve myself was by working at the game, working . . . working . . . working."*
>
> —Roy Campanella, Major League Baseball player[31]

> *"Our success [doesn't come] out of a computer. It comes out of the sweat glands of coaches and players."*
>
> —Tom Landry, NFL coach[32]

> *"Work, work, work. Whether a man spends his in an ecstasy or despondency, he must do some work to show for it."*
>
> —Henry David Thoreau, author, poet, philosopher, and naturalist[33]

"There is no such thing as natural touch. Touch is something you create by hitting millions of golf balls."

—Lee Trevino, PGA golfer[34]

"Nothing good comes in life or athletics unless a lot of hard work has preceded the effort. Only temporary success is achieved by taking shortcuts. Set goals and go after those goals with integrity, self-confidence, and a lot of hard work."

—Roger Staubach, NFL quarterback[35]

"Everything that God made valuable in the world is covered and hard to get to. Where do we find diamonds? Deep down in the ground, covered and protected. Where do we find pearls? Deep down at the bottom of the ocean, covered up and protected in a beautiful shell. Where do you find gold? Way down in the mine, covered with layers and layers of rock. You've got to work hard to get to them."

—Muhammad Ali, boxing champion[36]

"Working hard is very important. You're not going to get anywhere without working extremely hard."

—George Lucas, director, screenwriter, and producer[37]

"Nobody who ever gave their best regretted it."

—George Halas, football player, coach, and owner[38]

"If you don't have to work to get something, it probably isn't worth getting."

—John Wooden, college basketball coach

"Nothing will work, unless you do."

—Maya Angelou, author and poet[39]

"Elbow grease is the best polish."

—English proverb

"When you have completed 95 percent of your journey, you are halfway there."

—Japanese proverb

Doc Rivers, who coached for us with the Orlando Magic, had Patrick Ewing on the team during Ewing's final season as a player. Both men had also played together years earlier with the New York Knicks, so Doc was very familiar with Patrick's work ethic. He was amazed, though, when he saw something Ewing did during his final season, after the team had just gotten back to Orlando on a red-eye from Seattle, arriving at six in the morning. Ewing asked one of Doc's assistant coaches, Johnny Davis, to meet him at the gym.

"When?" Davis asked. "Later this evening?"

"No," Ewing replied. "Now."

So the two men went straight from the airport to our team's sports complex and practiced for an hour and a half.

"This is one of the 50 greatest players of all time at the end of his career," Doc Rivers marveled, "and he's working on his game. In fact, we had two days off before our next game and Patrick was there in the gym both days."

When Doc coached our Magic team, Ewing was on our roster along with a 7-foot rookie center named Steven Hunter. One day, Doc gave Hunter a call.

"Where were you yesterday?" he asked.

"What do you mean?" Hunter replied. "We had the day off."

Said Rivers, "Patrick Ewing didn't take the day off."

Steven Hunter wasn't the only rookie who had to learn what extreme work is, and how the extreme winners possess that attitude. My late friend Dr. Jack Ramsay once told me a story about bringing his Portland Trail Blazers' NBA team into Boston to play a game against the Celtics. "It was two hours before the game, and as we walked down the corridor toward the visitors' locker room, we could hear the swish of the net and an occasional bounce of the ball. One of my rookies asked what was going on, and without looking I told him it was Larry Bird getting ready for the game."

Eventually, as they got closer, they could see through the tunnel into a dimly lit court, and what they saw was a lone player shooting the ball and a ball boy retrieving it, over and over again. It was Larry Bird.

Allow me to remind you of that quote from Michael Jordan: "Championships are won while the stands are empty." That's Michael Jordan. That's Patrick Ewing. That's Larry Bird. They're all extreme winners.

You might believe that just working at something and being consistent at it is enough—but please don't think that. Think instead of what Thomas Alva Edison once said: "Being busy does not always mean real work. The object of all work is production or accomplishment and to either of these ends there must be forethought, system, planning, intelligence, and honest purpose as well as perspiration. Seeming to do is not doing."[40]

We like to call this working smart.

The late businessman James J. "Jimmy" Ling would often say: "Don't tell me how hard you work. Tell me how much you got done."[41]

In other words, working is not necessarily *working*. I've seen people, and you have too, sit in an office all day, staying busy, but accomplishing very little. They are expending energy, but they're really not putting an honest effort into what they're doing. The type of effort you put into your work can make all the difference.

I'm going to refer to Brian Tracy again. He said, "One of the most important habits you can develop . . . is the habit of working all the time when you work."[42] Tracy likes to quote an international placement agency called Robert Half International, which found that "the average employee works only 50 percent of the time. The other 50 percent of working time is largely wasted. It is spent in idle chitchat and conversation with coworkers, late arrivals, extended coffee breaks and lunches, and early departures. It is dribbled away making private phone calls, reading the newspaper, taking care of personal business and surfing the Internet. Only 50 percent of the time for which the average person is paid is actually spent on work-related activities."

If you're not going to put a 100 percent effort into the time you spend working, then chances are you're going to do the other thing that statistics have uncovered.

"Even worse," Tracy continued in his analysis, "when the average employee is actually working, he or she does the tasks that are fun and easy rather than the jobs that are hard and important. Most people major in the minors and work on low-priority activities. When you discipline yourself to focus on high-priority tasks and make every minute count, you will immediately separate yourself from everyone else and take full control of your career and your future."[44]

People notice effort. People appreciate effort. People remember effort. "I was a lousy football player," Richard Nixon observed years after his playing days at Whittier College were long over. "But I remember Chief Newman, our coach, saying, 'There's one thing about Nixon. He plays every scrimmage as though the championship were at stake.'"[45]

Eddie Payton played for four NFL teams in his five-year pro career, which meant he wasn't nearly as famous as his younger brother, the late Hall of Famer Walter Payton. From 1975 to 1987, Walter Payton played for the Chicago Bears and missed only one game. Walter wasn't very big, though. He was generously listed at 5-foot-10 and 200 pounds in media guides, yet he played big enough for Mike Ditka to call him the greatest football player he had ever seen. Ditka wrote the foreword to a book Eddie wrote about his brother, which he titled *Walter & Me*. In that book, Eddie focused on what we all already knew about Walter Payton—his extreme work ethic. But he got specific in that he talked about the effort Walter put into his work.

"I think Walter would most like to be remembered for the type of effort he gave every play," Eddie wrote. "He played like it was maybe his last play. He wanted that for people who watched, who may never get a chance to watch him again. He wanted to be remembered for giving his best on every play. It's amazing, when you go out and people see you do your best effort all the time and you do that in a professional manner with respect for the game, it seems to help you rise above the average guy who does something average, jumps up, pounds himself on the chest and says, 'Look what I just did.' Fifty thousand people say, 'You just did what you were paid to do.' Walter never did that. People appreciated him for the blue-collar effort he had and the manner in which he did it.

"He never really talked to me specifically about how he would like to be remembered. All he said was that he wanted to perform for the guy sitting in row double PP of the stadium, who works nine-to-five for minimum wage and brings his family, and that's the only place he can afford to sit. I want him when he leaves to say, 'I saw Walter Payton at his best.'"[46]

That's the way Arnold Palmer, winner of seven major golf titles, approached things. "I've always made a total effort," Palmer said, "even when the odds seemed entirely against me."[47]

Wayne Gretzky learned the value of effort the hard way, and it came when he was already an NHL superstar with the Edmonton Oilers, on his way to becoming the game's greatest player. The lesson arrived during the Stanley Cup Finals against the New York Rangers. Gretzky had just had another amazing regular season, scoring 71 goals while also getting a record 125 total assists to compile 196 points, which was good enough to win him his fourth Hart Trophy (given annually to the player judged most valuable to his team) and third Art Ross Trophy (given to the points leader). Gretzky's father wasn't all that impressed. Instead, what caught the elder Gretzky's attention is the way his son practiced when the Oilers were down 3–0 in the Finals to the Rangers.

"Why did you practice today?" his father asked him.

"Because we had to."

"Well, you shouldn't have," his father said. "You just wasted your time and theirs. You didn't give an effort."

It painfully showed in the next game, with the Oilers losing 4–2 to the Rangers and thus losing the Finals in a four-game sweep. The two men never talked about their exchange after that practice until later that summer, when they were at Wayne's grandmother's house and the old lady was hard at work in the yard.

"Look!" his father said, pointing to the woman. "Seventy-nine, and she's still working hard. You are 23, and when you're in the Stanley Cup Finals you won't even practice."

In remembering that lesson, Gretzky ruminated years later that it was a turning point. "Ever since then, the highest compliment anyone can give me is to say that I worked hard every day."[48]

Gretzky obviously passed that wisdom along to his son Trevor, who is a minor leaguer in the Los Angeles Angels' system. In the summer of 2015, I read an AP story about the younger Gretzky, who had this to say about his father and the work ethic he instilled in him: "All pro sports are the same. You work hard, and the guys who work the hardest and play the hardest come out on top. He's been telling me that since I was a little kid."

So work hard. Every day. Put effort into your work. Do a little more than you think you could. The railroad baron Edward H. Harriman once said, "Much good work is lost for the lack of a little more."[49] And be consistent. You'll be amazed at what you can accomplish and the goals you'll reach. The work-ethic motto that the Hall of Fame wide receiver Jerry Rice relied on simply said this: "Today I will do what others won't do, so tomorrow I can accomplish what others can't."

I'll leave you now with a poem from another man named Rice, Grantland Rice, who was one of America's great sportswriters. Rice was also a poet, and in many of his columns he would add poetry to his prose. This is Grantland Rice's poem titled "How to Be a Champion."

You wonder how they do it,
You look to see the knack,
You watch the foot in action,
Or the shoulder or the back.
But when you spot the answer
Where the higher glamours lurk,
You'll find in moving higher
Up the laurel-covered spire,
That most of it is practice,
And the rest of it is work.

Chapter 6

EXTREME RESPONSIBILITY

"We have so much room for improvement. Every aspect of our lives must be subjected to an inventory . . . of how we are taking responsibility."

—Nancy Pelosi, congresswoman [1]

Mike Krzyzewski is known as one of the all-time great college basketball coaches. He's been at Duke University since 1980, where he's won nearly 80 percent of his games. Winning, and winning consistently in the ultra-tough Atlantic Coast Conference, is quite a feat. But Krzyzewski hasn't just won, he's been an extreme winner—capturing five NCAA Championships and twice leading the USA to gold medals in the Olympic Games. In 2006, while still an active coach, Krzyzewski was inducted into the College Basketball Hall of Fame.

Accomplishing those many things and more, as well as the consistency Krzyzewski has displayed, requires a lot of character. But if you ask Krzyzewski what he thinks one of his foremost character traits is, he'll tell you that it's being responsible, it's being accountable. That might not sound like much. It might not sound as if it should be that important. But if you want to be an extreme winner, then extreme responsibility is a must.

Mike Krzyzewski learned that lesson when he was a plebe, a freshman, at the United States Military Academy at West Point. I've heard him tell the story of when he was just a 17-year-old kid from the tough South Side of Chicago, just learning the ropes as a cadet. At West Point, your uniform is required to be immaculate and your shoes always brightly shined, and that's just the way a young Mike Krzyzewski was dressed one morning on a cold, wintery January day. But while walking across campus, his roommate stepped in a puddle of mud and splashed it all over Mike's shoes.

Suddenly, Mike had a decision to make—should he go back to his dormitory room and rectify the situation, or should he take his chances with dirty shoes so as to make sure he got to his next class on time? Well, as it would be, an officer who was happening by stopped young Mike, and based on the deplorable condition of his shoes, he challenged him.

"Why are your shoes so muddy?" he asked.

"Officer," Mike blurted, "I was just walking across the campus and. . . ."

The officer didn't want to hear it. Instead, he rather pointedly reminded Mike that when challenged at West Point, you only have three responses:

1. Yes, sir.
2. No, sir.
3. No excuse, sir.

Since then, they have added a fourth response for a newer generation of West Point cadets. And that response is:

4. I do not understand, sir.

But back then, it was just the three, and in this case there was no excuse. After receiving demerits, Krzyzewski returned to his dormitory room furious over what had happened and especially furious with his roommate. But he calmed down and later, after several more weeks of training, he began to see more clearly what had happened and how he could benefit from it.

"When my roommate stepped in that puddle and splashed mud on my shoes, I had a choice to make," Krzyzewski said. "What my roommate did is something I had no control over, but the next event was my decision to make."

Today, Mike Krzyzewski is in his late 60s, and he would tell you that that event on the campus of West Point was a turning point in his life. Ever since then he has adopted this philosophy and clung to it: *This has been done well and I did it. This was done poorly and I did it. But either way I am responsible.* That's his belief system with life, and as Duke's basketball coach, he goes by this credo: "No matter what happens, it's my team. I'm responsible. There is no excuse. That's how I feel and that's how I act."

Responsibility, accountability, taking ownership of who we are and what we do . . . those are not popular topics in today's excuse-making culture. We live in a world of passing the buck and shifting the blame and taking credit for success but disappearing when there is failure. But I'm here to tell you that if you want to be an extreme winner, then you have to have extreme responsibility. The good news, though, is that you don't have to go to West Point to acquire it (although it definitely seems to help).

For years now, I've been hearing college coaches tell me that the lack of responsibility and accountability among students and student-athletes are growing concerns in the classroom and on the courts and sports fields. Because of that, we're seeing that it's also a growing concern in society. Unfortunately, all too often, that mind-set starts at home. When I was a youngster, if you were disciplined at school you got further disciplined at home. But now, parents blame educators or make excuses when their child is a discipline problem, which is why I feel that we've raised a generation that is largely unaccountable and irresponsible.

And when I tell you that college coaches—and also educators—tell me that responsibility and accountability are growing concerns, it's not hyperbole. Listen to what former college basketball coach John Thompson has to say:

> "The biggest problem that I see in college athletics is that the kid is never made responsible for his own actions, and he knows that and he plays it like the piano," John Thompson once told me on one of my radio shows, back when he was Georgetown University's basketball coach. "He knows that regardless of what happens with him, there is always somebody else that he can blame and the public will accept it. The most important thing you can give a child is a sense that he is responsible for himself with no excuses, regardless of the source of the problem. Then you'll be dealing with a strong kid.
>
> "All this crisis legislation in college sports in a sense stems from the kid having a lessened sense of responsibility for their own destiny. We blame everyone but the person who is most at fault. The colleges are part of the problem. The coaches are part of the problem. But nobody wants to go to the heart of the issue and say, 'This kid is a jerk. He needs to work harder.'"

Thompson said those things years ago, when news reports were churning out stories of kids killing other kids for a pair of Nike Air Jordan shoes. Thompson noted how fingers were pointing everywhere except where they needed to be pointed.

"I'll tell you how ridiculous it's gotten," Thompson said. "You hear people blaming Michael Jordan and John Thompson and Spike Lee when some kid goes out and shoots somebody to get a pair of tennis shoes. And the kid says, 'I never would have done it if I hadn't seen Michael Jordan wearing those shoes on TV.' Anybody who grew up in the streets knows that's bull. You wouldn't sell a lame excuse like that to one person in Northeast D.C. They'd laugh in your face if you said Spike Lee made you shoot somebody.

"The solution is for adults to get in their face and say, 'You got to get it done.' That doesn't mean we don't need social programs and more equality and opportunity. But the individual kid better understand that charity runs out fast. He'd better take responsibility for his life and survive."

John Chaney, who was the longtime basketball coach at Temple University, didn't believe he could depend on a player until he saw that they were responsible. He told me about a speech he once made to his players, telling them:

"I'm going on a recruiting trip next week. And guess what? My bag is already packed. It's got my clothes, my shirts, my socks, a toothbrush. And guess what? I don't even trust it. So I look in there, just to make sure. It's got a magazine in there and I don't even read it now. I'm saving it, so I have something to read on the train. And some of you guys, you have games and one sneaker's on the floor and one's on the bed, and you don't put your jockstrap in the bag. And I see you sneaking around in the locker room, going to the trainer, 'I forgot this. I forgot that.'"

Then Chaney added the punch line like a punch in the gut.

"Well, I wanna know who that is, because that guy is gonna cause me to lose games. He's the one who's not going to take a shot. When it comes time to take a big shot, he's not gonna do the job like he's supposed to. He's gonna fail, because that guy has already practiced failing."

He knew, like you should know, that extreme winners take responsibility. I've seen that again and again in sports and in life. As a former athlete in a team sport and now an NBA executive, I really appreciate the attitude of one of the great American female soccer players, Mia Hamm, who said: "I've worked too hard and too long to let anything stand in the way of my goals. I will not let my teammates down and I will not let myself down."[2]

Allow me again to refer you to a West Point product, though someone not as famous as Mike Krzyzewski. Retired Major General Joseph Franklin built a business called Frequency Electronics based on what is called the West Point Way. Those who are responsible, Franklin noted, live by honesty and integrity, which is something that is absolutely instilled in cadets at the academy. In fact, at West Point there is a Cadet Prayer that states: "Choose the harder right instead of the easier wrong."

This, Franklin says, should especially be true of those in leadership roles. Responsibility and accountability should start at the top.

To emphasize this, Franklin tells a story of something that once happened at West Point. One day, a senior came across a written authorization that evidently had been dropped on the ground. The authorization gave him privileges he shouldn't have had, and the senior knew it. But instead of doing the right thing, he took advantage of them. When the transgression was discovered, the senior was expelled. Franklin points out that in a similar situation, an underclassman might've been given a break, simply because he was likely still in the process of learning how to be responsible, how to do the right thing. But by the time you're a senior at West Point, you should know better. The same, he says, goes for business and for life.

Elizabeth Cady Stanton, an early leading figure in the women's rights movement, once said: "Nothing strengthens the judgment and quickens the conscience like individual responsibility."

There certainly must be something about West Point graduates that instills that kind of extreme responsibility because I can't imagine taking responsibility for anything more serious than the lives of other humans *and* the fate of a nation. But that's what West Point graduate and future general and president Dwight D. Eisenhower did.

June 6, 1944, wasn't just another day in human history. It's a day we've come to know as D-Day, the day the Allied forces invaded Normandy, France, during World War II. It was the largest seaborne invasion in history and obviously a pivotal battle in the war. But the day before D-Day, on June 5, 1944, General Eisenhower sat down and wrote a note that said if the invasion went wrong, it would be his fault. Then he stuck the note in his wallet. "He accepted responsibility even before it started," Alan Axelrod, author of the book *Eisenhower on Leadership*, told *Investor's Business Daily* in an interview. "He never blamed anyone else, but he also wanted to make sure those involved in the victory got credit for it."[3]

Impressive, isn't it? Perhaps it was Dwight Eisenhower whom British Prime Minister Winston Churchill was thinking of when he said that "the price of greatness is responsibility."[4] Either way, Churchill's statement is a profound one.

When you talk about extreme winning, it obviously doesn't get any bigger than the Allies winning that decisive victory at D-Day. But in everyday life, there are smaller victories to be won. And when you take extreme responsibility seriously, and you do so on a day-to-day basis, it can lead to big results.

That's the way Cal Ripken Jr. approached things. Ripken now holds the Iron Man record, playing in a string of 2,632 consecutive Major League Baseball games, breaking the previous record of 2,130 consecutive games played without a day off, which was set by the immortal Lou Gehrig. But do you know what fueled Ripken's durability? Answer: responsibility.

"My approach to the game was not to break Lou Gehrig's record of consecutive games," Ripken has said on different occasions. "It really was a culmination of many one-game streaks. I always felt that when you came to the ballpark, my responsibility to the team was to be available to the manager to play."

Notice that key word—*responsibility*.

Ripken said that the sense of responsibility to his teammates, and to his manager, was something his father instilled in him, adding that it was "one of those things that I felt was right principally. I felt that every player in the big leagues should come to the ballpark, and if the manager wants you to play and puts you in the lineup, you try to perform as well as you can and try to do the job. That was the approach I had."[5]

It's the type of approach that managers and coaches notice, and also greatly appreciate. They don't want excuse makers on their teams. They want players who are responsible and accountable.

Hall of Fame football coach Bill Parcells won two Super Bowls with the New York Giants with Phil Simms as his quarterback. Simms probably doesn't get the kind of credit and recognition normally afforded to two-time Super Bowl–winning quarterbacks. But to Parcells, Simms was gold. And Parcells told me why:

"The thing I loved about Phil Simms . . . is that he never made an excuse," Parcells said. "If something went wrong, he took it on his own shoulders. It was always his fault. Even if the receiver did something wrong, Phil would say, 'Hey, I'll get it to you. Try to deepen that route up a little bit,' or 'I was late with the throw' . . . even if he knew he was on time with the throw. He would make everyone around him feel that they were doing well, and he was the one who was holding them back. His teammates respected him for that."

I'm sure another Hall of Fame coach, Don Shula, would've loved having Phil Simms on his team. "The superior man blames himself," Shula once said, perhaps quoting Confucius. "The inferior man blames others."[6]

The amazing thing that I find really remarkable about Phil Simms is that he took responsibility to a higher level—to a really extreme level. Obviously, taking responsibility for one's own mistakes is rare today, but to take responsibility for someone else's shortcomings . . . that says something.

But that's what great leaders do.

Harry Truman's presidency wasn't viewed as significant in real time. But now, in looking back, most historians agree that he was one of our most effective presidents. As Franklin D. Roosevelt's vice president,

Truman definitely operated in the shadows. But when Roosevelt died, the spotlight shifted to Truman like an intense heat lamp. Truman was awed by the responsibility of the office, but he didn't shy away from it. Not hardly. His attitude was reflected by a little sign with four big words that he kept in prominent display on his desk: The Buck Stops Here.

That phrase has become synonymous with the man and his presidency. Truman never ducked responsibility or tried to shovel off his duties onto someone else. He wasn't one to make excuses. In fact, he never seemed to worry about being blamed for making mistakes. Many leaders are paralyzed by the fear of making mistakes. But if you have extreme responsibility, you don't fret about that. You simply do your best, and if it doesn't work, you own up to it. When you have that type of attitude, it really takes pressure off you rather than putting pressure on you. Ironically, that fed into Truman's other famous phrase: If you can't stand the heat, get out of the kitchen.

Truman's attitude reminds me of something Brian Tracy has said: "When you exert your self-discipline and willpower in the acceptance of personal responsibility for your life, you take complete control of your thoughts and feelings. By doing so, you become a much more effective, happy, and positive person in everything you do."[7]

Bobby Unser of the famous Unser racing family is one of 10 drivers to have won the Indianapolis 500 three or more times, but the only one to have won the most prestigious of all open-wheel races in three different decades. He ascribes to what he calls the pyramid of success, and he has some interesting theories about it.

"As you climb the pyramid of success, the space gets smaller," Unser has said. "As the space shrinks, you'll find some people quit climbing, while others get knocked off for one reason or another. I won't discuss quitting, because I don't know what that means. When it comes to getting knocked off the pyramid, there are many reasons. One of them is people aren't as accountable or responsible as they ought to be. They push accountability off on other people or other things. What they don't realize is that, by doing so, they are jeopardizing their ascent; not helping it. To get to the very peak of any profession requires accepting ever more levels of accountability and responsibility."[8]

Interesting comments from Bobby Unser, wouldn't you say? In fact, Unser is extremely passionate about being accountable and responsible. Just listen to what else he has to say:

> "It's not bad to fall, because everybody falls. You just don't want to fall too far. When things go wrong, as they sometimes do, if you are accountable you don't fall so far."[9]

As an example, when the Enron Corporation scandal erupted, Unser predicted that its leaders would fall far—very far, in fact—and that their climb back would be nearly impossible. That's exactly what happened. And remember, Enron was not just an elite energy company; it was an elite company—period. *Fortune* magazine named it "the Most Innovative Company in America" six years in a row. It annually raked in billions of dollars. But the fall of its leaders as a result of its scandal and subsequent bankruptcy was precipitous.

And today?

Former Enron founder, CEO, and chairman Kenneth Lay died of a heart attack. Former Enron president and COO Jeff Skilling is in the middle of a 14-year federal prison sentence. And former Enron CFO Andrew Fastow served a six-year federal prison sentence. All three lives suffered a mammoth fall. And all three skirted accountability and responsibility for what happened with Enron.

> "While trust and integrity [are] about being a person of your word through your actions, accountability and responsibility [are] about accepting the consequences of your actions," Unser said. "Some consequences are good and you get rewarded. Some consequences are bad and you are held responsible to correct the mistake or accept the result as it is. Being accountable is accepting the consequences of the decisions you make and the actions you take. It's not passing the buck or ducking. You learn to

accept a bad result, even if circumstances don't go your way. You can't go back and change the outcome. It's honoring your debts: paying people back what you owe them. It's the responsible delegation of authority; empowering people with responsibility to make decisions and take actions and to be accountable for the results of their decisions.

"The Unser way is not to duck responsibility, but to stand there and accept the consequences. By doing so you will develop a sharper focus, mature and become wiser."[10]

If you're wondering how being responsible can create a sharper focus, listen to what else Bobby Unser has to say.

"Have you ever wondered how people can 'grow up' so quickly when they are thrust into war at the age of 18?" he asked. "Or how suddenly a 16-year-old becomes the 'man' of the family because his parents were killed? You can't help but grow up when you don't have the choice but to grow up.

"Ducking responsibility is not an option. When you're in charge, you're in command. You mature in a hurry when you realize you're in charge, and you do so because you are accountable for your actions. There's no other way to put it. If you aren't accountable, you can't grow. If you don't grow, you'll never be successful. You mature through the process of accepting responsibility. As you learn to accept the outcomes of your actions (i.e., being a responsible person) you become smarter in the ways of living. You gain wisdom. Holding yourself accountable for your actions forces you to look at the deeper meaning of life, not the superficial meaning caused by lawsuits and blaming others for everything that goes wrong."[11]

Unser's thoughts were summed up nicely by Dr. Frank Crane, who was a Presbyterian minister, speaker, and columnist. Said Dr. Crane, "Responsibility is the thing people dread most of all; yet it is the only thing in the world that develops us, gives us manhood or womanhood fiber."[12]

Do you know where lack of accountability and not being responsible for one's actions started? In the Garden of Eden, that's where. When Eve ate of the tree of the knowledge of good and bad, and God questioned her about it, her response was, "The serpent deceived me, so I ate." And when God questioned Adam, he actually tried to shift the blame to God and also to his wife, saying, "The woman whom you gave to be with me, she gave me fruit from the tree, so I ate."[13]

So you can see from that account, from the first man and woman, just how ingrained it is in us to shirk responsibility.

But extreme winners know otherwise. Listen to what some of them have to say:

> *"The man who complains about the way the ball bounces is likely to be the one who dropped it."*
>
> —Lou Holtz, football coach[14]

> *"The greatest lesson of life is that you are responsible for your life."*
>
> —Oprah Winfrey, talk show host, media mogul, and producer[15]

> *"A man can make mistakes, but he isn't a failure until he starts blaming someone else."*
>
> —Sam Rutigliano, football coach[16]

> *"I've always felt it was not up to anyone else to make me give my best."*
>
> —Hakeem Olajuwon, basketball player[17]

> *"Keep your alibis to yourself."*
>
> —Christy Mathewson, baseball player[18]

> *"All my life, and particularly in the last 15 years, I've tried to develop a personal philosophy built on the belief that I cannot be free until I accept responsibility for what I do."*
>
> —Bill Russell, basketball player[19]

> *"In the final analysis, the one quality that all successful people
> have is the ability to take responsibility."*
>
> —Michael Korda, editor and writer[20]

> *"Ninety-nine percent of the failures come from people who have the
> habit of making excuses."*
>
> —George Washington Carver, scientist, botanist, educator, and inventor[21]

I really appreciate that last quote from George Washington Carver, because here was a man who, as John C. Maxwell noted, "was no stranger to adversity and could have easily made excuses for not succeeding. But that wasn't his way."[22]

Maxwell added that even though Carver was "born into slavery, he rose above his circumstances. He earned a B.S. and then an M.S. in agriculture from Iowa State College, and then he dedicated himself to teaching poor African-American farmers. He developed an extension program at Alabama's Tuskegee Institute to take the classroom to the people in the South, teaching agricultural methods and home economics. His research resulted in the development of hundreds of products made from crops, such as peanuts and sweet potatoes. He did all that despite working with limited resources and opportunities because of segregation. Where others might have offered excuses, Carver achieved excellence."[23]

Maxwell often uses George Washington Carver's example in his speeches and sermons:

"Unsuccessful people can always find reasons for why they are not doing well," Maxwell has said. "But successful people don't make excuses even when they could justify them. No matter what the circumstance, they make the best of things and keep moving forward. That's what it means to persevere. E. M. Gray noted, 'The successful person has the habit of doing the things that failures don't like to do. The successful person doesn't like doing them, either. But his dislike is subordinate to the strength of his purpose.' If you've allowed yourself to develop the habit of making excuses, make a commitment to change today. Trading excuses for excellence opens the door to many of the other positive tradeoffs you'll need to make to be successful."[24]

It's not easy. Again, we live in a culture that wants to point fingers in every direction except at oneself.

"We are taught you must blame your father, your sisters, your brothers, the school, the teachers—you can blame anyone, but never blame yourself," said Katharine Hepburn, who won a record four Academy Awards for her film work as an actress. "It's never your fault. But it's always your fault."[25]

It's always refreshing to be around the kind of person who is responsible and accountable. You gravitate to such people. That's the way sportswriter Wilt Browning felt around Hank Aaron.

At a Hall of Fame luncheon years ago, Browning told me a wonderful story about Hank Aaron that occurred back in 1966. Browning was writing for the *Atlanta Journal* at the time, and he was covering an Atlanta Braves–Pittsburgh Pirates game. In that game, the great Roberto Clemente singled to right field, where Aaron was playing. When Clemente took a wide turn, Aaron threw the ball to first, thinking that he'd catch Clemente as he tried to get back to the bag. Instead, Clemente took off for second base, and made it easily there. Later, Clemente scored the first run in what eventually was a 2–1 Pirates victory.

The next night, when Aaron saw Browning in the locker room, he barked at him: "What's the matter? What did I ever do to you?"

Browning was stunned.

"What do you mean?" he asked Aaron. "Have I done something wrong?"

"Listen," Aaron replied. "I read your story today and you never mentioned my name. I made a dumb play last night and you never said a word about it. You praise me when I do well; you have to criticize me when I mess up. If you do that we won't have any problems at all."

When Wilt shared that story with me years later, he was still shaking his head in amazement.

"Can you believe that approach?" he said. "I've never had a player say that to me before or since."

And again, how can you not gravitate toward a person like that? Wouldn't you like to have a man like that on your team? Imagine a team filled with players like that.

In his book, *Parcells: A Football Life*, Hall of Fame coach Bill Parcells recalled how, 10 minutes after his introductory press conference when he became head coach of the New York Giants, co-owner Wellington Mara said to him: "Bill, let's take a walk." Parcells trailed Mara down the stairs toward the team's locker room. Outside that room was a little alcove room. Mara took him in there and on the wall was a small plaque with an inscription on it, attributed to Emlen Tunnell, the first black player ever inducted into the Hall of Fame. The inscription said: "Losers assemble in little groups and complain about the coaches and the players in other little groups, but winners assemble as a team."[26]

I'm sure we've all seen that play out—in sports, in corporate America, in everyday life.

My friend Jay Bilas, the outstanding basketball analyst, has an interesting take on accountability.

"Most players believe that accountability means blame," he told me. "It doesn't. Accountability is being held to the standard you have accepted as what you want, individually and collectively. Trustworthy coaches and teammates can help you be at your best by challenging you to do your best even when you think you can't. For tough players and teams, accountability is an obligation coaches and teammates have to each other."

Jay told me something that Tom Izzo, the Michigan State basketball coach, once told him. Izzo said he was always taught that discipline is the greatest form of love you can show and that part of discipline is accountability. Asked Izzo: Where would a team be if they didn't hold each other accountable, if each player didn't take personal responsibility?

How true the quote is from French philosopher Voltaire, who is credited with saying: "No snowflake in an avalanche ever feels responsible."[27] But, of course, each snowflake does carry a measure of responsibility. And collectively, all those many snowflakes together carry much force. Sort of like teamwork.

One of the all-time great teammates was Steve Young, who plied a Hall of Fame career as the San Francisco 49ers quarterback. Listen to what he has to say:

> "Accountability! That's the big thing for me," Young said. "If you can breed that into a group of people it's amazing what you can accomplish. If every lineman, every wide receiver, every equipment manager, every traveling secretary, and everyone else on the team feels that if they do their job to the best of their ability the team will win . . . that's when you've got a really good shot at actually winning it. You need that buy-in from everybody, from top to bottom. It's rare, but when you achieve that it's pretty amazing.
>
> "With the 49ers we had accountability from the owner on down. There are certain elements that you have to have in order to be champions in this business, and the 49ers had them. You have to have the element of respect or love for each other that is built through breaking down cultural barriers that human beings have naturally. The organization has to be responsible to do that, to bring people together."[28]

Young said that the 49ers' culture started with accountability, and he learned about the concept of shared accountability through his 49ers' coach, Bill Walsh. Young was raised by his father to be accountable. He also came from a large family, and as the oldest sibling he was used to taking responsibility for others. But after taking over at quarterback for the legend that was Joe Montana, Young initially struggled. Walsh came to him one day and had a talk.

"Look," the coach said, "you're stealing accountability from others, and teams play much better if everyone is held accountable."

Said Young, "He helped me to understand that in a team setting everyone has to hold themselves accountable."[29]

Ron Gardenhire, the former manager of the Minnesota Twins, tells a story about one of his favorite players—Justin Morneau. It was the first exhibition game during the spring of 2009, and afterward Gardenhire found a note on his desk from Morneau. "Gardy," it said, "I forgot to run sprints after the workout yesterday. I'm fining myself." Next to the note was $100.[30] How's that for being accountable? Keep in mind that Morneau was the American League MVP in 2006. He could've tried to big-time it. But he didn't. He held himself accountable. He was responsible.

Again and again, we see that if you want to be an extreme winner, you have to have extreme responsibility and accountability.

Jim Collins is one of the foremost company consultants, and whenever he is working with one of his clients, this is a message he consistently tells them:

> "One notable distinction between wrong people and right people," he said, "is that the former see themselves as having 'jobs,' while the latter see themselves as having responsibilities. Every person in a key seat should be able to respond to the question, 'What do you do?', not with a job title, but with a statement of personal responsibility. 'I'm the one person ultimately responsible for x and y. When I look to the left, to the right, in front or in back, there is no one ultimately responsible but me, and I accept that responsibility.'"[31]

Hal Urban is an educator, writer, and speaker. One day in his classroom, he discovered that his students were being affected by a crippling disease that was preventing them from living as they were meant to live. He knew the disease was both deadly and highly contagious and that it also was a quiet killer. In fact, he doubted that any of his students even knew that they'd been infected. That's when he decided to do something about it.

"I told them there was an epidemic of EFWIC disease going around," Urban said.

The response was puzzled looks and a chorus of "huhs?"

He then told them that EFWIC was an acronym for "Excuses For Why I Can't."

The class was still puzzled.

That's when Urban rolled out about six feet of butcher paper and tacked it onto the wall, telling his class, "Every time you catch yourself making an excuse today, or hear anyone else making one, I want you to write it down. Tomorrow when you come in here, write all your excuses on this paper, which we'll call the 'Master Excuse List.'"

The next morning, the butcher paper filled up so fast that he needed to extend it a couple of more feet. The exercise continued throughout the week until the whole wall was covered with excuses for why people thought they couldn't do things. That's when Urban asked the class if anyone could explain why he considered habitual excuse making a deadly disease. For the first time that semester, the quietest kid in the classroom raised his hand.

"If we're always looking for excuses for why we can't do things," he said, "we'll never find the reason why we can."

"Hallelujah!" Urban exclaimed, raising his arms overhead, overjoyed at the comment. He added, "Those are as good as any words to live by that I've ever heard."[32]

And they are. Extreme winners are extremely responsible. And as Hal Urban's class and a young plebe named Mike Krzyzewski learned, extremely responsible people don't make excuses. *You* are responsible. *You* are responsible for *you* and for those who depend on *you*. *You* are responsible for *your* actions and you are responsible for the outcome of those actions. "Sooner or later everyone sits down to a banquet of consequences," said the writer Robert Louis Stevenson.[33] Or as another writer, Albert Camus, put it: "Life is the sum of all your choices."[34]

In closing, let me remind you of one of our favorite stories in American history, the one that concerns one of our Founding Fathers—George Washington. As the story goes, when he was a boy, young George chopped down a cherry tree. Later, after seeing what happened, George's father approached him.

"Who chopped down the cherry tree?" he asked.

According to lore, George replied: "I cannot tell a lie—it was I who chopped down the cherry tree."

Think about American culture today, and how we live in an age of spin doctors and apologists and professional excuse makers. We seem to have forgotten the words of another Founding Father, Benjamin Franklin, who said: "He that is good at making excuses is seldom good at anything else."[35] The spin doctoring and the blame shifting and the excuse making are a pervasive problem today. But it doesn't have to be with you. Take responsibility. Be accountable. And do those things to the extreme level. If you do, you'll be on your way to becoming an extreme winner.

Chapter 7

EXTREME POSITIVE ATTITUDE

"The difference between people who are skillful and merely successful, and the ones who win, is attitude. The attitude a person develops is the most important ingredient in determining the level of success."

—Pat Riley, basketball player, coach, and executive [1]

ome years ago, I called a news conference in Orlando and announced my resignation as the General Manager of the World. I explained to the media that for many, many decades I had been attempting to run the World. But I realized I wasn't getting the job done. Starving children in Africa, multiple wars daily plaguing the world, global warming, economic disparity, racial and religious strife . . . and on and on. As General Manager of the World, I simply wasn't getting the job done.

So I announced to the media that I was turning in my resignation, and I shared with them that from that day forward I was going to focus on the only thing in life I had any control over. It took me 60-plus years of living, I said, but I had finally figured out what the one thing was that I had control over.

My attitude.

Every minute of every day I, and only I, get to pick my attitude. I also get to choose the thoughts that feed my attitude. And what I've learned is that it's vital to pick a good one. I get to decide whether I'm going to have a good attitude or a bad attitude. And having a good attitude, I've learned, makes all the difference.

Of course, that story is fictitious. But the point it makes is real.

The extreme winners are constantly in a position where they're picking the attitude they're going to have. They consistently choose a good outlook, a positive approach to life. It's not something that is mandated; nobody is forcing them. It comes from within. And they've learned that with a good attitude and positive outlook, you can accomplish so much more than you ever thought. You can be significantly better in everything you do.

If you're going to be an extreme winner, you're going to have to over-come, and to overcome you're going to have to maintain and nurture a positive attitude. And that takes ongoing effort and work. Controlling your body is easy when compared to controlling your mind.

The great industrialist Andrew Carnegie once said that "a man who acquires the ability to take full possession of his own mind may take pos-session of anything else to which he is justly entitled."[2]

And John C. Maxwell, a leader in life-coaching skills, has shared this profound observation with me: "The major difference between successful and unsuccessful people is how they think."

In other words, the major difference between those who don't win and those who are the extreme winners so often resides in that six-inch piece of real estate that rests between the ears.

Several years ago, I came across some eye-opening statistics that I jot-ted down and saved. They came from a study on how the mind thinks. It pointed out that we average 60,000 thoughts a day. Of those thoughts, 40 percent focus on the future and 99 percent of those thoughts dwell on wor-rying about future concerns that never happen. The study also found that some 30 percent of the thoughts are about the past, which we know we can't change or do anything about. Another 12 percent are thoughts filled with doubt, and an additional 10 percent are worries about our health.

In other words, the study found that 92 percent of our thoughts are not pictures of our reality.

Ninety-two percent.

That left only 8 percent of our thoughts about things that were really happening. Those are staggering statistics, and it should tell us something.

When we waste our thoughts like that, we waste our time. And if we're not careful, we can waste our lives.

Norman Vincent Peale is generally regarded as the man who brought positive thinking to the masses. He authored *The Power of Positive Think-ing*, the landmark best seller which is something of a bible on the topic, selling more than seven million copies in 15 languages. But Norman Vin-cent Peale didn't arrive at positive thinking naturally. He had to push himself. As a young man, he wanted to become a preacher. But there was a problem, and it was a big one. He was petrified of public speaking. Realizing that the paralyzing fear of public speaking was all in the mind, he trained himself to think positively and found that it worked. He conditioned himself to replace negative thoughts, such as "I can't" and "I'm afraid," with positive thoughts. And not just general, abstract positive thoughts, either. Rather, he committed himself to having a positive word about everything. Norman Vincent Peale was also a pioneer in practicing visualization. He would rehearse his talks with confidence while imagining a receptive audience before him.

Eventually, he became one of the foremost motivational speakers the world has ever known. And in his 95 years, he wrote 46 books, started *Guideposts* magazine, influenced and inspired millions, and was awarded the Presidential Medal of Freedom.

Among some of my favorite quotes from Norman Vincent Peale are those that concern the way we think and act on our thoughts:

★ "The person who sends out positive thoughts activates the world around him positively, and draws back to himself positive results."[3]

★ "Shoot for the moon. Even if you miss, you'll land among the stars."[4]

★ "Change your thoughts and you change the world."[5]

★ "What the mind can conceive and believe, and the heart desire, you can achieve."[6]

★ "When you get up in the morning, you have two choices—either to be happy or to be unhappy. Just choose to be happy."[7]

How important are your thoughts to success? In his classic bestselling book, *As a Man Thinketh*, James Allen made this observation: "All that a man achieves or fails to achieve is the direct result of his thoughts."[8] That was the book John C. Maxwell read when he was fourteen. The entire book was a life-changer for him, but particularly that quote. When he became a personal-development coach, Maxwell wrote in one of his own books that Allen's statement made him realize that his own thoughts could make or break him. So he decided to adopt this motto: "I will think on things that will add value to myself and others."[9]

Maxwell is also a big proponent, as I am, of the belief that if you want to become a great thinker, you first need to become a good thinker. And in order to become a good thinker, you need to become a thinker. In other words, if you want your brain to work properly for you, then you need to exercise your mind. Albert Einstein would spend days, weeks, months pondering a problem. One problem. But look at us now. We're a nation sliding into a collective attention deficit disorder with all our electronic gadgets and their constant drain on our ability to focus and stay focused. When it comes to our ability to focus and concentrate, the inability to do so weakens our mind. And when it comes to our mind and our thoughts, we don't want any weaknesses.

"I believe the brain is like a muscle," said the tennis great Ivan Lendl. "And like any other, it can be improved."[10]

I agree.

In fact, my agreement with Lendl on this topic is passionate. I tell you that because this next paragraph might sound like a digression, but I assure you it isn't.

People who know me know my passion for reading, and I understand that not everybody shares that same passion. But I firmly believe that one of the best ways to keep our brains alert and strong is to be a lifelong reader. I'm not saying that all extreme winners are voracious readers, but I would encourage them to be that. The more exercise you give that muscle in your cranium, the better it's going to perform, particularly under pressure. The best way to do that is to attach a book to it. I truly believe that. I'm very bullish on encouraging people of all stripes, of all skills, to make a commitment to be lifelong readers. And I encourage you to do so too, from good books, from books you enjoy. Select books on topics you find fascinating. If you read an hour a day, then at the end of one week you'll have read a book. In a year, that's 52 of them. Ten years, 520 books. That's going to do wonders for that muscle in your skull.

Again, I know not everybody is a reader, but I would encourage you to invest some effort in it. And I would encourage everybody to exercise, not just your body, but also your mind. Never stop learning, particularly in your pursuits, your passions, your occupation, and your craft. The interesting thing about that is the more you learn, the more you realize how much there is yet to learn. That shouldn't discourage you. Rather, it should excite you. Approach what you do with endless curiosity. Nobody knows it all, but chances are there is someone out there who knows something more than you or perhaps has a different way of looking at the same thing you're looking at. Tap into that.

Martin Scorsese, who is one of the most influential filmmakers in history, gives this advice for up-and-coming directors: "I tell the younger filmmakers and young students to do it like the painters used to do it, or painters do: study the old masters, enrich your palette, expand your canvas. There's always so much more to learn."[11]

Attach yourself to experts, ask questions, observe, absorb. As President Woodrow Wilson once said, "I not only use all the brains I have, but all I can borrow."[12]

And while you're at it, share what you've learned with others. Be a teacher. You'd be surprised at how teaching others what you know, not only reinforces those things in your mind, but also forces you to think deeper about what you know. Thus, teaching becomes a form of learning, strengthening your thinking ability, your thought process, and yes, your knowledge of the topic.

Extreme winners are always learning, always sharing. In doing so, they're constantly stimulating and exercising that gray matter between their ears. The power of the mind cannot be overstated. So constantly train it to think positive thoughts, and regularly exercise it with stimulating reading and other ways of keeping it engaged and focused. And believe me, it's never too early to start that process.

I once heard a story about a young boy named Earl who grew up in Los Angeles during the Great Depression of the 1930s. Earl's mother made only $55 a month as a seamstress. But through her example, she showed Earl and his brother the importance of thinking positive thoughts, of being optimistic and cheerful no matter the circumstances. Those early lessons had a profound effect on him, because that young boy named Earl later became known as Earl Nightingale, one of the foremost proponents of positive thinking and the cofounder of Nightingale-Conant, which today is the world's largest publisher of personal development and self-improvement products.

In his bestselling book, *Earl Nightingale's Greatest Discovery*, Nightingale said this: "We can let circumstances rule us or we can take charge and rule our lives from within. A great attitude does much more than turn on the lights in our worlds; it seems to magically connect us to all sorts of serendipitous opportunities that were somehow absent before the change."[13]

It's true. A positive attitude, an optimistic outlook, can open doors you never even knew were shut. Here are a few of my favorite Earl Nightingale quotes about the importance of how we think:

★ "Whatever we plant in our subconscious mind and nourish with repetition and emotion will one day become a reality."[14]

★ "Picture yourself in your mind's eye as having already achieved this goal. See yourself doing the things you'll be doing when you've reached your goal."[15]

★ "Always keep that happy attitude. Pretend that you are holding a beautiful fragrant bouquet."[16]

★ "What's going on in the inside shows on the outside."[17]

A lot of people mistake positive thinking with forcing yourself to think happy thoughts, going through life blithely and blissfully unaware of the reality around you. That's not what it is. Life is hard. Achieving success is difficult. Becoming an extreme winner takes more than one or two qualities. Knowing that in advance means you have to attack the negative before it attacks you. You have to make up your mind—right now—that you're going to approach your life and your passions and your career with the right attitude.

Yes, there are obviously times when you're going to have to put up a front, a façade if you will; a happy face you outwardly show even though on the inside you're sad or perhaps even devastated. That's okay. Get in the habit of doing that. You'll be surprised at how even those times when you put up a front—a positive, upbeat countenance—can have a powerful effect.

"Once you replace negative thoughts with positive ones, you'll start having positive results," said singer-songwriter Willie Nelson.[18]

The sports psychologist Dr. Jim Loehr tells the athletes and corporate businesspeople he works with about what he calls the "Matador Walk." Think of a matador in a bullring, his life on the line, going against an animal that wants to maim and kill him. Is he afraid inside, nervous perhaps, maybe a little unsure? No doubt those thoughts creep into his head. But the matador walks around with extreme confidence, with what Dr. Loehr calls the matador walk—erect, shoulders back. His mind tells his body he's extremely confident and his body feeds that message back to his mind. That's not always easy to do when you're down set point in a tennis match, or facing an 0-2 count against a tough pitcher with two outs in the bottom of the ninth, or approaching your center to take the snap while looking at fourth-and-12 with five seconds left in the fourth quarter, your team trailing by five points.

But Dr. Loehr found, and you will, too, that when your mind commands your body to exude confidence, then your body will feed the same message back to your mind. And those positive, confident thoughts can in turn produce the results that will make you an extreme winner.

This is true in individual endeavors, as well as in leadership.

One of the most positive people sports has known, a man who built his reputation on positive thinking, is the Hall of Fame manager Tommy Lasorda. As a left-handed pitcher, Lasorda only had a brief playing career, but he worked his way up through the Los Angeles Dodgers' organization, eventually being named their manager in 1976. Over the next 21 years, Lasorda led the Dodgers to eight division titles and two World Series Championships. His success, he says, came from his attitude, from the way he thought, and the way he exuded his thoughts and attitude to his players.

"As a leader, the most important thing I did took place at the clubhouse door every day," Lasorda said. "Whether I was tired or discouraged or upset, I'd always put on a different face at the door. It was my upbeat, competitive, confident, enthusiastic face. If my players saw me down and depressed, that would have spread all over the clubhouse. It was the same way if my players saw their manager excited and optimistic. That would infect them and help them to play better."[19]

That's a leader.

And leadership, as we know, comes in all areas of life. So please don't think that thinking positive, confident thoughts is limited to athletics. The late basketball coach Jim Valvano once taught Pete Carroll the power of positive thinking, positive thoughts, and yes, positive words—even on job interviews. Carroll is one of the most upbeat, positive-thinking guys you'll ever meet. And an extreme winner, too. His Seattle Seahawks won Super Bowl XLVIII in 2014 and his Southern Cal Trojans won the BCS National Championship in 2004, making him one of only three coaches (Jimmy Johnson and Barry Switzer are the other two) to win both a Super Bowl and a college football National Championship.

Unbeknownst to many, Pete Carroll is a big basketball fan, and even into his early 60s, he still plays the game. In 1980–1982, Carroll was the defensive coordinator and secondary coach at North Carolina State, a tradition-rich basketball school. It was at that same time when Jim Valvano became North Carolina State's head basketball coach. The two incandescent and effervescent men—a cocksure New Yorker and a cool California kid—gravitated toward each other and became friends. In fact, they were close enough friends that Carroll once confided in Jimmy V that he was preparing for a job interview at another school.

Valvano told Carroll to meet him in his office, where the two men spent a Sunday afternoon talking about how to achieve goals. What Valvano impressed upon Carroll was the value of positive thinking, even in a job interview.

In his book, *Win Forever*, Carroll shares this talk he had with Valvano:

"Coach Jim Valvano told me that my goal should be to walk out of the interview with no negatives. Every comment, phrase, or story must be positive, and I had to be prepared to talk only about things that put me in the best light. No matter what the topic, it was my job to turn every answer into a response that highlighted my strong points. Like his point guard who controlled the court, or my middle linebacker who controlled our defense, I had to control the interview. He taught me that if they ask a question I couldn't answer I shouldn't answer it, but instead find a way to turn the question into something I could talk about comfortably, positively, and honestly. He explained the importance of being disciplined in that setting and avoiding any and all negative thoughts. If I spoke with positivity and confidence, it would be evident that I believed in myself, and that belief was what the interviewer would be looking for."[20]

Though Carroll didn't get that particular job he interviewed for, he never wavered in his belief about speaking and presenting yourself in a positive way. The next job he applied for, he got, and he kept moving up from there, until early in 2014 when he found himself sitting atop the football world.

Positive thoughts not only involve thinking positive thoughts, but visualizing positive scenes—and doing so in detail, in color, with sights and sounds and smells. Yes, you can even make your daydreams productive.

Brian Tracy, a leader in personal development, speaks a lot about positive thinking and the power of the mind, and particularly about positive visualization. "You can accelerate the process of becoming a highly productive person by regularly visualizing yourself as focused and channeled toward high achievement," he says.[21]

In other words, see yourself being successful, see yourself winning. If it's a sales pitch you're making, visualize making it superbly. Hear your words, and hear them not only in your head, but also aloud. See the face of your client, and see it light up. If you're a sprinter, see yourself breaking the tape at the finish line, feel it against your chest. The more sights, sounds, and smells you can incorporate into your visualization, the better.

"See yourself as a highly productive, efficient person," Tracy says. "Feed your subconscious mind with this picture until it is accepted as a command. Remember, the person you *see* is the person you will *be*. Your subconscious mind cannot tell the difference between a real experience and one you vividly imagine. If you create an imaginary picture of yourself performing in an efficient and effective way, your subconscious mind reacts exactly as if that is what you were actually doing at the moment."[22]

It's an interesting subject, and Tracy and many others have studied and researched it thoroughly. What they consistently find is that it consistently works. And they'll also tell you that positive visualization isn't just for athletes. You can flow it into all facets of your life. In whatever area you apply it to—sports, business, personal improvement, speech making, and so forth—you'll find that it's powerful and that it works across all platforms:

"Each time you replay this image of yourself performing at your best," Tracy says, "your subconscious mind records it exactly as if it were happening again. It then adjusts your words, actions, and behavior so that your actions on the outside are consistent with the picture you have created on the inside. Each time you remember an occasion when you were performing at your best, with confidence, your mind imprints it into your self-concept. The more often you see yourself as the very best you can possibly be, the more rapidly this becomes your automatic behavior. You program yourself for success by feeding your mind with positive pictures . . . either images that you create, or repeat pictures of some previous peak performance experience."[23]

Try it. Put it to the test. You'll be amazed.

Bobby Unser, the great open-wheel racer and a three-time Indianapolis 500 winner, learned to tap into the power of the human mind early in his life. When he was only 10, he would fall asleep while vividly dreaming of winning a road race in the Colorado Rockies called Pikes Peak. He learned that visualization and positive thoughts set him up for success. In later life, Unser preached with passion the power of positive thinking, along with positive visualization and goal setting:

"Look at your competition, look at the racetrack, look at the weather," he said. "Somebody's going to win and somebody's going to lose. Visualize all of that: the tires, the air pressure, the chassis. Don't be the guy who sits there and says, 'I don't know how it's going to be today,' and then they just react. The subconscious mind is the biggest energy producer and saver of money and effort that there is. It works for free. It will work all night long. When you go to bed, don't think about the bad stuff on the TV news. Go to sleep thinking about something you want to accomplish. Let the subconscious mind work for free. It's energy efficient."[24]

All those years Bobby Unser practiced those techniques as a boy led to big success as an adult: "When I got older," he said, "I would go to sleep thinking about the road, where it turns to the left, where it turns to the right, which are the fast areas. By the time I was old enough to race, my subconscious mind had worked on it for years."[25]

Positive thinking will help you overcome the unexpected obstacles that invariably arrive in your way. Obviously, none of us can prepare for every scenario. But you can prepare to be prepared to handle in the best way possible whatever obstacle or hurdle or setback might come your way. In other words, know that those things will happen and thus prepare in advance what your attitude will be when those tough times or situations arrive. The earlier you learn this, the better.

Kobe Bryant, the future Hall of Fame basketball player, was four years old when he learned about negative thoughts. He was living in Houston, where his father, Joe "Jellybean" Bryant, was playing for the Rockets in his final NBA season. Kobe had signed up for karate classes at a dojo there:

"One day, the master of the dojo came to me and said he wanted to put me up against a brown belt," Kobe recalled in a *Sports Illustrated* article. "I started crying. I told the master, 'That kid is so much bigger than me. He's so much better than I am.' The master said, 'You fight him!' So I stepped onto the mat, with my headgear on, my shiny red gloves. Kids were sitting all around the perimeter. I was so freaked out. I got my ass kicked, but I did get a couple of good licks in myself, and I remember sitting there at the end thinking, *It wasn't as bad as I feared it would be. It wasn't as bad as I imagined.* I think I realized then that your mind can wander and come up with the worst, if you let it."[26]

Don't let it. Think positive. And again, as it was with Kobe Bryant, the earlier you can learn this, the better.

Along those lines, let me tell you another story of a child. This one was born prematurely on a hot summer day in 1931, in a little hardscrabble West Texas border town named Fabens. That tiny baby boy didn't even weigh two pounds and barely survived his first night. Even still, the doctor said he wouldn't live much longer. His grandmother devised a makeshift incubator, wrapping the baby in blankets, placing him in a shoebox, and then setting him on the oven door. They weren't about to give up on the child.

The little boy had fight in him, they could tell, and soon the days he survived stacked up long enough to where they knew he would live. He grew up, but he never really grew much, only reaching 4 foot 11 and 100 pounds as an adult. Throughout his childhood, because of his small size, other kids picked on him mercilessly, but the one thing Billie always maintained was what he later said was a relentlessly positive attitude. He joined wrestling and boxing teams, plying a perfect record in school. He approached everything with a gritty, can-do spirit. After all, this was a guy who wasn't even supposed to survive his first day on earth. Well, that positive attitude pushed him to overcome obstacles and all the negative comments or looks he ever received.

He worked the family trade, as a sharecropper, one day telling his grandfather that he knew there had to be a better way to make a living, and that he was going to find it. Diminutive and drawn to horses, he became a jockey, first by working his way up from barn hand to an exercise rider and then to an apprentice jockey. Eventually, he became a full-fledged jockey and a great one, plying what eventually became a Hall of Fame trade throughout most of his life. By the time his career was over, he had won 8,833 races and more than $120 million in purses.

Today, William "Bill" Shoemaker is widely regarded as the greatest jockey who ever lived.

In his later years, even after a car accident left him paralyzed from the neck down, Shoemaker still maintained a full life, which included staying busy as a top-notch trainer. Through it all, his positive attitude never wavered. He once told an interviewer, "Sure I've been dealt a bad hand. So I'll just have to play it." There was no feeling sorry, no feeling negative. Shoemaker just kept moving forward with a can-do attitude. It's a wonderful example.

As the great newspaper publisher William Randolph Hearst once said: "You must keep your mind on the objective, not on the obstacle."[27]

That's what the extreme winners do, and that's what you can do.

In addition to battling your own thoughts, you'll often find yourself, like Bill Shoemaker, battling the negative thoughts of others. My colleague in writing this book, Peter Kerasotis, recalls covering the 1991 Sugar Bowl that pitted Notre Dame against the University of Florida. Leading up to that game, the story line was that the Fighting Irish didn't belong there by virtue of their three losses that season, and that the only reason why they made it to the Sugar Bowl to play against a statistically better Florida Gators team was because of the Notre Dame name. Other teams were said to be more deserving.

One night before the game, Notre Dame coach Lou Holtz was out to dinner. Holtz is normally a very positive, upbeat person. One of the

things he has preached is this sentiment: "Attitude is going to be critical the rest of your life. You're going to have people say negative things;
you're going to have people doubt you. Do not be discouraged by the 99
who don't believe in you. Be encouraged by the one person who does.
People are always going to be telling you that you can't do something."[28]
But Holtz's philosophy—and it's obviously a very sound one—was challenged that night before the Sugar Bowl, when Holtz was out to dinner
with his family. And the guy who challenged that philosophy was a waiter.

Holtz recalls that he was in a great mood that night, when the waiter
came over and recognized him.

"You're Lou Holtz, the head coach at Notre Dame, aren't ya?" he said.

"Yes, sir," Holtz replied.

At that point, Holtz took out his pen, thinking the waiter would be
asking for an autograph. Instead, he wanted to ask Holtz a question.

"What's the difference between Notre Dame and Cheerios?" the waiter
queried.

Puzzled, Holtz shook his head.

"I don't have a clue," he replied.

"Cheerios belongs in a bowl," the waiter said. "Notre Dame doesn't."[29]

It was actually the joke that was making the rounds in the weeks
leading up to that bowl game, but Holtz had not heard it, not until that
moment, and he admitted it put him in a bad mood. That's when his
wife, Beth, reminded him of his own philosophy on life, and admonished
him.

"You're going to let somebody you never met before, you're never going
to see again, doesn't care a single thing about you . . . you're going to let
him ruin this evening with your family?" Beth asked. "You're smarter
than that. You can't let other people control your thoughts."

Holtz pondered her words for a moment, and then snapped out of his
funk.

"You're right, honey," he replied. "He's not going to ruin this evening."

From that point forward, Holtz got himself into a great attitude, into
an even better mood than he was in prior to the joke. In fact, the coach

decided to have a little fun of his own. A little while later, Holtz called the waiter back and said he also had a question for him.

"What's the difference between Lou Holtz and a golf pro?" he asked.

"I don't have a clue," the waiter said.

"A golf pro gives tips," Holtz said.

If this were a text message, this is where we'd insert the LOL.

The point is: a potentially bad evening turned into one Holtz likes to laugh about today, retelling the story with good humor. He also used all the negative comments from the waiter and others about Notre Dame not being worthy enough to be in the Sugar Bowl as fuel for motivation. It worked. In that Sugar Bowl game, the Fighting Irish scored a big upset victory against the Gators.

"Life . . . it's not complicated," Holtz often says. "But attitude is critical."

It's so true.

And here is an echoing proverb from Dale Carnegie: "Happiness doesn't depend upon who you are or what you have. It depends solely on what you think."[30]

Something that walks hand-in-hand with positive thinking is optimism. If you have a positive attitude, and you apply it to various obstacles and setbacks you confront, you'll find that overall you'll be an optimistic person. You will have, as *Merriam-Webster's* defines it, "a feeling or belief that good things will happen in the future; a feeling or belief that what you hope for will happen." It is a great way to live, and people with an extreme positive attitude live that way.

Optimistic people are cheerful, upbeat, enthusiastic. They naturally see the good and the potential. They are the opposite of pessimistic people, who are doom and gloom, who always expect the worst and who walk around as if a dark cloud is always hovering overhead. We all know those types of pessimistic people, and we all know what a drag—and I mean that literally—they are to be around. We generally don't want to be around those types of people unless we have to be. But an optimistic person . . . well, we gravitate toward those types of people.

The great Minnesota Twins baseball player Kirby Puckett was that type of optimistic person. In 1996, Puckett was tearing up spring training with a .344 batting average, just days before the regular season was to start. Coming off a season where he hit .314 with 23 home runs and 99 runs batted in, it looked as if he was poised for another stellar year. But Puckett woke up the morning of March 28 without vision in his right eye. The diagnosis was glaucoma, and for the first time in his career he was put on the disabled list. Over the next three months he had three surgeries, attempting to restore vision in his right eye. It didn't work. So on July 12, he announced his retirement. He was only 36.

When he addressed the media, the ever-optimistic Puckett was his effusive, upbeat self.

"Kirby Puckett's going to be alright," he said. "Don't worry about me. I'll show up, and I'll have a smile on my face. The only thing I won't have is this uniform on."

And until the day he died—and way too young, at only 45—Puckett maintained a cheerful, upbeat disposition. At his Hall of Fame induction ceremony, Puckett told the crowd during his acceptance speech: "Don't feel sorry for yourself if obstacles get in your way. I faced odds when glaucoma took the bat out of my hands, but I didn't give in or feel sorry for myself. It may be cloudy in my right eye, but the sun is shining very brightly in my left eye."

What an inspirational, optimistic attitude to have.

Dwight Eisenhower was that way, too. In his book *Eisenhower on Leadership: Ike's Enduring Lessons in Total Victory Management*, author and historian Alan Axelrod shared this about the 34th president and former five-star general: "Just about everyone who knew and worked with Ike Eisenhower identified cheerful optimism as paramount among his leadership traits."[31]

Axelrod went on to relate some insight into that.

"Typical was his conduct during the grave crisis presented by the Battle of the Bulge in December of 1944. Gathering his top commanders for an urgent strategy conference, Ike began the session by saying, 'The present situation is to be regarded as one of opportunity for us and not of disaster. There will be only cheerful faces at this conference table.'"

The conclusion Axelrod reached about Eisenhower is that his "optimism wasn't blind faith and it wasn't a religion. It was simply the only feasible attitude. That's the way it must be for those of us who accept the leadership challenge. Without optimism the sale is lost before the prospect is approached, and the battle is lost before a shot is fired; yet Eisenhower never allowed optimism to stand in for reality."[32]

There are a trove of sayings Eisenhower had about optimism and its evil twin, pessimism. Here are two of my favorites:

★ "Pessimism never won a battle."[33]
★ "Optimism and pessimism are infections, and they spread more rapidly from the head downward than in any other direction."[34]

Eisenhower's British ally during World War II, Great Britain's Sir Winston Churchill, maintained the same optimistic outlook on life. "A pessimist sees the difficulty in every opportunity," Churchill said. "An optimist sees the opportunity in every difficulty."[35]

Be optimistic, and I guarantee you'll discover that optimism consistently trumps pessimism. It wins every time. You might even call optimism an extreme winner.

Steve Whitman, who played for the Alabama Crimson Tide in the late 1970s, once shared with me a wonderful insight into Coach Paul "Bear" Bryant and the optimism he infused into his team at halftime of a game against the Tennessee Volunteers. Alabama went into the locker room trailing their Southeastern Conference opponent 17–0. But what Whitman noticed with Bear Bryant was a coach walking back and forth, gleefully clapping his hands and smiling.

"He kept saying something like, 'This is great! This is great! We've got 'em right where we want 'em'."

Whitman couldn't believe what he was hearing, because not only had Tennessee thoroughly outplayed Alabama during the first half, the Volunteers also held that commanding 17–0 lead:

"Coach Bryant was totally calm, while we were more than a little concerned," Whitman said. "He just walked and clapped and kept talking about us having Tennessee right where we wanted them. I thought he had lost his mind. I thought that he thought that *we* were ahead. Then he started talking about how we had a chance to show what we were made of, a chance to show class. He said we had a chance to show a national audience what we were about. I don't think we talked much about strategy, other than Coach Bryant telling us our game plan was solid; that we just had to execute better."

The last thing Bear Bryant told his players was that if they won the second half there was no doubt they'd prove they had what it took to win a National Championship. Then, just before he left the locker room, Bryant told the team to sit and think about that for a few minutes. With only the players in the room, defensive back Don McNeal leapt to his feet and shouted, "Coach Bryant is right! I'm not going to quit and nobody on this team is going to quit!"

Whitman says the players practically broke down the doors as they exploded out of the locker room, eager for the second half to start. The result was dramatic. Alabama gained 235 second-half rushing yards and, as the expression goes, the Tide rolled to a 27–17 comeback victory. It pushed their record to 6–0, halfway to the 12–0 record and the National Championship they won that season.[36]

This leads me to another thing that positive thinking and optimism feed into, and that's motivation. If you're negative, if you're pessimistic, you're going to be nearly impossible to motivate, as well as motivate others. But if you're optimistic and you have a positive attitude, you'll find this not only feeds into self-motivation, but also the ability to motivate others.

Jim Calhoun, the former basketball coach at the University of Connecticut who won three National Championships, believes that all coaches have to be "a hellacious motivator to develop your talent every day, so that it performs at a peak level. Not a decent motivator or even a good motivator, but a hellacious motivator . . . somebody who is working 24/7 to get his people in a winning frame of mind."[37]

Notice what he ended that statement with: *a winning frame of mind.*

We should all develop that winning frame of mind, doing so with positive thoughts and ebullient enthusiasm and optimism. And while it's good to be motivated and to motivate others, we all need the ability to stoke the flames of motivation that burn within us.

What will help you do that is optimism amplified, which is what I refer to as hope. Hope is what gives your life and work meaning, and we all need meaning—a deep meaning—to our lives and in what we do. The extreme winners have learned that without hope, you cannot exist. Studies tell us that we can go 40 days without food, eight days without water, and four minutes without air. Allow me to add to that with the thought that we can go only two seconds without hope. When hope perishes we are through. Extreme winners always keep hope alive. They're never defeated, even when the odds seem insurmountable. Hope is always there, vibrant and full of vitality. The word "hopeless" isn't even in their vocabulary.

Hopelessness.

To me it's the most depressing word in the English language.

This team is hopeless. My children are hopeless. The situation is hopeless.

The extreme winners never view it that way. There is always, always, always hope. When you have that positive attitude, when you exude optimism, when you always carry hope with you, you'll find that it brings you back to living your life as an ultra motivated person. You won't have to rely on someone else to motivate you. You're self-motivated. It comes from within, and you're constantly fueling the fire.

I'm going to refer to author and historian Alan Axelrod again. Listen to what he wrote about Sir Edmund Hillary, a New Zealander who along with Tenzing Norgay became the first two men to reach the summit of Mount Everest.

Wrote Axelrod: "There was a quality that he admitted set him apart from many others. He expressed it in a single word: motivation. Physical fitness and technical skill were certainly important in mountain climbing, he observed. But a 'sort of basic motivation, the desire to succeed, to stretch yourself to the utmost is the most important factor.'"[38]

Sir Edmund Hillary's source of motivation? Aiming high. He believed it was better to aim high and fail than to aim for the middle and succeed. It was that possibility of failure that fueled his motivation. If he felt certain of success, then he also felt his motivation wane.

"Why do something if you know you will succeed?" he asked.[39]

While I didn't know Sir Edmund Hillary personally, there is no doubt in my mind that he held a positive attitude that he would succeed. There is no doubt in my mind that he was optimistic in his outlook and that he learned everything he could about the task he had at hand. All of that, combined with the specter of failure, motivated him to reach the peak of the highest mountain in the world—Mount Everest.

Make sure you put those same tools in your toolbox, the ones you'll need in order to become an extreme winner—a positive attitude, optimism, being a learner and a teacher, hopefulness, and self-motivation.

If you do, you'll be amazed at the peaks you'll reach.

Chapter 8

EXTREME GOALS

"What keeps me going
is goals."

—*Muhammad Ali, boxer* [1]

The city of Orlando of today is not like the Orlando of the mid-1980s. The Walt Disney World that seems such an established epicenter of entertainment now was only a teenager when I arrived in Orlando in 1986, barely 15 years old. Epcot was not even four years old, scarcely out of diapers. Only a handful of years earlier, the University of Central Florida was known as Florida Tech, a fledgling 23-year-old school playing lower-division college sports. And speaking of lower-division sports, the city itself had never had a true major league sports team. Instead, it had a steady diet of big league wannabe teams playing in alphabet soup acronym sports leagues.

So why would I move to Orlando in June of 1986 thinking I could help bring an NBA franchise to the city? Because, as Chapter 1 tells us, I had an extreme dream. But what was it that made that extreme dream a reality? I hope this chapter will impress upon you the power of extreme goals.

When we announced in the summer of 1986 that we were going to try to bring an NBA team to Orlando, we were viewed as the longest of long shots—both nationally and no doubt also in the NBA league office. So how were we going to get in the hunt? How were we going to get the national media to take us seriously? How were we going to get the NBA's attention?

I'll be honest with you. When I started on that journey in 1986, I didn't know the answer.

But I learned, and I learned quickly, that it was going to take deposits —specifically, $100 deposits on season tickets. That was what was going to grab people's attention. So that was my goal, to get $100 deposits toward season tickets on a team that didn't exist, in a city where there had never been a real major league sport, where there was no arena to play in, and at a time when the NBA had not yet agreed to add more teams. I went on a speaking tour of the city, speaking to every group that would listen to me. Rotary, Kiwanis, Lions, Chamber of Commerce, churches . . . it didn't matter. Wherever there was a lectern, I preached the power of $100 season-ticket deposits and I preached it with all the extreme passion I could muster.

To my delight, convincing people to plop down a hundred bucks for a deposit on season tickets soon created a buzz in the city. We got off to a quick start, and from that point in June until the NBA's league meetings in September it was all about goal-setting. Our first goal was simple: let's get 2,000 season-ticket deposits. After we reached that goal, it was let's get 3,000. Then 4,000. We were setting goals by increments of thousands. When we got to 5,000, oh my goodness, we made a big deal of that. In fact, every time we reached a goal we'd call a news conference at the Chamber of Commerce, where we'd tear up the old number and post a new number. Momentum steamrolled, and soon it became overwhelming.

As I think back on that time, it reminds me of something I once read from an NFL assistant coach named Jeff Davidson. He said, "The wonderful thing about reaching goals is that as you reach one goal you mobilize the atmosphere for reaching another." Or as the American philosopher and psychologist John Dewey once observed, "Arriving at one goal is the starting point to another."[2]

It's so true. And that's how it went for us. We never stopped setting short-term goals while keeping our eyes on that extreme long-term goal of bringing an NBA team to Orlando. When the league meetings took place in Phoenix that September, we were in a position to tell the NBA that in 90 days we had reached our goal of 14,000 season-ticket deposits, which was about double of what any other city that was vying for a franchise had accomplished. Rest assured, it got the NBA's attention. And the rest, as they say, is history. The NBA awarded Orlando a franchise, and in 1989 we played our first game in a new arena (which is a whole other story).

That journey taught me something. It was through that experience of goal-setting that I learned a great lesson about the power of goals, about achieving them and then moving on to the next goal, and the next goal, and the next goal, and the . . . well, you get the idea. You see, we are driven and motivated by goals. Goals are powerful motivating forces, and I've made it a point to tap into that power on a consistent, everyday basis.

As I write this, I am a 75-year-old man battling cancer. More importantly, I'm a man with goals. Extreme goals. I don't live my life thinking about the finish line. Years ago, I set a goal to get to 100 books published. The book you're reading now is that book—my 100th. Now my goal is 200. I had a goal to run 100 marathons. I got to 58 when multiple myeloma tapped me on the shoulder and told me I wasn't going to run them anymore. But the goal was there, and I was striving to reach it.

And that's an important thing to know about goals. We need to review them constantly and revise them when necessary. Reality, like my cancer diagnosis, may demand that we settle for something a little less than what we were aiming for. That's okay. It's okay to reach for the stars and get to the moon. The key, however, is to aim high. Always aim high. You'll surprise yourself if you do. And more often than not, you'll find that you will reach the stars.

Writer and editor Dave Branon recalls a story that illustrates the value of aiming high with our extreme goals. He and his son and two sons-in-law went on a guy outing once. What they decided to do was go to a firing range and practice shooting. "While shooting," Branon said, "all four of us discovered that on one of the firearms the sight was set too low. If we aimed using the sight, we hit the bottom of the target. We had to aim high in order to hit anywhere near the bull's-eye." Later, Branon pondered that. "Isn't life like that?" he mused. "If we set our sights too low, we really don't accomplish all that we can. Sometimes we have to aim high in order to reach a desired goal."[3]

So aim high, and, even more importantly, please aim at something. Have a goal that you're shooting for. One of Zig Ziglar's most famous sayings that he often repeated in his motivational speeches was, "If you aim at nothing you'll hit it every time."[4] Or as former Beatle George Harrison sang on the last single he released before his death: "If you don't know where you're going, any road will take you there."[5]

The metaphor of a road is a good one. Reaching your goal is a journey, a road with twists and turns, roadblocks and wrong routes. To keep you focused on where you need to go and what is required to get there, you'll absolutely need to put your goals down in writing, and you'll need a deadline. Because without a deadline, which I recommend you also put down in writing, we tend to just drift along on the current of procrastination; we tend to find ourselves taking off-ramps into all sorts of time-wasters. Deadlines prevent that. And really, when you think about it, a goal is a dream with a deadline.

Legendary sports agent Mark McCormack once observed these two powerful ingredients regarding goals:

★ No. 1. "Write it down. Write it down anywhere, but get it down in writing. Writing it down is the first step of any action. It articulates your desire to do something. It is a reminder when you get swamped. It eliminates the excuse that you forgot. But most important, writing it down is a commitment—a signed contract that gives you the momentum to achieve your goals. Goals give you a reason to compete and do more. Without them, you just wander in the woods."

★ No. 2. "The second thing about goals is that they require deadlines. These can be flexible. You don't abandon a worthwhile goal simply because you don't achieve it by New Year's Day. The beauty of writing down a deadline is it anchors your goal in the real world—namely, in the framework of time. When time is the issue, I've found people become very practical. Suddenly, their goals become sensible rather than pie-in-the-sky."[6]

Live by those two goal-setting guidelines, and I promise that you'll live a productive, abundant, exciting life. That's because goals—extreme goals—are powerful. Goals keep you going; they keep you energized; they keep you focused; they keep you alert and alive. Up until you take your last breath you should always have goals.

In his book *The Influential Leader: 12 Steps to Igniting Visionary Decision Making*, John Edmund Haggai highlighted the significance of goals as they relate to our health. He wrote: "Some of the world's leading medical experts emphasize the importance of goals as a deterrent to sickness and as a stabilizer of health." After referring to a book titled *Getting Well Again* that he called "groundbreaking," Haggai noted that in the book:

> "[T]he authors argue that goal-setting and striving constitute one of the most important and successful therapies in combating cancer. They say that setting new life goals constitutes the most effective tool for getting patients well. As they conceptualize and visualize their reasons for living, patients reinvest themselves in life. Psychological satisfaction depends on feeling that your life is worthwhile. In turn, that feeling is reinforced strongly if you can point to goals you have recently attained. Even if you have not completed your mission, you know that certain key stages have already been reached."[7]

So never stop setting goals and never stop believing that you can achieve them. When Chuck Daly coached the Orlando Magic for us, he often said he never achieved success in his coaching profession until he reached his 50s. In fact, he was just a month shy of 59 when he won his first NBA title. And you might have heard Joe Torre during his Hall of Fame acceptance speech, talking about when he got fired from his second managerial job, this one with the Atlanta Braves. During his 18 seasons as a very good player, reaching the World Series eluded him. Torre always seemed to be getting to the wrong team at the wrong time. Then he tried managing and got fired not once, but twice. It was that second time that knocked him for a loop.

"I was very depressed," Torre admitted.

In talking with his wife, Ali, she asked him, "How do you want to be remembered?"

Torre thought and replied, "Someone who never realized their goal."

As he recounted that conversation at Cooperstown, Torre admitted, "I was feeling sorry for myself."

That's when Ali went into action.

"All of a sudden she slapped me into reality," Torre said.

How?

With four words.

"What are you, dead?"

Joe Torre was 44. He went into broadcasting, working in that medium for six years, before getting the St. Louis Cardinals managerial job in 1990. In 1995, he was fired again—a third time. The next year he became manager of the New York Yankees, prompting one of the city's tabloids to greet the hire with the headline: Clueless Joe.

Torre promptly went on to win four World Series titles in the next five years. He was 56 when he won his first one. Not dead. Several years later he became a cancer survivor. And he was very much alive when he was enshrined into the National Baseball Hall of Fame at the age of 74.

That struck me, because again, I'm 75 and currently living with cancer. Even now, I believe in the power of long-term goals and the positive benefits they can bring to you—both psychologically and physiologically. I'm especially convinced of it because I saw it in action. Coach John Wooden taught me that lesson back in 2010, when he was 99 years old. Coach Wooden was a frail man by then. He had just gone into the hospital and he wasn't going to come out. But while there, he was working on the next book he was writing—a coffee-table book filled with pictures. The day before he died, Coach Wooden was proofing that book, approving pictures. Six weeks after he died, the book came out. That was his final effort. Right up until the end of his life he was setting goals and extending himself toward those goals. He lived life right up to the end of his life.

So set goals. Live your life right up to the end. And remember, no matter how young or how old you are, without goals you're just wandering, guessing, stabbing in the dark. As sports psychologist Dr. Rod Gilbert often says, "If you don't know where you are going, you might end up where you are headed." Which is to say—nowhere. Sadly, you can waste a life that way. In his book *Everything I Know About Success I Learned from Napoleon Hill: Essential Lessons for Using the Power of Positive Thinking*, Don M. Green wrote: "You can have high goals, develop good plans, and have a pleasing personality and many other desirable qualities. But to be truly successful, you must have discipline. Without discipline you will be among the majority who will look over their lives and think about 'what could have been.'"[8]

Reaching and striving for goals—both short-term and long-term—will prevent regret. "A man has to have goals—for a day, for a lifetime," said Ted Williams,[9] the greatest hitter the game of baseball ever knew. Yes, goals will infuse meaning into your life, and when your life has meaning it naturally leads to happiness. That's what one of the world's great thinkers observed. "If you want to live a happy life," said Albert Einstein, "tie it to a goal, not to people or things."[10] And as the sports agent Mark McCormack said, write it down. I've heard Brian Tracy say in his motivational speeches that "only 3 percent of the population has written goals, and everyone else reports to those people."

Here are some of my other favorite quotes about goals:

"The tragedy of life doesn't lie in not reaching your goal. The tragedy lies in having no goal to reach."
                              —Benjamin E. Mays, minister, educator, and scholar[11]

"People with goals succeed because they know where they are going."
                              —Earl Nightingale, motivational speaker and author[12]

"Give me a stock clerk with a goal and I will give you a man who will make history. Give me a man without a goal and I will give you a stock clerk."
                              —J. C. Penney, businessman and entrepreneur[13]

"The person who makes a success of living is the one who sees his goal steadily and aims for it unswervingly."
                              —Cecil B. DeMille, film director and producer[14]

"The most important thing about having a goal is having one."
—Geoffrey F. Abert, author[15]

"After climbing a hill one finds many more hills to climb."
—Nelson Mandela, revolutionary, politician, and philanthropist[16]

"Before you begin a thing remind yourself that difficulties and delays quite impossible to foresee are ahead. You can only see one thing clearly, and that is your goal. Form a mental vision of that and cling to it through thick and thin."
—Kathleen Norris, author[17]

When you have clear, well-defined goals, you'll find that those extreme goals will push you more than any human. It will come from within. In his book, *The Champion's Mind: How Great Athletes Think, Train and Thrive,* Dr. Jim Afremow wrote of an experience that legendary University of North Carolina women's soccer coach Anson Dorrance once had. It was early in the morning, and Coach Dorrance was driving into work when off in the distance he saw one of his players doing extra training in the lonely morning hours. He later left a note at that player's locker that said: "The vision of a champion is someone who is bent over, drenched in sweat, at the point of exhaustion when no one else is watching."[18]

The player whose locker he left the note on was Mia Hamm, who would go on to achieve her goal of becoming the greatest player in the history of her sport.

There is no magic, secret formula. You set a goal and then you consistently work hard to achieve it. It's challenging, but being challenged is good.

"I don't think men are worth a darn unless you have a challenge in your life," said the Hall of Fame basketball player Jerry West. "I think the thing that has always driven me is people telling me 'no.' When I was little, people told me I couldn't do this and couldn't do that. I've always looked at it differently. I take 'no' as meaning 'yes.' I've always been a goal-setter. When you set goals, you get knocked down a lot. Goals allow you to get out of bed. I set lofty goals. It makes you extend yourself. It makes you reach a bit higher, and it stretches you. Everything you want to accomplish, you won't accomplish without goals."[19]

If you saw Rory McIlroy after his sensational wire-to-wire victory at the 2014 British Open, you saw a cool customer who refused to succumb to the enormous pressure of being a young man from Northern Ireland who was vying for what has to be for him the most prestigious of all golf tournaments. What you didn't see was McIlroy's burning desire simmering deep within him, ignited some seven years earlier when he set a long-term extreme goal to win that tournament. After winning the British Open, McIlroy talked about it with ESPN's Tom Rinaldi. During the interview, ESPN showed a close-up of McIlroy's face when he was presented the prestigious Claret Jug with the words: "The winner of the gold medal and the champion golfer of the year is Rory McIlroy."

At that point, McIlroy looked heavenward, smiled, then looked down as emotion clouded his face. Rinaldi picked up on that.

"There was a shot of you during the trophy presentation," Rinaldi said. "As the words 'champion golfer of the year' were said, you looked up. What was going through your head?"

McIlroy smiled, shook his head, still in almost disbelief that those words were real, and then released an audible sigh.

"I've been on that 18th green at Carnoustie when Padraig Harrington [a fellow Irishman] was announced as the champion golfer of the year in '07, and I was receiving the silver medal [as the Leading Amateur]," he said. "I remember thinking to myself, *I want to hear those words said about me. I want to be the champion golfer of the year and receive the gold medal and the Claret Jug.* Seven years later it came true."

Keep in mind, when McIlroy set that goal he was a pudgy 18-year-old amateur. Talented, yes. But barely a blip on golf's radar. Still, he set winning the British Open as his extreme goal and applied extreme work toward it. Seven years later, he achieved his extreme dream; he reached his goal.

"It's done by a lot of hard work, determination, making myself a better links player," he said. "There's *a lot* of things that went into it."

Kobe Bryant, the great Los Angeles Lakers basketball player, spent his formative basketball years in Europe, where he learned what he calls "extreme fundamentals: footwork, footwork, footwork, how to create space, how to handle the ball, how to protect the ball, how to shoot the ball." But back in the United States, when he was living in Philadelphia, he found that the game was more flash than substance. At an Adidas-sponsored ABCD basketball camp, Bryant, just 16, recalled in a *Sports Illustrated* article, "I wasn't the strongest kid at that camp. I wasn't the fastest. I wasn't the most athletic. I was probably the most skillful, but that didn't matter. It was all about 360 windmill dunks."[20]

A skinny kid, young Kobe really didn't stand out. But he set the goal to return to that ABCD camp that next year and not leave without being recognized as the best player there. Toward that goal he would awaken early for 5 AM workouts. Being the best player in camp, however, was only his short-term goal. His long-term goal was to be the best player in the country. As he explains, "When I went back to ABCD the next summer, I was ranked third, behind Tim Thomas and Lester Earl. I told myself, *I'm not leaving this camp until I'm No. 1. I'm not leaving!* Back then, if you were a highly rated player, you could stay in a nice hotel. I shacked up in dorms. I could tell that the game meant more to me than everybody else. Other guys could leave it afterward and detach from it. I couldn't. It stuck with me. I thought about it all night. They let players vote on who was the best, and one day this kid was eating breakfast across from me. He said, 'Hey, have you seen number 143? Have you seen that kid play? He's unreal. I'm voting for him.' He didn't know it because I was so skinny, but that was me. I was 143."[21]

And so it was that number 143 became No. 1 at the Adidas ABCD camp.

But it didn't end there. Following his senior season at Lower Merion High School in Philadelphia, where Kobe Bryant led the Aces to their first state title in 53 years, he was named the Naismith High School Player of the Year, the Gatorade Men's National Basketball Player of the Year, a McDonald's All-American, and a *USA TODAY* All-USA First Team player. He then turned pro at 17, becoming the first guard ever drafted into the NBA straight out of high school.

He set extreme goals, achieved them, and, if you know Kobe Bryant, you know he's still setting goals—both short-term and long-term goals.

I can't emphasize enough the importance of both those types of goals. Once you set a long-term goal, break it down into short-term goals. There is an old saying that goes like this: *Mile by mile it's a trial, yard by yard it's hard, but inch by inch it's a cinch.* It's true. I smiled when I saw a headline in *Investor's Business Daily* atop an article on Neil Armstrong, the first man to walk on the moon. The article related Armstrong's journey and all the small goals he reached before achieving that truly extreme goal of walking on the moon. The headline said: He Took a Million Steps to Make His Giant Leap.

It's doubtful that your destination is the moon. I know mine isn't. But whatever it is, know clearly your destination but focus on what is in front of you. Achieve your long-term goal with a steady succession of short-term goals. Bestselling author E. L. Doctorow once said that "writing a novel is like driving a car at night. You can only see as far as your head-lights, but you can make the whole trip that way."[22] My writing partner, Peter Kerasotis, tells me that one of his favorite books on writing is *Bird by Bird: Some Instructions on Writing and Life*, by Anne Lamott. In her book, and in many of her speeches, Lamott tells the story of her brother, just 10 at the time, who had three months to write a school report on birds. But he hadn't done it, and it was due the next day. Recalled Lamott, "He was at the kitchen table close to tears, surrounded by binder paper and pencils and unopened books on birds, immobilized by the hugeness of the task ahead. Then my father sat down beside him, put his arm around my brother's shoulder, and said, 'Bird by bird, buddy. Just take it bird by bird.'"[23]

Hence, the title of Anne Lamott's bestseller and also a great lesson on breaking up your big goal into smaller ones.

When he was a player, Michael Jordan knew the value of setting an extreme goal, seeing the big picture, and then breaking that down into manageable parts with short-term goals. One example of that is Jordan's scoring average. During most of his NBA career, Jordan kept his scoring average right at 32 points per game. He was consistent that way, automatic, like clockwork. No matter what the personnel was like around him, he always got his 32 points.

A reporter once asked him how he managed that kind of consistency, and Jordan replied, "I simplified it a few years ago. Thirty-two points per game is really just eight points a quarter. I figure that I can get that in some kind of way during the course of the game."[24]

The late sports agent Mark McCormack applauded inwardly when he heard Jordan say that.

"It's as clear and elegant an explanation of how to set a high standard for yourself and how to achieve it," he once wrote. "You start with the end result (32 points) and break it down into its most easily doable components (eight points per quarter) and then focus on each of the components. If you're successful with each component you'll achieve your goal."

McCormack then added: "It's a wonder more people don't adopt this strategy. I wonder how many starters in the NBA, with half of Jordan's talent and the same amount of playing time, could average 16 points per game if they broke down their scoring goals to four points each quarter. I wonder how many of these highly disciplined professionals even think in terms of quarters rather than a full game. If professional basketball is anything like the professional workplace, the number is probably not very high. My impression is that most people in the workplace are not particularly goal-oriented, or if they do have goals, they are not particularly smart about how to achieve them."[25]

But you *can* be smart.

Paul J. Meyer, founder of the Success Motivation Institute, lived a life where he helped motivate people. Here are his three key philosophies on goals:

1. **Make your goals meaningful to you:** Too often, the goals we are told to achieve are someone else's goals and as a result we are not internally motivated to achieve them. People reach for the minimum, the standard, and the average rather than aspiring to reach the maximum heights of which they are capable.

2. **Visualize your own success:** There is nothing that increases your passion and desire for achievement like controlled and directed visualization. Something unique and amazing happens when you practice looking into the future to see yourself in possession of your goals. You become so excited, so motivated, and so passionate to reach them that nothing can deter you or draw you off course.

3. **Work harder than ever before:** Be willing to work harder and longer without complaining. No goal exerts enough power to produce passion and desire unless you are willing to invest much of your time and effort in bringing it to fruition. When you have invested a part of yourself in the achievement of some worthy purpose, your passion and desire know no bounds.

The one other philosophy I'd like to add to that list is what many experts recommend and what you've already seen mentioned a couple of times in this chapter—and that is this: write down your goals. Tap them into your tablet, your phone; ink them into your planner or put pen to paper . . . whatever. In some shape or form, put it down in writing. There is power in that. And again, that's not a personal belief; it's a widespread one.

Said Isiah Thomas, a Hall of Fame basketball player who helped the Detroit Pistons win two NBA titles:

"One way to make sure you take your goals seriously is to write them down and keep them in a place where you can review them on a regular basis, maybe on a nightstand next to your bed, or taped to the bathroom mirror. There is something about putting your goal on paper that validates it and gives it power. If you write them down and keep them where you can see them or refer to them, often your goals will translate into actions and accomplishments. There is nothing easy about achieving your dreams, but by setting goals and constantly working toward them, in spite of distractions and frustrations, your life will pick up positive momentum."[26]

As you can see, setting and achieving extreme goals takes effort. So I'm going to share with you two important ingredients—extreme self-discipline and extreme habits.

If you're going to achieve extreme goals, you're going to need extreme self-discipline that is consistent enough to become an extreme habit. The ability to discipline yourself is how you build a bridge that will transport you from goals to achievements. You can't rely on other people to discipline you, nor should you want to. I can't emphasize that enough. I've never seen an extreme winner in any sport or field who was not fanatical about goals and who was not extremely self-disciplined. They didn't have to wait around for people to set goals for them, and it doesn't come to the point where people have to discipline them.

And let me say this about self-discipline. A lot of people tell me that they just don't have the discipline, and my response is: oh, yes you do. Everyone on planet Earth has the same amount of discipline at their disposal. It's all there, waiting for you to tap into it. The question is: Have you decided to use it? So please don't tell me you don't have it. You do. And I argue that point, and I argue it vehemently, all the time. You *do* have it. You just have to decide to have that extreme self-discipline.

I love former college basketball coach Bobby Knight's four-step definition of self-discipline. He says that self-discipline is (1) doing what has to be done, (2) doing it when it has to be done, (3) doing it the best it can be done, and (4) doing it that way every time you do it.

To do that, you have to work at self-discipline every day. *Every day?* Yes, every day. Think about just one decision we all have to make every day, and that is: What are we going to eat? I don't know about you, but I'm constantly tempted by a 14-inch pizza, a bubbly Pepsi, and tiramisu for dessert. And when I say I'm tempted, I'm *tempted* . . . every . . . single . . . day. I'm sure you have similar temptations every day, designed to detour and derail you from your goals. Decisions. There are hundreds to make every day. And it's so easy to make the wrong one. It is so much easier to decide to blow off the workout today and tell yourself you'll get back at it tomorrow and do a double workout. Uh, no you won't. But that's what we think when the alarm clock goes off and we just want to roll over and get another hour of sleep.

I'm a firm believer in investing today in what will pay dividends tomorrow. And again, it takes self-discipline to make that investment every single day. It's a lot easier to curl up on a couch and watch TV for a couple of hours than it is to read a 700-page biography on Winston Churchill. But for what I do, that biography on Winston Churchill is going to benefit me a lot more with my speaking and with my writing than those two mindless hours in front of a TV set will. Or for that matter, aimlessly surfing the Internet.

When you have clearly defined goals, you're ridden with guilt if you allow something to take you away from that goal. Conversely, you're elated when you persevere and reach your goals. You feel great. You pat yourself on the back, and rightfully so. *I did it; I read 700-plus pages on Winston Churchill. It took me three months. It was not a quick read. It was not an easy read. But I did it.* It's such a euphoric feeling to achieve a goal. It becomes addictive, in a good way. It motivates you to be self-disciplined.

And did I say you need self-discipline every day? Allow me to revise that. You need self-discipline every minute of every day.

Here are some of my favorite quotes on self-discipline:

> **"Without discipline there's no life at all."**
>
> —Katharine Hepburn, actress and winner of four Academy Awards[27]

> **"The disciplined person . . . is the truly free person. We give our players discipline to make them free."**
>
> —Dean Smith, Hall of Fame basketball coach[28]

> **"The alternative to discipline is disaster."**
>
> —Vance Havner, minister[29]

"The first and best victory is to conquer self."

—Plato[30]

"Success is tons of discipline."

—Brian Tracy, personal and professional development trainer[31]

"If you don't learn anything but self-discipline, athletics is worthwhile."

—Paul "Bear" Bryant, Hall of Fame football coach[32]

"When you are tough on yourself, life is going to be infinitely easier on you."

—Zig Ziglar, author and motivational speaker[33]

"For every disciplined effort there is multiple reward."

—Jim Rohn, author and motivational speaker[34]

"Without self-discipline, success is impossible."

—Lou Holtz, Hall of Fame football coach[35]

When you're self-disciplined you accomplish so much more toward your goals. You don't procrastinate. You'll find that you have more time, rather than less. "Some people regard discipline as a chore," said the actress Julie Andrews. "For me it's a kind of order that sets me free to fly."[36] Goals also breed self-discipline. Eric Heiden, the top athlete of any single Winter Olympics who also set 15 world speed-skating records, wrote in his book, *Better, Faster, Stronger*, that "goals aren't necessarily for the good days, but for the bad days. Any one of a number of goals may be the trigger that gets you out the door."

Like everything else we've discussed with regards to becoming an extreme winner, the sooner you can develop self-discipline, the better. And if you don't develop it, then it can easily lead to problems at some point in your life.

When I was raising my big brood of children, which at one point was 18 under the roof, I was responsible for the discipline in the home. There were rules and regulations. There were assignments and chores. And there were consequences.

I was the disciplinarian for the simple reason that they were not ready to discipline themselves. My message, therefore, was constant and pointed. I'd tell them that there is going to come a point where I'm no longer the disciplinarian. When you leave here at 18—and they all left, either for college, the armed services, or the workforce—I will not be there to discipline you. I will not be there to judge and deliver the punishment. So you'd better be ready to discipline yourself, because if you can't you're going to end up in trouble and then a higher authority has to do the disciplining. After 18, if you can't discipline yourself and someone else has to do it, then it becomes a very harsh form of discipline that you don't want any part of.

During those times of counsel with my children, I often thought of one of Coach John Wooden's favorite sayings: "Discipline yourself, and others won't need to."[37]

So when my children left home one by one, I'd pray that dear ol' dad's words followed them. Discipline yourself. That means not succumbing to negative peer pressure. That means saying no when you know it's the wrong thing to do and everybody in your crowd is saying, *Ah, this sounds like great fun. Let's go do it.* And you know it's not even close to being the right thing to do. Will you have the self-discipline to say no, or will you get swept up like a broken tree branch flowing downstream, heading straight for a cataclysmic waterfall?

In raising so many children, I've come to believe that at a certain point, perhaps at 16 or 17 years old, if young people don't understand that they have to provide discipline themselves—that is, self-discipline—then the chances are their goals will not become a reality.

That might sound like a digression, delving into teenagers and peer pressure. But we all face peer pressure, no matter how old we are. Remember, when you have an extreme dream, which was the first chapter of this book, I cautioned you that your friends and family will likely try to talk you out of it. They'll want you to stick with something tried and true, which is easy to do. After all, we're prone to go with the flow and take the easy road to disaster instead of the more difficult road to success. Even Jesus recognized that. The Great Teacher said, as recorded in Matthew 7:13–14, "Go in through the narrow gate, because broad is the gate and spacious is the road leading off into destruction, and many are going in through it, whereas narrow is the gate and cramped the road leading off into life, and few are finding it."[38]

One of the nice byproducts of being goal-oriented is that you almost by default are self-disciplined—and vice versa. And both lead into something else, which is where extreme habits come in. When you're developing good habits, you'll find yourself getting into a good rhythm, a groove. You get up at the same time every morning, work out at the same time, keep a schedule. It's that way in every aspect of life.

"The individual who wants to reach the top in business must appreciate the might of the force of habit," said the billionaire industrialist J. Paul Getty. "He must be quick to break those habits that can break him, and hasten to adopt those practices that will become the habits that help him achieve the success he desires."[39]

Even with good habits, you're never home free. Those habits can get disrupted quickly. There's an enormous amount of focus needed. You can't take your eye off the goal, your eyes off the prize. It's so easy to start wandering and drifting, to get careless and sloppy, to lose interest, to mail it in. Bad habits are always nipping at our heels. It's been said that the worst boss you can have is a bad habit. It's also been said that bad habits are like a comfortable bed . . . easy to get into, but hard to get out of.

So develop good habits, be extreme about it.

Brian Tracy, in his book *The 100 Absolutely Unbreakable Laws of Business Success*, wrote about a businessman named Herbert Gray, who spent 11 years searching for what he called "the common denominator of success." After studying thousands of successful people, Grey concluded that "successful people make a habit of doing the things that unsuccessful people don't like to do." The interesting thing is that successful people don't like to do the same things that failures don't like to do, but successful people do them anyway because they know that this is the price they have to pay for success.[40]

There is the famous quote from the old English poet John Dryden that many of us who write books and give motivational speeches often quote. Said Dryden: "We first make our habits, then our habits make us."[41] Here are several other quotes on habits that I especially like:

> *"We are what we repeatedly do. Excellence, then, is not an act, but a habit."*
>
> — Aristotle, Greek philosopher[42]

> *"In truth, the only difference between those who have failed and those who have succeeded lies in the difference of their habits."*
>
> —Augustine "Og" Mandino, author[43]

> *"Do something every day that you don't want to do. This is the golden rule for acquiring the habit of doing your duty without pain."*
>
> —Mark Twain, author and humorist[44]

> *"A bad habit never disappears miraculously; it's an undo-it-yourself project."*
>
> —Abigail Van Buren, advice columnist[45]

> *"Men do not decide their future. They decide their habits, and their habits decide their future."*
>
> —Mike Murdock, pastor[46]

People who have studied habits will tell you that bad habits are extremely difficult to break through sheer willpower, but what works better is exchanging a bad habit with a good one. That's what Benjamin Franklin once did. In his autobiography, Franklin wrote about his technique for eliminating his bad habits and replacing them with good ones, and how empowering that was. At the same time that he was eliminating a set of behaviors that worked against him, he acquired another set of behaviors that worked for him.

Benjamin Franklin found that forming good habits took repetition—sustained repetition—but that the effort was well worth it. It takes time to develop good habits and seemingly no time at all to fall into bad ones. That's why constant vigilance is needed. But the more you apply yourself to good habits, the stronger they'll become. Author and motivational speaker Hal Urban puts it this way. He says that at the beginning a habit is like a thread, but through repetition enough threads intertwine until they become a cord, a rope, a chain, and finally a cable.

I like to think of it as a threefold cable—your extreme goal, your extreme self-discipline, and your extreme habits. Wind them together and it will be an unbreakable tether, tying you to that ultimate goal of becoming an extreme winner.

Chapter 9

EXTREME PERSEVERANCE

"God bless perseverance.
Because it is not easy."

—*Junot Diaz, author and professor* [1]

It is thought that the seed of Walt Disney's extreme dream of an amusement park—and not just any amusement park, but one that would be a magical kingdom—was planted when he was a boy in Kansas City. Young Walt would peer through the fence at an amusement center known as Electric Park and dream an extreme dream that never left him.

When he lived in Southern California, Disney would go to Griffith Park in Los Angeles and sit on a bench eating peanuts, watching as children rode the merry-go-round, dreaming of a place where parents and children could have fun together. He'd visit other area amusement parks, asking the children which rides they liked best, and why. Sketches of his idea for an amusement park were found in his Burbank studios as early as 1932, when Disney was a 31-year-old animator.

But there were obstacles—both internal and external. Amusement parks had lousy reputations. Most of them were carnivals with sleazy undertones. Even Walt's wife, Lillian, a creative and stylish soul, didn't see his fascination, much less share his dream. Said Walt, "Lillian used to say, 'But why do you want to build an amusement park? They're so dirty.' I told her that was just the point —mine wouldn't be."[2]

The dream accelerated through the years, even while his successes in other areas of entertainment not only blossomed, but made him wealthy. Eventually, Disney attached a name to his idea—Mickey Mouse Park. Other family members, like his brother Roy Disney, vehemently opposed him. In fact, Roy referred to Mickey Mouse Park as "that screwball idea."[3] But even in the face of family opposition and other serious roadblocks, Walt refused to abandon his dream; he kept persevering. "I couldn't get anybody to go along with me because we were going through this financial depression," he once said. "But I kept working on it, and I worked on it with my own money. Not the studio's money, my own money."[4]

It became, as one of Disney's animators, Ward Kimball, recalled, "An obsession. It's all he thought about."[5] One of his artists, John Hench, who lived near the studio, recalled "seeing Walt across the street in a weed-filled lot, standing and visualizing all by himself."[6] Disney's visualization grew, eventually to the size that he was no longer envisioning a park, but rather a kingdom—one that would be magical.

By 1950, Disney was painstakingly researching parks, fairs, zoos, circuses, and amusement parks; the match he lit as a child was now a blazing—if not consuming—flame. He interviewed patrons. What did they like? What didn't they like? What entertained them? Enthralled them? What left them feeling cheated?

Disney interviewed workers, where he again ran into naysayers. He told workers of his intent to build a meticulously clean park where people paid an admission to get in, rather than at various rides and attractions. He reasoned that charging an admission would keep out the drunks and lowlifes. And he would staff the park not with the typical carnival type of worker, but with well-groomed, friendly people. The reaction? Laughter. Scornful, derisive laughter. *A clean park run by so-called nice people? Ha!* They predicted he'd be broke within a year. "You can't keep cleaning the restroom all day," they told him. "That costs money! And you can't charge admission—nobody will come. And you don't hire 'nice people'— you hire people who work cheap."[7]

Disney never wavered. He kept at his extreme dream with dogged perseverance. In 1951, he and Lillian took a cruise to Europe, where they found themselves on the same ship with Art and Lois Linkletter. Walt had met Art several years earlier, and it was on the cruise that a close friendship developed. On their European trip, the two couples visited the famous Tivoli Gardens in Copenhagen, Denmark. Its cleanliness, courteous workers, beautiful flower gardens, fine restaurants, a few rides, lights, nightly fireworks, and wholesome family atmosphere awakened Walt Disney's dream. Disney later recalled how Tivoli Gardens was "spotless, brightly colored, and priced within the reach of everyone. The gaiety of the music, the excellence of the food and drink, the warm courtesy of the employees—everything combined for a pleasurable experience."[8]

Linkletter recalled something else. "As we walked through it, I had my first experience of Walt Disney's childlike delight in the enjoyment of seeing families and in the cleanliness and the orderliness of everything. He was making notes all the time—about the lights, the chairs, the seats, and the food. I asked him what he was doing, and he replied, 'I'm just making notes about something that I've always dreamed of—a great, great playground for the children and the families of America.'"[9]

Back in America, it wasn't going well financially. Disney's studio was awash in debt. But Walt persevered with his dream, against the advice of experts, investors, advisors, and family members. "Walt," Roy Disney told his brother, "we're in the motion picture business, not the roller-coaster business." Eventually, Roy went from trying to change his brother's mind to simply changing the subject. "Whenever I'd go down and talk to my brother about the park, he'd suddenly get busy with financial reports," Walt said. "So I stopped bringing it up around Roy."[10]

Meanwhile, Walt continued to assemble funds. He drained his personal bank account. He borrowed money from banks. He borrowed $100,000 against his life insurance. He sold his vacation home at Smoke Tree Ranch in Palm Springs, California. He was still millions of dollars short. Again, those around him told him to quit. He wouldn't. He went to the two biggest TV networks, NBC and CBS, and tried to sell them on his Disney programming and also his idea of Disneyland. They very much wanted in on the former, but wanted no part of the latter. He went to upstart ABC, and they turned him down.

In the fall of 1953, Disney went back to ABC, this time with a detailed proposal and aerial rendering of the park. Finally, ABC put up a half-million dollars and cosigned bank loans for another $4.5 million. With other investors, an ownership group assembled $6 million, barely more than a third of the $17 million needed. Only after his TV show became a smash success did the remaining money finally flow in. Even then, people—like Walt's friend Art Linkletter—still harbored doubts. Shortly after excavation began in Anaheim, California, Disney gave a quietly appalled Linkletter a tour. "We drove around this remote spot in Orange County," Linkletter said. "I looked around and I couldn't believe it! We were miles away from any major population center. I wondered if Walt had lost his mind! I thought, 'My gosh, he wants to put a bunch of roller coasters out in the middle of these orange groves? Ridiculous!'"[11]

It was so ridiculous that when Disney tried to convince Linkletter to buy some of the surrounding land (since Disney couldn't afford to do so himself) Linkletter politely declined. Years later, Linkletter calculated that every step he had taken that day would've been worth $3 million, had he just taken his friend's advice.

And today? Well, you know the rest of the story. Walt Disney's unwavering, single-minded perseverance led to Disneyland, Disney World, and all sorts of ancillary theme parks and family-themed resorts—a recreational and entertainment empire worth billions.

Of course, you know what Walt Disney attributed it all to. Perseverance. Except he didn't call it that. He didn't even call it extreme perseverance. Instead, he coined his own word—stick-to-it-ivity. Through all the years, the decades, through all the opposers and naysayers and scorners and mockers, he stuck to his extreme dream.

So I ask you: What is your extreme dream? And are you willing to apply extreme preparation, focus, passion, work ethic, responsibility, positive attitude, and goal-setting to it? If so, you'll still need another ingredient en route to becoming an extreme winner—extreme perseverance.

You'll need stick-to-it-ivity.

Let me tell you about someone else in the entertainment business—Sylvester Stallone. From the time he entered the world, Stallone had it rough. His mother struggled during his birth, forcing her obstetrician to employ two pairs of forceps to extract him from his mother's womb. It left the lower left side of Stallone's face paralyzed, leading to what looks like a perpetual snarl and slightly slurred speech. In school, he was taunted.

At home, his parents divorced when he was a boy, which led to a childhood of instability.

As an adult, Stallone had a hard time producing a steady income, so much so that he once had to sell his dog so he could pay his electric bill. When he wrote his script for the movie he wanted to call *Rocky*, he took it from studio to studio, enduring rejection after rejection. Finally, United Artists offered him $125,000 for it, but only if he agreed to abandon his idea of starring in the movie. He was a virtual unknown, and United Artists thought that maybe an actor like Robert Redford or Burt Reynolds would be better suited to play the role of Rocky. Stallone refused. United Artists sweetened the pot—first to $250,000 and then to $325,000—if he would just agree to let them cast someone else for the lead.

But Stallone had an extreme dream, and he persevered.

Finally, United Artists relented, but only if he took $35,000 and a percentage of the profits as salary. Stallone agreed.

Rocky was filmed at the low-budget cost of $1 million. It grossed over $200 million, won three Oscars (including Best Picture), and its sequels have raked in more than a billion dollars. And by the way, Stallone used what he made from his first *Rocky* movie to buy his dog back.

The point, of course, is to never quit, to persevere.

I have one more entertainment industry story to share with you. This one is about George Lucas. As a young screenwriter and director, Lucas wasn't happy with his first two films, the second of which was *American Graffiti*, because of the way the studios re-edited them over his objections. In fact, he was convinced that his first film, *THX 1138*, flopped because of the studio's re-editing. So, on the heels of the financial success of *American Graffiti*, Lucas told 20th Century Fox that he not only wanted more control over his third film, he also wanted ownership of sequels. In addition, he said he would cut $500,000 from his directing and screenwriting fee. The studio balked. Lucas battled and persevered until he got what he wanted, what he believed in.

That film was *Star Wars*, and it launched a cultural phenomenon and one of the most successful series of movies in filmmaking history.

In addition, Lucas created the Indiana Jones franchise. Years later, this is what Lucas shared with *Investor's Business Daily* about his secret to success:

> "If you want to be successful in a particular field of endeavor, I think perseverance is one of the key qualities. I haven't met anyone (who is successful) who hasn't been able to describe years and years and years of very, very difficult struggle through the whole process of achieving anything whatsoever. There's no way to get around that."[12]

It sounds as if Lucas is not just describing perseverance, but extreme perseverance.

> "The secret is not to give up hope," Lucas added. "It's very hard not to. If you're really doing something worthwhile, I think you will be pushed to the brink of hopelessness before you come through to the other side. You just have to hang in through that. You need to have a deep passion for it, because you're going to have to overcome a lot of hurdles. You have to find something you love enough to take a lot of risks, to be able to break through the brick walls that are always going to be placed in front of you."[13]

Interestingly, it was *Star Wars* that catapulted an itinerant, 35-year-old actor who supported himself as a carpenter into international fame and a long and lucrative film career. That actor was Harrison Ford, who later mused, "I realized early on that success was tied to not giving up. Most people in this business gave up and went on to other things. If you simply didn't give up, you would outlast the people who came in on the bus with you. Sometimes the only reason you get the job is that you're the only one left. I didn't make a living acting until I was 35. Tenacity is critical."[14]

What's interesting about those anecdotes you just read is that we all enjoy reading and hearing about the journey, while the result becomes more of an exclamation point at the end of a powerful sentence. It's the story that is often most interesting, the journey rather than the destination. But it's the journey that connects the key steps that will take you to becoming an extreme winner. And I'm sure you're seeing by now that these 12 steps/chapters are closely linked and intertwined. It's a process, and that process takes time. Never lose sight of that. Walt Disney and George Lucas never did. For them, it took "years and years"—as Lucas so aptly noted. Anything worth achieving is worth persevering for. I believe throughout human history there have been so many dreams not realized, battles not won, potential greatness left untapped, because people gave up too soon.

"Most people give up just when they're about to achieve success," said the billionaire businessman H. Ross Perot. "They quit on the one-yard line. They give up at the last minute of the game, one foot from a winning touchdown."[15]

"Many of life's failures," said the inventor Thomas Edison, "are people who did not realize how close they were to success when they gave up."[16]

So don't give up. Don't quit trying. Don't give in.

"You may have to fight the battle more than once to win it," said former British Prime Minister Margaret Thatcher.[17] Another former prime minister, Winston Churchill, put it this way, "If you're going through hell, keep going."[18]

Churchill is one of my favorite historical figures—such a shining example of persevering. And because he's now a gigantic historical figure, people forget that although he is recognized as one of the world's greatest orators, he had a speech impediment. He also, after numerous setbacks, did not become Britain's prime minister until he was 65. Through it all, he persevered with a never-quit attitude that served the Allied forces well during those tense, touch-and-go moments that were pivotal during World War II. Churchill later said with conviction, "Never give in, never give in, never, never, never—in nothing, great or small, large or petty—never give in except to convictions of honor and good sense."[19]

To be sure, Churchill isn't the only historical giant with a never-quit attitude.

When you think of Bill Gates, you think of Microsoft—right? Does anybody remember that before Microsoft, Gates headed a company called Traf-O-Data, which was a flop?

You can hardly go anywhere in the world today without seeing a KFC, or as it was called in my day, Kentucky Fried Chicken. But there was a time when a fellow named Harlan David Sanders, now known as Colonel Sanders, drove thousands of miles, persevering in his search of someone willing to partner with him on his secret recipe. It wasn't until he was in his mid-60s when Sanders' fast-food fried chicken restaurant began franchising and became a success.

Henry Ford filed for bankruptcy twice before finding success with his Ford Motor Company.

The litany of failures in Steve Jobs' career is legendary. So is his enduring legacy that is his Apple brand, which is why Jobs was once able to say with fervent certainty, "I am convinced that what separates about half of the successful entrepreneurs from the unsuccessful ones is pure perseverance."[20]

Perhaps you've heard of a female author whose book manuscript was rejected a dozen times before one British publisher took a chance on it for the equivalent of about $2,000. Her name is J. K. Rowling, and her perseverance paid off to the tune of more than a billion dollars, thanks to her Harry Potter books and movies.

Legend has it that back in 1954, after just one performance at the Grand Ole Opry, the manager there fired the singer and told him, "You ain't goin' nowhere, son. You ought to go back to drivin' a truck."[21] Perhaps you've heard of the singer, a hard-headed young man who persevered through that rejection. His name was Elvis Presley. Years later, Elvis made the statement: "When things go wrong, don't go with them."[22]

And who can ever forget Coach Jim Valvano, dying of cancer, giving that passionate speech at the ESPY Awards? "Don't give up! Don't ever give up!"

The list, of course, goes on and on. There is no shortage of motivating stories of perseverance that we can tap into to get us moving forward toward achieving our extreme goal. And as you push forward, know that sometimes you can push through adversity easily, sometimes not. It's said that when Elvis Presley was told to go back to driving a truck, he cried all the way back to Memphis from Nashville. And that's okay. If you didn't care so much about your extreme dream, it wouldn't hurt so much when someone rejects you. So expect rejection, and expect it to knock you down. Expect it to slow you down. The point is, as with Elvis Presley, don't let it stop you. Keep getting up and keep moving forward.

Think of yourself as a shark. A shark must always continue to move forward, otherwise it dies. Sometimes a shark might be zipping along through the water, and sometimes it might be barely crawling. But either way, as long as it's moving forward, it stays alive. The same for us and our dreams. Sometimes you might be zipping along toward fulfilling your dream, and at other times barely crawling. But either way, the important thing is to keep moving forward. Persevere. Confucius said, "It does not matter how slowly you go, as long as you do not stop."[23]

Here are some of my other favorite quotes on perseverance:

"Life is not easy for any of us. But what of that?
We must have perseverance and above all confidence in ourselves.
We must believe that we are gifted for something and that
this thing must be attained."

—Marie Curie, the first woman to win a Nobel Prize[24]

"Perseverance is not a long race; it is many short races one
after another."

—Walter Elliot, British politician[25]

"By perseverance the snail reached the ark."

—Charles Spurgeon, preacher[26]

"Great works are performed not by strength but by
perseverance."

—Samuel Johnson, English writer, poet, and essayist[27]

"We can do anything we want to if we stick to it long enough."

—Helen Keller, author, political activist, and lecturer[28]

"Perseverance, secret of all triumphs."

—Victor Hugo, French poet, novelist, and dramatist[29]

"Perseverance is the hard work you do after you get tired of doing the hard work you already did."

—Newt Gingrich, politician, historian, and author[30]

That last quote from Newt Gingrich is particularly illuminating because achieving your extreme dream and reaching your extreme goal is, once again, a process. It's not an all-at-once thing. And sometimes, along the way, you achieve things that you never even allowed yourself to dream that you would.

I'm sure Lou Gehrig never thought he'd play an astounding 2,130 consecutive baseball games. But he did exactly that by persevering through injuries and adversities, playing one game at a time. When it came to an end, and Gehrig underwent a battery of tests to determine why his body was failing him, x-rays found that he had persevered and played through at least 17 bone fractures. Yet, he never stopped. It took the dreaded and incurable amyotrophic lateral sclerosis to stop him. It's quite a testament. That's not to say we should persevere through broken bones. But can we persevere when someone tells us we can't? When we feel like giving up? When we don't think we have another try in us?

Those in sales know the power of perseverance, perhaps better than people in any other profession. A study once conducted by the National Retail Dry Goods Association unearthed interesting statistics. It found that unsuccessful first attempts led almost half of all salespeople to certain failure. But it found that those who persisted and persevered were richly rewarded. Here is what the statistics showed:

★ 48 percent of all salespeople make one call and stop.

★ 25 percent of all salespeople make two calls and stop.

★ 15 percent of all salespeople make three calls and stop.

★ 12 percent of all salespeople go back and back and back and back. They make 80 percent of all sales.

Success rarely comes overnight, and it rarely comes without consistent, persistent effort. The great American radio commentator Paul Harvey once said, "You can always tell when you are on the road to success. It's uphill all the way."[31] But that's good. Think of it this way: people who frequent gyms know the benefits of putting their treadmill on an incline. It's harder that way, for sure. But the end result is that they become fitter and stronger.

Why is that so important? Because of what one of the great figures of the 20th century, Nelson Mandela, once said: "After climbing a great hill, one only finds that there are many more hills to climb."[32]

So keep climbing.

I know it might sound like a trite platitude, but there are two sayings that are oft-repeated for a reason, and I'm fairly sure you've heard them both. One is: Winners never quit, and quitters never win. And the other is: When the going gets tough, the tough get going.

Eddie Arcaro had plenty of opportunities to quit. It's believed that his 250 consecutive losses as a horse racing jockey to start his career, without so much as one win, is a record in futility. But Arcaro didn't give in, and eventually he broke through, becoming the biggest money winner in 1948, 1950, 1952, and 1955. By the time he retired, Arcaro had won 4,779 races.

So again, just because you've heard many times those two sayings about *winners never quitting* and *when the going gets tough*, don't allow your eyes and mind to gloss over them without absorbing their simple, yet powerful, message. And it really is that simple. As the famous crooner Frank Sinatra once mused, "There is something to be said for keeping at a thing, isn't there?"[33] Yes, there is. But if you want something more poetic about that ability to dig deep within yourself, this is what Elisabeth Kubler-Ross, a psychiatrist and author, once said: "People are like stained-glass windows:

they sparkle and shine when the sun is out, but when the darkness sets in their true beauty is revealed only if there is a light within."[34]

Speaking of light, I'm going to defer to Thomas Edison again. Edison, who once described genius as "1 percent inspiration and 99 percent perspiration,"[35] tested more than 3,000 filaments before settling on carbon for the incandescent lightbulb. As we're likely well aware, Edison's journey toward making a lightbulb is legendary, and the takeaway is that he refused to quit. He persevered through thousands of failures. Tellingly, when he was once asked if he ever got discouraged by all of his many failures, Edison replied, "Those were steps on the way. In each attempt, I was successful in finding a way *not* to create a light bulb. I was always eager to learn, even from my mistakes."[36]

One thing that's particularly special about persevering is how it can, and often does, inspire others. If you're in a leadership role, never underestimate how your stick-to-it-ivity will inspire those whom you're leading. In fact, we're all inspired by stories of people who showed extreme perseverance. I dare say that at this point in reading this chapter, you have felt surges of inspiration by some of the anecdotes, quotes, and life experiences you've just read about. And perhaps one day your story, your example, will inspire others.

Bob Richards persevered years ago to become a track and field star, winning a bronze and two gold medals over three successive Olympic Games. Talking to youngsters once at a Sunday school class in Long Beach, California, sharing his story, Richards kept getting interrupted by an overweight girl with thick bifocals. She kept jumping up and down during his talk and saying, "I'm going to be a great tennis champion. I'm going to be a great tennis champion." Years later, when Richards recounted the story, he said, "She was the girl most unlikely to succeed at tennis of any girl you have ever seen in your whole life. I felt like saying, 'Well, honey, go into apple dunking. You would make the greatest apple dunker that ever lived.' But I could not say it."[37] The overweight girl with the thick bifocals was named Billie Jean Moffitt, who later became known as Billie Jean King—the greatest women's tennis champion of her time.

A young Bob Pierce, who later founded the renowned relief organization known as World Vision, was inspired by a clergyman who told him:

"I have studied leaders and organizations. I have devoured biographies and autobiographies. I have immersed myself in history. I have carefully observed the contemporary leadership of my day. I've come to the conclusion that one factor distinguishes the organization that wins. It's staying power. In many cases, organizations headed by leaders more qualified by virtue of educational achievement, name recognition, natural gifts, and powerful relationships have withered and died, while those of seemingly lesser advantages went on to spectacular achievement. The latter simply exercised staying power. When they were hanging on the ledge, ready to crash into the abyss, fingers bleeding as their nails were pulled off from their fingers, the people who won were those who just kept clinging."[38]

So keep clinging to your dreams, and cling with all the tenacity and extreme perseverance you can muster. Remember, these are your *dreams*; this is what you want to do. I once heard the brain researcher John Assaraf say that if you're interested, you'll do what's convenient, but if you're committed, you'll do whatever it takes. It's so true.

The interesting thing about pushing through and persevering during hard times is that the more you do it, the more determined you are to continue to do so. As the Hall of Fame football coach Vince Lombardi once said: "The harder you work, the harder it is to surrender."[39] In other words, not only do you get used to pushing through adversity, you've persevered so many times that you refuse to let the next obstacle that comes along stop you.

Of course, the opposite is also true. The more you surrender and quit, the easier it becomes to do that the next time there is an obstacle or a tough time. "Once you learn to quit, it becomes a habit,"[40] Lombardi also said.

Another Hall of Fame football coach, Bear Bryant, thought along the same lines. "If a man is a quitter, I'd rather find out in practice than in a game," Bryant said. "I ask for all a player has, so I'll know later what I can expect.[41] The first time you quit, it's hard. The second time, it's easier. The third time, you don't even have to think about it."[42]

If you don't quit, even after you've failed, your success will be that much sweeter. Along those lines, I was struck by what Joe Torre said in the summer of 2014, at his National Baseball Hall of Fame induction speech. And allow me to preface this by saying that it might seem odd that I'm going to attach what Joe Torre said on that day with what the late writer Truman Capote once said—but bear with me. Capote, author of the iconic book *In Cold Blood*, once said that "failure is the condiment that gives success its flavor."[43] So I thought of Capote's comment when I listened as Torre, at this most momentous moment in his life, when he achieved immortality in his sport, talked about all his failures in his managerial career, and how his wife once talked him out of quitting that journey altogether. As mentioned in Chapter 8, before he ever became the New York Yankees manager, and before he ever led them to four World Series titles, Torre had been fired by the New York Mets, Atlanta Braves, and St. Louis Cardinals, which were the only organizations for whom he had played. He thought his managerial career was over, but it wasn't. He persevered in the face of failure, which is what he focused on in his induction speech, and which is why he made this statement: "I want to tell you kids, I got fired three times."

Torre was also 55 years old when he was offered the Yankees' managerial job, which was generally perceived at the time as his last chance as a baseball skipper.

So if you fail, try again. If you fall down, get up. If you fall down again, get up again. Pretty soon, you'll get used to getting up, and you'll do it reflexively, without thinking. Not only does quitting not become an option at that point, it's not even a consideration. The same goes if you're knocked down, or even kicked to the ground. Get up. Again and again . . . get up!

Even the animal kingdom recognizes the importance of that. In his book *A View from the Zoo*, Gary Richmond wrote about once watching the birth of a giraffe. Giraffes give birth standing up, so Richmond was shocked when at birth he saw a male giraffe calf fall 10 feet from his mother's womb. And not only that, but the calf hit the ground flat on its back, with a loud, dusty thud. Then the real shocker came. Richmond watched as "the mother lowered her head to see the baby; then moved until she was towering directly above the calf." After about a minute of observation, "the mother giraffe swung her great, long leg outward and booted her lying baby through the air. The calf sprawled head over heels across the ground, puzzled and protesting."

Gary's head spun toward the zoologist standing next to him.

"What's that all about?" he asked.

"She wants it to get up," he said. "And if it doesn't get up, she's going to do it again."

Sure enough, the process was repeated again and again. And again and again the calf struggled to get up, but couldn't.

Finally, after being kicked around numerous times, the calf struggled to its feet and with wobbly, spindly legs stood up for the first time, amid hearty cheers from the zoo's animal care staff.

Guess what happened then?

To Richmond's horror, the mother swung her majestic leg and kicked the calf off its feet. It seemed so brutal, and Richmond could barely watch, but the whole scene was frighteningly fascinating.

Again, Richmond turned to the zoologist. The calf had gotten up. So why did the mother kick it to the ground again?

Explained the zoologist, "She wants it to remember how it got up."[44]

The lesson: Don't forget how to get up. And no matter how many times you're kicked to the ground, keep getting up. You've done it before and you can do it again . . . and again and again and again.

It reminds me of one of King Solomon's proverbs, found in the Bible at Proverbs 24:16: "For the righteous one may fall seven times, and he will get up again."[45]

There is a special beauty to persevering and pushing through a rocky time in our life. The British Poet Laureate Alfred, Lord Tennyson put it this way: "The brook would lose its song if we removed the rocks."[46]

The other thing about tough times is that it *will* expose your weaknesses. And that, too, is actually good. When under pressure, is your exposed weakness anger, apathy, or maybe alcohol? Whatever it is, that weakness threatens to derail your dream, or it can give you an opportunity to fix and strengthen it. When we're going through tough times, when we're under stress, it reveals a lot about who we are. Almost always, it gives us knowledge of something to work on and turn into a strength.

"People need trouble, a little frustration, to sharpen the spirit on, toughen it. Artists do," said the Nobel Prize–winning author William Faulkner. "I don't mean you need to live in a rat hole or gutter, but you have to learn fortitude, endurance."[47]

Engineers, when testing a new product, will conduct a stress test to determine if there are any weaknesses. If a weakness is exposed, it's immediately addressed and often it becomes the strongest part of a product. Cardiologists perform stress tests to determine if there are any weaknesses in the heart so that they can be attended to. When a bad storm hits a house, it'll often expose a weakness—loose roof shingles, windows that need sealing, or perhaps an unhinged shutter. The result is that that weakness is addressed; that section of the roof, that window, that shutter not only gets repaired, it becomes stronger than it was before.

Thus, I'm convinced that you should welcome setbacks, embrace failures, look forward to obstacles. It will test who you are; and when you pass those tests, it will strengthen your resolve, redouble your efforts, sharpen your focus, and force you to adapt and innovate and address any weaknesses. It will also help you to face the next test, the next challenge, the next storm in your life.

Resistance makes you stronger. Isn't that why we go to the gym and lift weights? Birds can't fly unless they have the resistance of the wind. A boat can't motor through the water if not for the resistance against its propeller. Take whatever comes against you and use it to move forward, not backward.

Said *Gone with the Wind* author Margaret Mitchell, "Hardships make or break people."[48]

Instead of thinking obstacle, think opportunity.

"Obstacles don't have to stop you," said the great Hall of Fame basketball player Michael Jordan. "If you run into a wall, don't turn around and give up. Figure out how to climb it, go through it, or work your way around it."[49]

I was reminded of Jordan's wall metaphor when I read Dudley Rutherford's wonderful book *Walls Fall Down*. In it he writes: "How many of us are willing to put in the time to endure hardship and testing in order to become extraordinary at something? How many of us are willing to spend countless hours in a gym taking shots well into the night as Michael Jordan was known to have done? The phrase 'practice makes perfect' would be better stated 'perseverance makes perfect.' That's because everyone who has ever been great at anything has had to consistently persevere through challenges and hardships."

One of the great obstacles that causes people to give up is not just failure, but the fear of failure. Some people are so worried about failing, or even simply making a mistake, that they never do anything great. But remember this: Babe Ruth, who not only hit 714 career home runs, but was the first baseball player to hit 30, 40, 50, and 60 home runs in a single season, struck out a staggering 1,330 times.

So don't fret about failure. Abraham Lincoln didn't. "My great concern is not whether you have failed," the 16th president said, "but whether you are content with failure."[50]

Here are some other quotes about overcoming the fear of failure that I appreciate:

> *"You may be disappointed if you fail, but you are doomed if you don't try."*
>
> —Beverly Sills, opera singer[51]

> *"Failure is simply the opportunity to begin again, this time more intelligently."*
>
> —Henry Ford, industrialist and founder of Ford Motor Company[52]

"When one door closes, another opens. But we often look so long and so regretfully at the closed door that we cannot see the one that has opened for us."

—Alexander Graham Bell, scientist, engineer, and inventor[53]

"Never confuse a single defeat for a final defeat."

—F. Scott Fitzgerald, author[54]

"If you're not failing every now and then, it's a sign you're not doing anything very innovative."

—Woody Allen, director, screenwriter, and actor[55]

"I believe anybody who is not afraid to fail is a winner."

—Joe Torre, Hall of Fame baseball manager[56]

"If you fell down yesterday, stand up today."

—H. G. Wells, writer[57]

"I have not failed. I've just found 10,000 ways that don't work."

—Thomas Edison, inventor and businessman[58]

"Success is not final; failure is not fatal; it is the courage to continue that counts."

—Winston Churchill, British prime minister[59]

"Success is stumbling from failure to failure without loss of enthusiasm."

—Winston Churchill, British prime minister[60]

"There is only one thing that makes a dream impossible to achieve: the fear of failure."

—Paulo Coelho, author of the international best seller *The Alchemist*[61]

So don't be afraid to be all that you can be, even if it means persevering through failure. It'll build in you character, a trait often missing in today's world, and one we often think of in terms of morality. But perseverance, and the mental toughness needed for it, is a character trait. The best-selling author James Michener once said that "character consists of what you do on the third and fourth tries."[62]

So keep trying, keep pushing, keep persevering.

I recently saw a billboard in downtown Orlando. There was a picture of the actor John Wayne and a great quote from him that said, "Don't much like quitters, son."

If you maintain a tenacious, dogged stick-to-it-ivity, I guarantee you'll accomplish things that will amaze you. You'll soar to heights you never thought possible, achieve even your most extreme dreams, and yes, build your own magic kingdom.

Chapter 10

EXTREME COMPETITION

*"You have competition
every day because you set such
high standards for yourself
that you have to go out every day
and live up to that."*

—Michael Jordan, basketball player and owner [1]

Graham Spurrier was probably the last man you'd think of as being an extreme competitor, if only because his name was preceded by the occupational title of Reverend. Not only was the Reverend Graham Spurrier deeply religious, he was also a gentle man as well as a gentleman. But he found it difficult to hide his fiercely competitive streak when it came to sports. His wife, Marjorie, used to tell how Graham had a bad habit of throwing his tennis racquet in spasms of frustration. Years later, when Marjorie saw her son, the college football coach, throwing his visor during his own fits of frustration, she would wince knowingly.

Steve Spurrier inherited much from his father, not the least of which was his burning desire to compete and to win. During young Steve's formative years, when the family lived in Newport, Tennessee, his father started Little League baseball there so that his two sons could play the sport and also so that he could coach them. Several years later, when his father coached Steve in a Babe Ruth baseball league, the boy was well-versed in his father's philosophies regarding competition—philosophies that became a part of him like a genetic code. So when, on the first day of Babe Ruth baseball practice, Graham Spurrier gathered his young team along the right-field line, Steve knew exactly what was coming next:

"Okay," Graham Spurrier said, "how many of you boys believe in the saying, 'It's not whether you win or lose, but how you play the game?'" Steve watched as every hand shot up. Every hand, that is, except his. Graham Spurrier observed the group of boys, hands held aloft, and kept his gaze on them for several seconds without speaking.

"You can put your hands down," he finally said, "because I don't believe that statement. It does matter whether you win or lose. That's why they keep score. There's going to be a winner and a loser in every game. Any time you keep score, you're supposed to try and win. So we're going to play by the rules, and we're going to play fair. But we're going to try and win."

More than 40 years after that lesson, Steve Spurrier sat in what was then his football office at the University of Florida and told my cowriter Peter Kerasotis that story and the impact it had on him and his approach to competition.

"I believe that what separates the good coaches from the great ones is that the great ones hate to lose," Spurrier said. "I think I inherited that from my dad. He was a competitor. He could not take losing. I think you need to be that way as a coach. Once a coach or player gets used to losing, and it doesn't hurt them anymore, then they're going to be losers."

It's interesting that Coach Spurrier, who is one of the all-time great college football coaches and a man credited with reshaping the style of play in the vaunted Southeastern Conference, described it as *hating to lose*.

Throughout my career in sports, I've heard that phrase many times. For whatever reason, extreme competitors will often say that they hate losing more than anything else. Not uncommon is a comment Jimmy Connors made during the peak of his tennis prowess. Explaining what fueled his extreme competitive desire—and Connors was, if anything, a ferocious competitor—the tennis legend said: "I hate to lose more than I love to win."[2] It is why, years later, when retired professional athletes rewind their memories and hit the pause button on certain career moments, it seems to be the failures that they go straight to, especially those times when they lost and they know they could've and should've won. For them, the losses linger longer than the wins. It hurts. And it should. Ask golfing great Arnold Palmer about the seven major championships he won, and he'll invariably ruminate about the times he didn't win the one major that eluded him—the PGA Championship. He finished second three times in that major—in '64, '68, and '70—and those close to him will tell you that it is a bitter disappointment to him.

It's an interesting dichotomy between the two opposite ends of the emotional spectrum that are winning and losing, and it is part of the beauty of competition—that the outcome doesn't reside in some sort of middle ground. It's why we eschew ties, and why we insist on tie-breakers.

And when I say that winning and losing reside at the opposite ends of the emotional spectrum, it is not hyperbole. Perhaps you remember the long-running TV show that began in 1961 and lasted until 1998, called *ABC's Wide World of Sports*. If so, you're no doubt familiar with, and can likely recite, those well-known words from announcer Jim McKay's iconic intro, where he intones: "The thrill of victory and the agony of defeat."

Yes, it's that black-and-white.

You either win or you lose.

I know there is a movement afoot to downplay competition, and to say that everyone is a winner just by entering the race. Unlike what happened with Steve Spurrier's father, I know there are youth sports leagues that don't keep score, and that there are schools that want to give every kid a medal or a ribbon just for being there. On a micro level, I get it. I also get that on a macro level it isn't just unrealistic, it's unrealistic at Pollyannaish proportions. It's been said that while schools may have done away with winners and losers, life has not.

Life is competition. Against others. Against yourself. Against the forces of nature. Against your aging body. We compete every day, whether we realize it or not—and really, whether we like it or not. For those who doubt that, Ann Landers disagrees. The advice columnist once wrote this: "Anyone who believes that the competitive spirit in America is dead has never been in a supermarket when the cashier opens another checkout lane."[3]

While the competitive spirit in America isn't dead, I know there are some who would like to kill it, or at least diminish it. I know there are those who say that just getting in line is what's important, just joining the race. But whatever line you're in, someone is at the head of it; and whatever race you're in, someone is leading it. Who better for that to be than you? According to his son, the legendary football coach Vince Lombardi would have hated to see this societal shift away from keeping score and the de-emphasizing of competition.

"My father equated competition with what made America great," Vince Lombardi Jr. said. "He believed that the virtues and qualities learned through competitive athletics were the very qualities needed to succeed in life, and he encouraged parents and institutions to place more emphasis on competitive sports. He practiced what he preached. When he was a high school coach, he frequently made a speech titled, 'I'm Raising My Son to Be an Athlete.'"[4]

In that speech, Lombardi's father implored fathers to push their sons to play a game, any game, if only because it would help those boys to grow into leaders. And no doubt, given the evolving roles of gender in society, Lombardi's father would have the same things to say about daughters today. Having raised 19 children, I would agree.

Even worse than downplaying competition is that some have sought to demonize it, which raised the ire of Harvey Mackay, the motivational and business guru who wrote the best seller, *Swim with the Sharks Without Being Eaten Alive*. Listen to what Mackay says, and please listen closely, because his words cut to the heart of what competition is:

"Our image of corporate villainy is so pervasive, businesses are loath to present themselves as profit-hungry, competitive enterprises to anyone but the stockholders. The truth is, human beings compete for profit, love, prestige, prizes, power, and esteem. We compete in sports, love, business, and every other form of human activity. We thrive on competition. We do it for a living, and we do it for recreation. We do it for all the things we want and just for the sheer love of competing for its own sake. Sure, let's admit it, there's an ugly side to competition: greed, boasting, self-seeking, one-upmanship, but doesn't the good outweigh the bad?

"Without competition we would still be driving unsafe gas guzzlers. The Japanese slammed Detroit to the pavement and forced us to improve. Without competition, we never would have a space program. John Kennedy's promise to put a man on the moon was the result of the Russians seizing the initiative. Without competition, there would be a one-size-fits-all soda pop, one brand of television, and, worst of all, one flavor of politician.

"Competition has shaped every facet of our society. It is the essence of motivation. Competition is the reason salespeople sit in the open, in the bullpen, where they can track each other working . . . or not working . . . instead of being tucked away in an office. It's the reason we set annual sales goals and post monthly standings. It's the reason we get results. Competition is what drives performance in every field. Good guy images are fine, as long as we see them for what they are: advertising fluff. Let's stop treating competition as if it were wrong."[5]

Mackay pretty much touches all the bases, doesn't he? If you're in business, in sales, in scientific research, in software development, in sports, or just in this great game of life, it's all an ongoing competition, with every day bringing with it a series of wins and losses.

And again, as Jim McKay aptly put it in his *ABC's Wide World of Sports* intro: one is thrilling, the other agonizing. You love one, and you hate the other. And be assured, there is a mixture of both. Whenever Jimmy Connors and so many other athletes say that they hate to lose more than they love to win, they're acknowledging that both elements— both emotions—are present to some degree. And both push them. It's just that one pushes them more, which is fine.

Interestingly, love and hate are probably the two most powerful emotions known to us as humans. So whenever you're competing, tap into them, and whichever one works best for you—either loving to win or hating to lose—then especially mine that vein.

For Jimmy Connors, it was hating to lose. Same with Hall of Fame baseball pitcher Bob Gibson. I once heard one of Gibson's former teammates, Mike Shannon, say this about the great pitcher: "He was a fierce competitor; not because he wanted to win, but because he despised losing."

And then there is the other end of the spectrum. For the newsman Mike Wallace, in that fiercely competitive world of big-time broadcast journalism, it was all about loving to win. In fact, fellow journalist Peter

Jennings once said of Wallace, "He loves to win in such a way that it gets the competitive juices going in everybody else."

For Derek Jeter, winner of five World Series titles with the New York Yankees and maybe the greatest shortstop to ever play the game, it was probably an equal combination of both. One of the great stories about Jeter, and perhaps one of the most insightful, occurred after the Yankees lost Game 6 of the 2001 World Series by a lopsided 15–2 score. In that game, a journeyman relief pitcher named Jay Witasick surrendered a whopping nine of those runs, eight of them earned, in just $1\frac{1}{3}$ abysmal innings. With the score 15–0, Yankees manager Joe Torre pulled Jeter along with catcher Jorge Posada and first baseman Tino Martinez from the game to rest and prepare them for the critical and decisive Game 7.

When he went into the team's clubhouse to change from his spikes to turf shoes, Jeter overheard Witasick say, "Well, at least I had fun." Jeter snapped. Posada later told *Sports Illustrated* writer Tom Verducci, "Derek just jumped all over him. Derek couldn't believe what he was saying. He was really, really hot. That was the angriest I've ever seen him." Some time later, when Verducci questioned Jeter about the incident, and asked if he remembered it, the future Hall of Famer nodded. "I remember," he said, his agitation rising again with the memory. "Fun? I can't relate to it. I'll never forget that. *At least you had fun?* I'll never understand it. I don't want to understand it."[6]

Rather, what Derek Jeter understood, and what he always understood, is that it comes down to winning and losing, and that you compete to achieve the former and to avoid the latter. And the fun? The fun, of course, comes from winning. (As a footnote, that postseason performance was the last time Witasick ever pitched in a Yankees uniform, while Jeter went on to play for the pinstripes 13 more seasons, eventually retiring in 2014 with five World Series rings, the most hits in franchise history, and his ticket to Cooperstown punched.)

For Jeter, and other extreme competitors, there are no gray areas; no ambiguity. The goal is so clear that it can be distilled to one three-letter word, the one I wrote about in the introduction of this book, when the great Hall of Fame quarterback Johnny Unitas signed his autograph for a woman with that one small but powerful word—win.

"It's just winners and losers," sings rock poet Bruce Springsteen on his song "Atlantic City," before adding, "and don't get caught on the wrong side of that line."

The Hall of Fame baseball manager Leo Durocher defined it with a rhetorical question that is more of a statement. Asked Durocher, "What are we out at the park for, except to win?"[7]

Another baseball manager, Gene Mauch, once said about Gene Autry, his team's owner with the California Angels. "You have to bear in mind that Mr. Autry's favorite horse was named Champion. He ain't ever had one called Runner Up."[8]

While competition pervades all areas and aspects of life, we know that sometimes the consequences of the outcome are minor, and at other times major. Regarding the latter, General Omar Bradley once observed: "In war, there is no second prize for the runner-up."[9]

Another wonderful thing about competition is that when your competitor pushes you, you also find yourself pushing yourself. Jesse Owens, who won four Olympic gold medals in track and field, once observed, "I love competition. It makes me run faster."[10] And the Hall of Fame baseball manager Tony La Russa said, "Competition is a good thing. It brings out the best in players."[11] That's so true. Competition brings out the best in you. It breeds improvement, a betterment of yourself. It also reveals who you are. Said Pat Riley, winner of nine NBA titles as a player, assistant coach, head coach, and executive: "Once you're a competitor and involved in trying to win, what comes out of you is what you are."[12] Embrace that. Country music singer Reba McEntire certainly has. I once heard her say on a talk show: "I always feel pressure from young artists, and I like that competition."

I'm going to take that a step further and say that we shouldn't just *like* competition, we should *love* it. You see, what runs parallel with winning and losing is competing. It's the third rail on the track that takes us to becoming an extreme winner, and it's an important one—vitally so.

You may love to win more than you hate to lose, or vice versa, but what you must unequivocally and unabashedly and uncompromisingly love is competing.

"I love competition," said the late NBA coach Bill Musselman. "I don't know why, but a lot of people don't like competition. They'd rather go set up a business down the block, where there's no competition. I want my business where there's three other guys doing the same thing."[13]

Longtime print journalists will tell you that one of the saddest things that happened to their industry, aside from the way the Internet has decimated it, is when cities and towns went from having two, three, or more newspapers to just one. That loss of competition took the edge away from their profession. Those ink-stained scribes loved competing against the other guy or gal covering the same beat. In the end, the ones who won more of those head-to-head, day-to-day battles were the ones whose newspapers stayed in existence while the others folded. That's life in general. Not everyone in the race gets a medal. All too often, what most people get is a pink slip or a sign on their company's front door that says: Going Out of Business. In fact, it's been said that there are two kinds of companies: those that are competitive and those that are closed.

I once saw a plaque on a businessman's office wall that I'll share with you. It said:

> "My competitors do more for me than my friends do. My friends are too polite to point out my weaknesses, but my competitors go to great lengths to advertise them. My competitors are efficient, diligent and attentive and they make me search for ways to improve my products and service. My competitors would take my business away from me if they could. If I had no competitors, I would be lazy, incompetent, and inattentive. I need the discipline they force upon me. I salute my competitors. They have been good to me. God bless them all."

That is the real world. In whatever you do, in whatever business you're in, whatever product you're producing, whatever service you're offering, whatever sport you're competing in, there is always going to be someone striving to do it better than you. And that's a good thing.

"Nothing focuses the mind better than the constant sight of a competitor who wants to wipe you off the map," said D. Wayne Calloway, who was the former chairman and CEO of PepsiCo.[14]

Competition ramps up your energy, narrows your focus, streamlines your goals, and gives everything you do the weight of purpose.

Competition simply makes everything better. It makes your business better. It makes your product better. It makes *you* better. Where would Coca-Cola be without Pepsi? Where would Apple be without Samsung? Where would McDonald's be without Burger King? Where would Visa be without MasterCard? Answer to all the above: Not as good. And while we're asking questions, here are a few more. How great did Wilt Chamberlain make Bill Russell, and vice versa? How great did Joe Frazier make Muhammad Ali, and vice versa? How great did Martina Navratilova make Chris Evert, and vice versa? How great did Arnold Palmer make Jack Nicklaus, and vice versa? How great did Magic Johnson make Larry Bird, and vice versa?

The better the competition, the better you become.

"An athlete doesn't get good by playing against someone she can easily beat," said Donna Lopiano, the founder and president of Sports Management Resources. "If you win against someone who is not very good, you are little better than not very good. Always seek competition against someone better than you are. Always seek the most demanding challenge. When great players practice, they envision themselves in the most difficult and challenging situations, so there are no surprises or nervousness when they actually find themselves in that situation." Lopiano went on to say that successful athletes "want to play against the best and are always looking for an extraordinary challenge. These athletes want to play against the best because they know this will make them better. By elevating their game, they will know how good they can be."[15]

Or, as a Bible proverb states: "Iron sharpens iron."[16]

It was that type of mind-set that made Joe Cribbs, a journeyman football running back, much better than he would have been otherwise. "When I see a guy, and he is super, I'm not going to say he is the best," Cribbs said years ago in an interview. "I'm going to say, 'I'm going to be better than he is. I'm going to compete with him.'"

And when you're an extreme competitor like Joe Cribbs, the desire to compete never leaves you, especially if during your career you had a specific rival. That was the case with Joe DiMaggio and Ted Williams, two Hall of Fame baseball players whose games were always being compared against each other, with the debate always raging as to who was the best. And make no mistake, DiMaggio and Williams were aware of the debate and competed against each other in their own way, even long after their playing days were over. There is a wonderful story along those lines that the late sportswriter Joe Falls used to tell. As the story goes, Falls called DiMaggio on his 70th birthday and had a half-hour conversation with him. The following spring, he ran into Williams and told him about how DiMaggio engaged him on the phone for a half-hour. Williams, who was 66 at the time, barked back at Falls, "When I'm 70, you call me and I'll give you an hour."

Competitions don't have to be acrimonious. One of the all-time greatest sports rivalries was Arnold Palmer and Jack Nicklaus, and they remained friendly through it all. Not social, buddy-buddy friends. But friendly. Here is what each of them have said in interviews.

Arnold Palmer: "The competition has been there from the very beginning. In my mind, it will go on for as long as we live. We don't socialize, we don't spend a whole lot of time together, but Jack and I have a deep-seated respect for one another. If you stop and reflect upon how long we've been at it, I think we've gotten along pretty well over the years. I consider us friends."

Jack Nicklaus: "Arnold and I have had a rivalry in everything we've done. We're competitive in golf, we're competitive in business, and we've been competitive in endorsing products. I've said it before and I'll say it again. . . . I don't like to be beat by Arnold, and I'm sure he feels the same way about me. There is no one in the world I'd rather beat than Arnold."

I'm sure you'd find similar comments from Larry Bird and Magic Johnson. And I'm sure that all those who've been involved in great rivalries will admit that they not only benefitted from fierce competition, but also looked forward to it. That's really the one common denominator with all the great champions I've seen and had the good fortune of being around and knowing. Without exception, they are all extreme competitors. Instead of shying away from competition, they seek it and embrace it.

"I just like competition," Nicklaus plainly said. "I enjoyed the challenges of each guy who came along. Every time. Arnold Palmer first, and Gary Player, and all of a sudden Tom Weiskopf, Tom Watson, Lee Trevino, and Johnny Miller. There was always somebody who came along posing a challenge. I always enjoyed that."

Why? Because it propelled him to work harder, made him better. When you love to compete, you'll love doing whatever it takes to compete well . . . and to win. That extra set in the weight room, that extra mile of roadwork, that extra bucket of practice balls, that extra 100 swings in the batting cage, that extra hour in the office . . . none of it will seem like a burden. "How do you spot a true competitor—that unique individual who possesses a special quality called the will to win?" John Wooden once queried. "Easy. The competitor with the will to win also has the will to work."[17] And a desire to do the work. To put in the practice time. To sacrifice. You'll want to do it, because you absolutely believe that it is all worthwhile.

That's always been the way Tiger Woods approached golf and his preparation to compete. His love of competition fuels everything he does behind the scenes.

"I love to mix it up," Woods said. "I like to go toe-to-toe, eyeball-to-eyeball. That to me is fun. That's what we as players practice all those hours for, all those hours in the gym, all those miles on the road, to be in that position, to feel that rush, to win."[18]

When you envision that goal in your mind, when you see that end result, it'll fan your competitive flames. NASCAR driver Jeff Gordon felt that way.

"The thing that caught my attention with racing early on was seeing the checkered flag wave and experiencing what it's like to win," Gordon said. "That brought out the competitive edge in me. From that point on it's never been the same. It's always just looking for that checkered flag. I'm not a speed demon. I'm not a guy who likes to go fast. It's about just trying to make the car go faster than anyone else."[19]

The other thing about extreme competitors is that they want the pressure; they want to be in that moment when the game is on the line. Derek Jeter wanted the bat in his hand, or that ground ball hit to him. Players like Michael Jordan and Larry Bird wanted the ball in their hands when their teams were down to one shot that they needed to make to win. The sportswriter Dave Kindred noticed that about Bird. "Larry Bird always wanted the last shot. He believed he would make it," Kindred wrote, noting that at the NBA's annual 3-point shooting contest during the All-Star break, Bird would not-so-kiddingly ask, "Who is going to be second this year?"

Extreme competitors, because they also have extreme focus, an extreme work ethic, and an extreme positive attitude, always believe they are going to make that shot, get that hit, complete that pass, sink that putt. That's why they want the spotlight when it's burning the brightest.

"It was more than just confidence," Kindred wrote about Bird, although he could've been speaking about any number of extreme competitors. "To take that last shot, when that one shot means victory or maybe defeat, is to expose yourself to the possibility of pain. It is a proposition so frightening to many folks that they find ways to avoid it."

But if you've employed and implemented the nine extreme steps leading up to this chapter, you won't be afraid of competition, especially when you realize that it's unavoidable; that it pervades every aspect of life. Here are just a few of the wide-ranging thoughts on the topic:

"Honest competition is a wonderful thing, as central to the American way of thinking as anything."

—Arnold Palmer, golfer[20]

"I can't say, 'It doesn't matter if you win or lose.' It's not true. You go in to win."

—Katarina Witt, Olympic gold medal–winning skater[21]

"Brains without competitive hearts are rudderless."

—Vince Lombardi, football coach[22]

"No competition, no progress."

—Bela Karolyi, gymnastics coach[23]

"Without competition, we all would become mediocre. Competition keeps you going one step further, and that's the way to get ahead. Competition promotes the very best kind of discipline. It forces you to do a little more, to give a little extra. As we athletes say, 'It raises the level of your game.'"

—Mary Lou Retton, Olympic gold medal–winning gymnast[24]

"In business, the competition will bite you if you keep running. If you stand still, they will swallow you."

—William S. Knudsen, automotive executive[25]

"The breakfast of champions is not cereal. It's the opposition."

—Nick Seitz, golfer[26]

"You are shaped by your competition. You measure yourself against your toughest rival."

—Bobby Bowden, football coach[27]

"There is nothing I love as much as a good fight."

—Franklin D. Roosevelt, 32nd U.S. President[28]

"The only thing better than a little competition is a lot of competition."

—General David Petraeus[29]

"I'm convinced the only thing that separates champions is the individual's competitive drive. The people who survive and then flourish are the ones who love to compete . . . maybe even live to compete."

—Joe Montana, football player[30]

That last quote from Montana is profound, and accurate. The loss column—for teams, for individuals, for businesses, for life—is filled with people who were smarter, faster, stronger, better, and more talented. Meanwhile, the win column is filled with people who were more competitive.

As great as he was, perhaps the greatest ever, I don't think Michael Jordan was the most talented or athletic basketball player there ever was; but he was probably the greatest competitor. In fact, he's one of the all-time greatest competitors in any arena. MJ was always competing—against himself, against others, in real games, in practice, playing cards on the team plane, it didn't matter. Former ESPN sportswriter Bill Simmons once described Jordan as "homicidally competitive." Wrote Simmons in an August 13, 2012, ESPN.com piece: "Jordan loved beating people so much that he couldn't stop doing it. He had to beat people at everything: golf, poker, half-court shots, even whose bag came out first in baggage claim."

Yes, Jordan loved to compete, and he certainly loved to win.

"I play to win, whether during practice or a real game," he once said matter-of-factly. "And I will not let anything get in the way of me and my competitive enthusiasm to win." Extreme competitors like Jordan are constantly manufacturing some sort of way to compete, injecting small competitions into larger ones, small battles into bigger ones. Said Jordan: "When you're a competitor and want to win, nothing is trivial."[31] And for Jordan and other extreme competitors, it's always great fun, too. That's probably why, during one of my many conversations with the basketball coaching legend John Wooden, he told me this about Jordan: "He's one of the greatest competitors I've ever seen, in any sport, and he looks like he's always enjoying it."

Extreme competitors like Jordan don't have an on-off switch. They're always on, and their competitive desire crackles as if a current of electricity was flowing through them. My writing partner Peter Kerasotis recalls a Los Angeles Rams training camp in the summer of 1986, with Rams players going through a morning of preseason physicals and other perfunctory tests—except that they weren't perfunctory to the team's star running back Eric Dickerson.

"They were doing these hand-eye coordination drills," Kerasotis says. "A light would appear on a board, and they'd have to quickly tap it and look for the next light that emerged, and then tap it. The entire exercise was timed. Well, Dickerson turned this seemingly unimportant drill into a team competition to see who could come up with the best time. As I recall, it was Eric Dickerson."

Keep in mind that this was two seasons *after* Dickerson set the single-season rushing record of 2,105 yards—a record that still stands. At that point in his career, what did a simple little hand-eye coordination drill mean to him? Answer: an opportunity to compete.

Kerasotis also recalls chatting once with former NFL wide receiver Cris Collinsworth's wife, Holly, and her bemused take on how her husband had turned their home into a houseful of little competitors. Holly said they rarely had any problem getting their four kids ready for school, because Cris had made every part of the mundane morning rituals—from the getting out of bed to the brushing of teeth to the eating of breakfast—into various types of competition.

One of the great stories about the power of competition occurred about a hundred years ago. The industrialist Charles M. Schwab kept trying to get his factory steel workers to be more productive. But time and again, none of his efforts worked—not even the threat of firing.

According to Dale Carnegie's book *How to Win Friends & Influence People*, this is the account of what happened:

"This conversation took place at the end of the day just before the night shift came on. Schwab asked the manager for a piece of chalk, then, turning to the nearest man, asked:

" 'How many heats did your shift make today?'

" 'Six.'

"Without another word, Schwab chalked a big figure six on the floor, and walked away. When the night shift came in, they saw the six and asked what it meant. The big boss was in here today, the day people said. He asked us how many heats we made, and we told him six. He chalked it down on the floor.

"The next morning Schwab walked through the mill again. The night shift had rubbed out six and replaced it with a big seven.

"When the day shift reported for work the next morning, they saw a big seven chalked on the floor. So the night shift thought they were better than the day shift, did they? Well, they would show the night shift a thing or two. The crew pitched in with enthusiasm, and when they quit that night, they left behind them an enormous, swaggering 10. Things were stepping up.

"Shortly this mill, which had been lagging way behind in production, was turning out more work than any other mill in the plant."

Schwab's strategy was to create competition—a rivalry between teams of workers—and see what happened. Later he told Carnegie, "The way to get things done is to stimulate competition."[32]

And when you can stimulate a team of people, the results are dynamic. The great WNBA player Maya Moore told sportswriter Richard Deitsch in an October 21, 2013, *Sports Illustrated* article: "I love to compete, and when you have the talent, the discipline, the work ethic, and teammates who do the same thing, winning follows you around."

All of us—and I mean all of us—are born with some type of competition coursing through our veins. Use that competitive drive within you to your advantage. That's what extreme competitors do. Extreme competitors love to compete and will even find and invent areas to create competition.

That's certainly the way Cal Ripken Jr. was. People remember him for his Iron Man record in baseball, playing 2,632 consecutive games. But those who were close to him will tell you that he was an extreme competitor —in everything. Baseball writer and ESPN analyst Tim Kurkjian has some great stories about Ripken. One was told to him by pitcher Mike Flanagan, who was Ripken's former teammate. Flanagan recalled that he was a competitor in a variety of sports, but once he became a pro baseball player, he lost his desire to compete in other sports—if only because devoting his energy to baseball was so demanding. Not so with Ripken. "It didn't matter anymore if I won in Ping-Pong," Flanagan told Kurkjian. "But it matters to him. Basketball is a perfect example. I've played basketball many times with Ripken [and] I learned more about him playing basketball than I ever did watching him play baseball."

Ripken would play pickup games over the winter in a small, dank gym in Baltimore.

"There were no fans, there was no money to be made, and he played every game like it was his last," Flanagan said. "He dived for loose balls, he admonished teammates for dribbling with their heads down, and he was the best help defender ever. In pickup games, with nothing on the line and no one waiting to play the next game, he would harass me defensively all the way down the court until his offensive player arrived. 'Would you leave me alone?' I once yelled at him. 'Can't you stop trying for one second?' 'No!' he said."

That was early in Ripken's pro baseball career. Kurkjian's other story comes later in Ripken's career, and it highlights that even after he became an established All-Star, his competitive fire still burned hot. As Kurkjian's story goes, at the old Metrodome in Minneapolis there was a tunnel leading from the visitors' dugout to the clubhouse that was long and steep. It had 11 steps, then a six-foot landing, another 11 steps, another six-foot landing, and then a final 11 steps. Every time after Ripken finished his pre-game infield, he would sprint up the stairs and leap through the series of steps and landings and do so in just six strides—an incredible feat. But then, before one game, teammate Rene Gonzales also accomplished the feat in six strides.

"That was unacceptable to Ripken," Kurkjian wrote. "He couldn't stand to not be the best; not even for one night. So he went back to the bottom and did it again. He made it in five. Why? Why would a guy who was closing in on Lou Gehrig's record of 2,130 consecutive games feel the need to play such a stupid, childish, meaningless game, 45 minutes before the start of a Major League game? What if he turned an ankle as he lunged on that last flight?"

Why?

Kurkjian answered: "The tunnel game was about the love of competition, the common denominator shared by all the greatest players."

Competition, after all, is competition.

One of Coach Jerry Sloan's all-time favorite players was John Stockton. Playing for Gonzaga University in his hometown of Spokane, Washington, the 6-foot-1 Stockton was a relative unknown coming out of college in 1984. The Utah Jazz decided to gamble a 16th overall pick on him, considering him a project. What they got in return was not only one of the greatest point guards in NBA history, but one of the game's fiercest competitors, which is what Sloan so loved about Stockton. It wasn't that Stockton was competitive in games, he was competitive in everything. For example, at the end of practices when players are fatigued, coaches will run suicide drills—which, quite frankly, players hate. Running suicides is a great way to increase endurance and speed, but there is obviously a reason why they are called suicides. In the drill, players start at the baseline and run to the foul line, touching it, before returning back to the baseline, where they quickly touch that before running to half-court, touching it and back, before finally running the full length of the court and back at full sprint.

Most players endure the suicides with a goal of just getting done with them. But not John Stockton, who thrived on what he clearly saw as another avenue of competition. "In 19 years, John Stockton never once lost a suicide drill in practice," Sloan said. "Well, there was one day. He was sick, but he still ran it. That's the important thing. John didn't need all the attention that comes with making All-Star teams or getting his name into headlines. He just liked to play basketball. He loved to compete."[33]

That fiery desire to compete and win, and doing whatever it takes to do so, is likely why Stockton holds two all-time NBA records that might not be considered glamorous in the eyes of a casual fan, although coaches love players who excel in these areas. Stockton holds the NBA record for both assists and steals—and by a wide margin, too. Not surprisingly, John Wooden used to say that the one player he most enjoyed watching was John Stockton, and the only player whom he'd pay to see.

And again, Stockton was a little-known point guard coming out of college. "Nobody thought that he was going to be this good," said Frank Layden, his first NBA coach. "Nobody. But the thing was, you couldn't measure his heart."[34]

That's the thing about being competitive. You can't really quantify it. It's an intangible. It doesn't show up on a stopwatch or a weight-room wall or in any kind of measurable way. Pat Summitt, the great women's college basketball coach at the University of Tennessee, explained it this way: "You can't always be the most talented person in the room, but you can be the most competitive."[35]

And when you can combine extreme competitiveness with some of the other things we've discussed—like extreme work ethic, goals, passion, and perseverance—then you have the Michael Jordans and Tiger Woodses—the legendary giants in sports.

Nobody can deny Tiger's enormous talent, especially during the peak of his golfing career. But notice what he said during one of the more revealing interviews he ever did, and certainly a very engaging one. It was for a *60 Minutes* segment, and this is the exchange Tiger had with the late Ed Bradley.

"I love to compete . . . whatever it is," he told Bradley. "You and I could be playing cards right now and I'd want to kick your butt."

"You'd wanna win?" Bradley said.

"No, I'd wanna kick your butt," Tiger emphasized. "There's a difference. It's just in me. I don't know why. I enjoy competing."

Tiger not only wants to kick butts, he wants to kick his own butt. You see, with extreme competitors there is also that inner competition, against themselves, to be better than they were before.

Shortly before his death in 1994, Richard Nixon was having a conversation with his former speechwriter William Safire. The former president was quite the sports fan, so it's not surprising that Nixon tapped into sports to shed light on the two ways we most often compete—against others and against ourselves.

"Sterling Marlin won the Daytona 500 a couple of months ago by twenty-three-hundredths of a second, going over 180 miles per hour," Nixon noted. "And in the Winter Olympics in Norway, the American alpine skier Tommy Moe won the downhill by just four one-hundredths of a second. Pretty slim margins of victory. But consider this: Sterling Marlin had another car on his tail the whole time; the competition was right there in his rearview mirror. If he thought about letting up, the other guys were always there to remind him. But Tommy Moe, the downhill skier, was alone. He couldn't see the competition whizzing along next to him. Nothing to remind him, except an inner voice whispering at him to push the limits."

Here are a few more voices, speaking—not whispering—about pushing our limits. Listen to what they tell us:

> *"I do not try to dance better than anyone else. I only try to dance better than myself."*
>
> —Mikhail Baryshnikov, dancer, choreographer, and actor[36]

> *"The person I've always competed hardest against is myself. My objective is to be the best possible Terry Bradshaw."*
>
> —Terry Bradshaw, quarterback[37]

> *"To be your best, you must compete with yourself."*
>
> —Rev. Richard C. Halverson, minister[38]

> *"The best way to beat the competition is to compete against yourself."*
>
> —Julian Hall, businessman and entrepreneur[39]

> *"The principle is competing against yourself. It's about self-improvement, about being a better person than you were the day before."*
>
> —Steve Young, quarterback and NFL analyst[40]

"Put yourself in competition with yourself each day. Each morning, look back upon your work of yesterday and then try to beat it."

—Charles Sheldon, minister[41]

"Our business in life is not to get ahead of others, but to get ahead of ourselves . . . to break our own records, to outstrip our yesterday by our today."

—Stewart B. Johnson, Vermont governor[42]

"The game has such a hold on golfers because they compete, not only against an opponent, but against the course, against par, and most surely against themselves."

—Gary Player, golfer[43]

"Eventually you learn that the competition is against the little voice inside you that wants you to quit."

—George Sheehan, runner, physician, and philosopher[44]

"Don't bother just to be better than your contemporaries or predecessors. Try to be better than yourself."

—William Faulkner, writer[45]

"The only competition worthy a wise man is with himself."

—Anna Jameson, writer[46]

Rick Fox, who from 1991 to 2004 played for either the Boston Celtics or the Los Angeles Lakers, was around two of the all-time greatest NBA competitors—Michael Jordan and Kobe Bryant. Like Jordan, Fox also played basketball for Dean Smith at North Carolina. Interesting that Fox saw in Jordan and Bryant the two types of competition we've been discussing here—with others and with yourself.

"There are no two other individuals I've known who act like they do," Fox said in Phil Jackson's book *Eleven Rings*. "To them, winning at all costs is all that matters, and they demand that everyone around them act the same way, regardless of whether they can or not. They say, 'Find somewhere inside yourself to get better, because that's what I'm doing every day of the week, every minute of the day.' They have no tolerance for anything less: none."

But here's the difference that Fox noticed between Michael and Kobe.

"Michael had to win at everything," he recalled. "I mean, he couldn't drive from Chapel Hill to Wilmington without making it a race. Whether you wanted to compete or not, he was competing with you. But I think Kobe competes with himself more than anything else. He sets barriers and challenges for himself, and he just happens to need other people to come along with him."[47]

Which one are you? Are you one who competes against others? Against yourself? Both? If you haven't yet discovered the answer, now is the time. Find your inner Michael Jordan, find your inner Kobe Bryant, find your inner you. It is in us to compete. It is in you. Dip your bucket into your competitive well and draw up all your competitive juices.

Do that, and you'll be an extreme competitor.

Chapter 11

EXTREME DESIRE

*"The starting point of
all achievement is desire."*

—Napoleon Hill, author [1]

ome years ago, I was having lunch with Tom Smith, who at the time was our athletic trainer for the Orlando Magic, and he told me a story of what he encountered at our team's training facility a year earlier. It was summertime, the offseason, so Tom didn't show up too terribly early at our facility—about 9 AM. As he walked in, he noticed the lights were already on with a lone figure working out.

That sure looks like Kobe Bryant, Tom thought to himself.

Of course, it couldn't have been.

Could it?

Tom moved in closer, got a better look, and saw that it was indeed Kobe Bryant, the superstar guard for the Los Angeles Lakers at *our* training facility in Orlando on an off-season summer morning.

"Kobe!" Tom exclaimed. "What are you doing here?"

"I'm on vacation with my family," Kobe replied.

"No, no, no, I mean what are you doing *here*? What are you doing *here*, right *now*?"

"My family and I, we're staying at one of the Disney World resort hotels. I got permission to come here in the mornings and work out."

In his conversation, Tom ascertained from Kobe that he was rising at 6 AM, driving 30 to 45 minutes across town to our facility, working out, and then heading back to clean up, be with his family, and as Kobe said, "We're in the parks by 11 AM."

Incredulous, Tom asked him how many days during his family vacation he was planning on doing this.

Kobe looked back at him equally incredulous.

"Every day," he stated, as if his reply should have been a foregone conclusion.

When Tom relayed the story to me, he was still shaking his head, still incredulous.

"There is a reason," he intoned, "why *that* guy is so good."

There certainly is. There are, in fact, a variety of reasons. One of the foremost of them is that Kobe Bryant, like all extreme winners, has extreme desire.

What is extreme desire? You can describe it a number of ways, with a variety of adjectives. It's having drive. It's being dedicated and determined. It's consistency, being someone others can rely and count on—consistent especially because of the commitment you've made, which means you are dependable. It's endurance. It's being a fighter. It's working on the little things, over and over, until you're fundamentally sound. It's wanting—demanding, in fact—to be challenged every day. Those with extreme desire have all the G words; they are gamers, grinders, they have grit and guts. They also have the three Hs—heart, hunger, and hustle. They're intense. They're relentless, resolute, and have resolve. They're willing to sacrifice and they refuse to stop when they hit obstacles. They don't retreat. They don't quit. They don't surrender. Those with extreme desire are mentally tough that way. Plucky. I love that word—plucky. Mostly, I love people who approach what they do with extreme desire. They're invigorating to be around, and their determined attitude is infectious.

Do you want to be that type of person? Do you want all the aforementioned adjectives and attributes ascribed to you?

Then read on.

As you've no doubt noticed in a lot of these chapters, many of these qualities don't just feed into each other, they bleed into each other. If you're an extreme competitor, you're going to have extreme desire. And to have extreme desire, you must already have an extreme goal.

I started this chapter with an anecdote about Kobe Bryant, not because it was an anecdote that illustrated the point, but because Kobe is an athlete who epitomizes—and perhaps even personifies—extreme desire along with a good handful of the other attributes we've mentioned. And Kobe developed all those things at a young age. When he was a teenager, Bryant set the goal of leading his high school team, the Lower Merion High Aces in the Philadelphia suburbs, to its first state championship in 53 years. His desire to achieve that goal was extreme, as you will see. In the semifinals of Bryant's senior season, Lower Merion was to play Chester High, a team that had already beaten them twice in the state semifinals with Bryant on the squad. To make the odds appear even more insurmountable, Lower Merion High basketball coach Gregg Downer recalled a practice leading up to the game when there was a collision on the court.

"I look over and see Kobe lying on the floor in a pool of his own blood," Downer said. "He's got a broken nose heading into one of the most electric games in a long time. We spent a couple of days frantically trying to find a mask that would fit him. The day of the game, he warmed up with the mask on. But in the locker room right before we went out onto the court, he ripped it off in front of everybody. He threw it against the wall and yelled, 'I'm not wearing this thing! Let's go to war!' He scored 39 points. We won."[2]

Three days later, thanks to Kobe Bryant's unquenchable desire to be a champion, Lower Merion High won the state title.

So exactly how important is approaching what you do with desire? The late artist, poet, and writer Kahlil Gibran said this about it: "Desire is half of life, indifference is half of death."[3]

Gibran's quote reminds me of a story passed down through the millennia about the Greek philosopher Socrates, who was one of history's great thinkers and a founding father of Western philosophy. There are various versions of this story. This is the one I like:

According to legend, a young man approached Socrates and asked about the secret to success. Socrates in turn asked the young man to meet him at the river the next morning. Once there, Socrates had them walk side by side into the river until the water reached the young man's neck. That's when Socrates pounced on him, dunking the young man under water. The young man struggled, but Socrates was strong and he kept him submerged until the young man started turning blue. Only then did the philosopher pull his head out and watch as the young man gasped violently, taking heaving breaths of air. After a few moments, Socrates asked him:

"What did you want most when you were under water?"

"Air," the young man replied, still gasping.

"That is the secret to success," Socrates said. "When you want success as badly as you want air, then you will get it."

That's what you'll see again and again with successful people, with extreme winners; they approach their sport, their craft, their business as if their life depended on it. People with extreme desire do not rely on talent. In fact, they go about their profession as if they have no talent, as if they have to overcompensate in other areas because of a lack of talent. Those types of people stand out, not because of what they do, but because of who they are.

That's the way Michael Jordan was when he played for the Chicago Bulls, winning six championships. Bulls team owner Jerry Reinsdorf once told Jordan that he reminded him of Jake LaMotta. Jordan shot Reinsdorf a quizzical look. "Who?" Reinsdorf explained that LaMotta was a relentless middleweight boxer in the 1940s and 1950s who, although he did lose fights by technical knockouts, nonetheless was never knocked off his feet. LaMotta's legend is that he would stand there and take blow after blow, refusing to go down. "You had to kill him to beat him," Reinsdorf said. "He refused to lose." LaMotta's life was later depicted in the Martin Scorsese film *Raging Bull*, starring Robert De Niro. When Reinsdorf spoke to a writer named Adam Fluck about the Jordan-LaMotta analogy, he said this about his superstar player: "There probably have been players with similar skills to his. The thing that separated him from all the other athletes I've ever seen was his desire to win."[4]

My cowriter Peter Kerasotis was at the 1997 NBA Finals between the Chicago Bulls and Utah Jazz and witnessed Jordan's heroic performance in Game 5 at Salt Lake City (and believe me, neither Kerasotis nor I feel comfortable using the word *heroic* for an athletic performance, but this rises to that watermark). The series was tied at 2–2 when Jordan became extremely ill. It was reported that he had the flu, but now Jordan says he believes he was the victim of food or drug poisoning, perhaps deliberate.

Whatever it was, Jordan hid how seriously ill he was. Only years later did he reveal the gravity of the situation, telling Rick Weinberg for an ESPN.com piece[5] that he awoke in the middle of the night, sweating profusely, shaking uncontrollably, and feeling as if he was going to die. "I was scared; I didn't know what was happening to me," Jordan said, adding that he felt "partially paralyzed." Nauseated, and with the room spinning, Jordan summoned the Bulls' medical personnel, who flatly told him there was no way he would play in Game 5.

From Jordan's perspective, however, there was no way he was *not* going to play in Game 5. Never mind that he had already accomplished so much in his career—four NBA championships while winning the Finals' MVP Award each time to go along with nine scoring titles, four season MVP Awards, and two Olympic gold medals. His desire to win championships, and to play in that Game 5, was overwhelming—extreme. No matter what he accomplished, or how much he accomplished, Michael Jordan always believed at his core that he still had something to prove. The fact that Utah forward Karl Malone had won the season MVP award over him only fueled Jordan even more. Besides, although the series was tied at 2–2, the Jazz had won two in a row. The Bulls needed to stop their momentum, which was something Jordan felt was his duty to do.

Not play?

He may as well not breathe.

For the next 24 hours, Jordan was bedridden, taking IV fluids while trying to stave off dehydration. His weight dropped several pounds. He missed Chicago's practices the day before and also the day of Game 5. Then, three hours before tipoff, he willed himself out of his hotel bed and dragged himself to the Delta Center.

His teammate Scottie Pippen will never forget what he saw when Jordan entered the team's locker room. "The way he looked, there's no way I thought he could even put on his uniform," Pippen recalled. "I'd never seen him like that. He looked bad—I mean really bad."

Several times in the first quarter, it looked as if Jordan—unsteady and clearly not close to full speed or strength—would faint. Several of his shots weren't just off, they were *way* off. Utah took advantage, taking a commanding 29–16 first-quarter lead and building on it early in the second quarter until they led by 16 points. Jordan kept pushing himself and his teammates, forcing himself to drive his body beyond normal thresholds. Somehow, someway, he scored 17 second-quarter points, prompting play-by-play announcer Marv Albert to describe what he just saw as "a heroic performance by Michael Jordan." Whatever he was able to summon was enough to pull Chicago to within four points at half-time—53–49. In the Bulls' locker room, Jordan was fed more fluids and draped in cold towels. He looked spent, as if that second-quarter effort drained everything he could possibly give. Nobody would've been surprised had he sat out the second half. But again, Jordan dragged himself onto the court. His third quarter, though, resembled the first. Again, he looked as if he would pass out, his arms often dangling at his side like loose ropes. He hunched over during timeouts, his hands on his knees, clutching the bottom of his shorts for support.

"In between every possession, when there was a dead ball, you could just see it on his face, how drained he was," Bulls teammate John Paxson recalled years later. "But then when the play would start, he'd summon something from within."[6]

Early in the fourth quarter, the Jazz stretched their lead to 77–69, and again Jordan willed himself back into the fray, nailing a 12-foot jumper that sparked a 10–0 Bulls run. He orchestrated the offense, seizing control when he could, passing precisely to teammates at other times, all while clearly exhausted. Still, with nothing but fumes in his tank, he continued to mash the gas pedal.

"I don't know how I got through the fourth quarter," Jordan said afterward. "I was just trying to gut myself through it."[7]

He did. And with 3:55 remaining in the game, the Bulls tied the Jazz at 81–81. With the score still tied with less than a minute left to play, the focus of attention was obviously on Jordan. That's when he nailed a three-pointer that TV announcers described as sticking "a dagger" in the Jazz. The Bulls went on to win, 90–88, in what Marv Albert called "a courageous, classic performance." Jordan's 38 points wasn't only the game high, it doubled the output by the next leading scorer—Karl Malone with his 19 points. The loss deflated the Jazz, who succumbed in Game 6 by a 90–86 margin, giving the Bulls their fifth NBA title and Jordan his fifth Finals MVP award.

Here is what I love, though. As Jordan wobbled off the court after that Game 5 turning point, literally carried along by Scottie Pippen, he was stopped by courtside reporter Ahmad Rashad and asked for his thoughts. "It's all about desire," Jordan told Rashad. "We wanted it real bad. And me as the leader, I had to come out and do my best. Somehow I found the energy to stay strong. I wanted it really bad."

Like most everyone else, Bulls head coach Phil Jackson described what he and the nation had just witnessed as "a heroic effort, one to add to the collection of efforts that make up his legend."

A little later, speaking to the media, Jordan said playing that game "was probably the most difficult thing I've ever done. I almost played myself into passing out just to win a basketball game. If we had lost, I would have been devastated."

But *why*? Why play when he was that ill? Why play to almost the point of losing consciousness?

Jordan repeated the same thing he had told Ahmad Rashad, telling a larger contingent of media members, and really all of us, what it boiled down to for him.

"It was all about desire," he said.

Extreme desire, to be sure.

I find it particularly interesting that Jordan focused on his desire, and not on his obstacle. And it was only years later, after his retirement, that he divulged just how sick he was that night. That's a hallmark of extreme winners.

If you followed Derek Jeter's career you'll know that he was loathe to talk about injuries. Whenever he was asked about them, the Yankee shortstop's stock answer was: "I don't talk about injuries, because I think it's just making an excuse for yourself. You either play or you don't."[8] And from Jeter's perspective, if you're playing, then there is nothing else to talk about. His attitude reminds me of a saying I really like: You're either going to find a way, or you're going to find an excuse.

Love him or loathe him, George Steinbrenner was a find-a-way type of guy. The late New York Yankees owner took over the once-proud but moribund franchise in 1973. During Steinbrenner's tenure until his death in 2010, the Yankees won seven world championships. One of Steinbrenner's old college fraternity brothers, Charlie Glass, was once asked how he'd account for his friend's success. "He had this great drive," Glass said. "You can do a lot of amazing things if you just try. That's why so many people don't do a heck of a lot. They just give up. George just doesn't give up."[9]

That's the same motto that the late college basketball coach Jim Valvano inspired us with: "Don't give up. Don't ever give up."[10] When you have extreme desire, that'll be your attitude. To complement that, here are a few of my favorite quotes about desire:

"The starting point of all achievement is desire.
Keep this constantly in mind. Weak desire brings weak results,
just as a small amount of fire makes a small amount of heat."
—Napoleon Hill, author[11]

"My attitude is never to be satisfied: never enough, never."
—Duke Ellington, jazz pianist[12]

"Desire is the most important factor in the success of any athlete."
—Willie Shoemaker, jockey[13]

"People who are successful simply want it more than people
who are not."
—Ian Schrager, entrepreneur, hotelier, and real estate developer[14]

"What does it take to be a champion? Desire, dedication, determination, concentration, and the will to win."

—Patty Berg, golfer[15]

"Dwell not upon thy weariness; the strength shall be according to the measure of thy desire."

—Arab proverb

"The starting point of all goal attainment is desire. You must develop an intense burning desire for your goals if you really want to achieve them. Only when your desire becomes intense enough will you have the energy and the internal drive to overcome all the obstacles that will arise in your path. The good news is that almost anything that you want long enough and hard enough, you can ultimately achieve."

—Brian Tracy, personal and professional development trainer[16]

"In my experience there is only one motivation and that is desire. No reasons or principle contain it or stand against it."

—Jane Smiley, author[17]

"A young woman may have a putting touch, a tee shot that devours fairways, iron shots that rattle flagsticks; and she may win. But she won't continue winning; not without the B.D.—the Burning Desire."

—Betty Hicks, golfer, golf coach, aviator, and author

I love the story that scout Art Stewart tells about Hall of Fame baseball player George Brett. In his book *The Art of Scouting*, Stewart writes about Brett's last big league game in 1993. His Kansas City Royals baseball team was in Arlington, Texas, and the reporters there asked how he'd like his last at-bat to go. Everyone was expecting Brett to talk about hitting a home run or a game-winning RBI in the ninth inning. But he didn't say any of those things. "I want to hit a ball back to the pitcher," Brett said, "and run as hard as I can to first base."

You play the game that way, down to your last at-bat, if you play with extreme desire.

Bobby Unser is one of the most successful open-wheel racecar drivers ever. He is one of only 10 drivers to have won the Indianapolis 500 three or more times. In addition, he's one of only two to have won the Indianapolis 500 in three different decades—in 1968, 1975, and 1981. His list of accomplishments is numerous, but his basis for them is very simple. In fact, in can be boiled down to one word. Listen to how Unser explained it:

> "If any one word or thought sums up both my racing and business career, it's this: Desire! That's the one secret, the great equalizer in every person's career. Not education. Not being born with hidden talents. Desire! Nothing fuels success like desire. Whatever you elect to do in your life or career, let your passion dictate where you make your turns. Let the fuel of desire drive you through the tough times, and propel you upward during the good times. You'll discover that your belief in what you do is more important than any of the obstacles thrown in your path. The taste of victory will then endure forever. . . . If you do what's in your soul, success will come. It is guaranteed and in the end you'll realize that it wasn't the financial reward that drove you there. It was a deep, burning feeling. It was desire."[18]

It is what coaches notice right away with players. It's what Frank Reich noticed about Peyton Manning when Reich was the Indianapolis Colts quarterbacks coach. Reich described Manning this way to a *Sports Illustrated* writer: "He has a relentless desire to be great."[19] Catch that? A *relentless* desire.

Rick Dempsey, a career baseball man, has seen this type of relentless desire throughout his life. And when I say that Dempsey is a career baseball man, it isn't an exaggeration. The 1983 World Series MVP is closing in on a half century in professional baseball—24 major league seasons as a catcher and the rest as either a coach or broadcaster. Dempsey said that one of the first things he'll look at with a ballplayer is his work ethic. Why?

Because, he said, "it tells me about his desire." If you have that desire—that extreme desire —an athlete will "go out on the field when there's nobody else around, and be working on something by himself. They just have a burning desire to play at a higher level, and it just sticks out."[20]

Years ago, one of those types of baseball players was a shortstop in the Boston Red Sox organization. Jim Thrift, who was then a scout in the Cincinnati Reds organization, was scouting a game at Fenway Park. Scouts often get comp seats next to family and friends, and on this day Thrift told me he was sitting next to "an attractive young woman who had more than a passing interest in one of the Red Sox players. She said to me, 'I can't really believe the desire he has. He has the best desire for personal achievement I've ever seen. It's constant. I hope he doesn't mentally burn out.' The young woman was Mia Hamm. The Red Sox player was Nomar Garciaparra."

During his baseball career, Garciaparra was the AL Rookie of the Year in 1997, a six-time All Star and a two-time AL batting champion. As for Hamm, she later became Garciaparra's wife.

Did you pick up on how Mia Hamm not only noticed Garciaparra's extreme desire, but also that he was constant? That's important, because consistency is so key. I heard Pat Riley, who has been part of nine NBA championships as a player, assistant coach, head coach, or front office executive, describe it this way: "The key to success is to learn to do something right and then do it right every time."

I once heard the great pitcher Tom Seaver tell a story about his manager with the New York Mets—Gil Hodges. "One day in 1968, he called me into his office at Shea Stadium. You didn't want to go into his office because you didn't know if you'd come out alive or with broken bones. I can joke about it now, but I was thinking, 'My God, I hope he doesn't break my neck.'" Seaver had pitched that day against the San Francisco Giants and allowed a 7–1 lead to evaporate to a 7–6 lead before hanging on for the win.

"Your approach today was very unprofessional," Hodges told Seaver. And then he explained why. "It doesn't matter if there are 5,000 people in the stands or 55,000 people, or if it's Tuesday night in Los Angeles or Saturday afternoon in Chicago, or if you're leading by one run or six runs, or if we're two games ahead or 18 games behind. Your approach to your business is the same all the time. You must stay focused and professional and maintain all those intangibles that go into consistency and have respect for your job."

Seaver, who received the highest-ever percentage of Hall of Fame votes, never forgot that.

"I'm fortunate that I got that advice in only my second season," he said, "because I would benefit from it for eighteen-and-a-half years."

If you ask the Hall of Fame quarterback John Elway, who definitely approached his craft with extreme desire, what he was most proud of during his football career, he'll tell you it was "hanging in there and being consistent." If you listened to any of Derek Jeter's numerous news conferences during his farewell tour season with the Yankees, the one thing he consistently said that he was most proud of was "being consistent." Jeter's manager, Joe Girardi, noticed it, too. "The consistency," Girardi said. "It's really amazing." Football coach Eric Mangini has said that "anytime you marry hard work with consistency, you've got a real shot at being successful."[21]

Consistency naturally leads into dependability, which is another trait that another football coach, Hall of Famer Bill Parcells, says is so vital. I had Parcells on my radio show, and this is what he shared with me: "What I tell my players is, 'Whatever ability you have, you need to be the same player every day.' I'm not looking for a guy who's over here one day and over there the next. I'm looking for a guy who is dependable, reliable . . . whatever his ability is . . . whether it's real good or maybe not so good. If he's a dependable player, he is going to be pretty much the same guy every day. If he can do that, I know what to expect from him and I know how to use him. If I know how to use him, he represents a value to my team."

At his 2014 Hall of Fame induction, the former Chicago White Sox slugger Frank Thomas pointed to a coach who instilled consistency in him as his key to success, and that staying dedicated to that creed was paramount. "I had a special love for this man—Walt Hriniak. My favorite hitting coach of all time," Thomas said. "I thank you for being honest from day one. You taught me to only want to be the best. You would always say to me, 'Anyone can be good, Frank. But the special ones want to be great.' Our work sessions were very consistent every day. It didn't matter if we were 10–for–10 or 0–for–10. It was the same process every day. No freelancing. Consistency and dedication were what made you tick, and I'm so grateful for your tutelage."

Michael Jordan summed it up this way: "Success is something you have to put forth the effort for constantly; then maybe it'll come when you least expect it."[22]

Again, if you're consistent and dependable it's almost always because you're attacking what you do like Jordan did with extreme desire. I'll give you an example. One of the most mundane things in baseball is running out a ground ball when you know that it's a sure out. In fact, one of the great criticisms fans will have with pro players is not running all out on ground balls. That wasn't the case with Robin Yount, who was inducted into the Hall of Fame in 1999. Gordon Lakey, the Philadelphia Phillies' director of Minor League Scouting, once told another Hall of Famer, Peter Gammons, that he timed Yount running to first base on numerous occasions over a three-year period, and that the fastest he ever timed him was 3.9 seconds, and that the slowest was 4.0 seconds.[23] Not surprisingly, Yount's Hall of Fame plaque describes him as someone whose "extraordinary work ethic made him a bastion of consistency."

Dan Plesac, a former pitcher and now an analyst for the MLB Network, was a teammate of Yount's, and he told ESPN's Tim Kurkjian a revealing story about Yount, and how in his 18-year career he never saw anybody play the game harder. Plesac told Kurkjian how one day he saw that Yount was hurt so badly he couldn't even walk. But when he looked at the lineup card, there was Yount's name. Later, during batting practice, Plesac approached Yount.

"Why are you playing today?" he asked.

"Remember when you were in elementary school and you said you were sick so you didn't have to go to school," Yount said to Plesac.

"Yeah, I did it all the time."

"Remember how much easier it was to do it the second time?" Yount asked.

"Yeah."

"Well, don't do it the first time."[24]

Yount's mind-set reminds me of a quote from the Hall of Fame manager Casey Stengel, who said: "Play every game as if your job depended on it. It just might."[25]

Perhaps you've wondered what would propel an athlete to not just play every game as if his job depended on it, but to simply play *every* game—game after game after game—until he had played 2,632 consecutive games without taking a day off. That was Cal Ripken Jr. He played through injuries and illnesses. He played through frustration and fatigue. He played through it all, and after his career was over, even Ripken wondered where that kind of desire came from. Was he born with it? Or did he develop it? Listen to his self-evaluating answer:

> "I'd like to say that my desire to play baseball every day was only because I loved the sport. But it was more than that. I also had a deep-seated desire to get things done, to achieve, to win. It was like a fire burning inside that propelled me forward. I don't know if such a force is totally genetic, or if it's learned in some way. Perhaps a little bit of both. I do know that many successful people have experienced the same feeling. And I also know that I had it when I was very young, that I had it at the age of 17, when I signed my contract with the Orioles, and that I had it for 21 Major League Baseball seasons. As a matter of fact, now that I'm retired and embarking on an entirely new career in business, I still have it. When I was a kid, this feeling was like a powerful force inside my body. It pervaded everything I did."[26]

Arnold Palmer was that way as a kid, too, mostly because his father, Deacon Palmer, instilled it in him. "My father always said to me: 'You don't have to be the biggest and the strongest. Having natural ability can even be a detriment if you take it for granted. Your dedication has to be 100 percent. It won't happen if you're doing it because someone said you ought to. You have to have that burning desire.'"[27]

That's not to say that talent and ability don't matter. They absolutely do. But again, extreme winners don't rely on talent and ability, because no matter how good your talent and ability are, it only gives you an opportunity to be great, not a guarantee. Taking what you have and constantly challenging yourself to be better is what will make you great. It is what extremely driven people do. "It's a great challenge to be better than your opportunities," said the actress Sarah Jessica Parker.[28]

Athletes who want to be extreme winners don't rely on their vertical leap, their 40-yard-dash time, their hand-eye coordination, or any of those things that can be measured with a stopwatch or tape measure. Like Michael Jordan, they summon something from within that can't be measured. They summon something from that organ that does double duty pumping blood. I love the way Muhammad Ali described the balance between ability and desire. "Champions have to have the skill and the will," Ali said. "But the will must be stronger than the skill."[29]

So if you've wondered where extreme desire comes from, I hope you're seeing by now that it comes from your heart. By its definition, desire is something that speaks to something we long for, which, again, springs from the heart. When somebody in the athletic arena puts in that extra effort, digging deep, we say that they had a lot of heart or showed a lot of heart. When someone perseveres when most would have given up, we say that it took a lot of heart. We reference the heart in expressions a lot more than we might realize, and obviously for good reason. My pastor David Uth likes to say that "until our hearts are in it, neither are we." Interestingly, Michael Jordan said that "heart is what separates the good from the great." The greatest wide receiver the NFL has ever known was Jerry Rice, whose remarkable 20-year career ended at the Hall of Fame in Canton, Ohio. But do you know where it began for Jerry Rice? "It starts with your heart," he has often said. "I was not the fastest. I was not the biggest. But I was going to outwork you. I was going to solely commit myself 100 percent, and I think that's why I had so much success on the football field, because I just devoted myself to the game."

Did you pick up on that? Rice *devoted* himself to the game. Devoted, devotion—yet another word (or words) attached to the heart.

Rice also exuded another word that begins with a D, another important aspect of extreme desire—determination. He talked about that in his Hall of Fame speech, saying, "I played the game with a lot of determination, a lot of poise, and a lot of pride. I enjoyed hard work and the dedication and the preparation I had to make to try to be one of the best receivers to ever play the game. I felt I had to prove myself every year. I never got complacent."

One of the best compliments you can give an athlete is to say he or she is a gamer, a grinder. Their motor never stops running. They never give up, never give in. Pete Rose was probably the greatest grinder the game of baseball has ever known. The all-time hits leader wasn't the biggest, strongest, fastest, or most talented player of his era. Heck, Rose was never the biggest, strongest, fastest, or most talented player on any of the teams he played on. But he played with such grit, such determination, such drive, such desire, that he became known by the nickname Charlie Hustle. He was a grinder, and not all athletes are. In fact, that nickname, Charlie Hustle, was initially given to him derisively by the pitcher Whitey Ford during a spring training game in 1963, when Rose ran all-out to first base after drawing a walk. Ballplayers who weren't hustlers, who weren't driven, who weren't grinders, no doubt felt that Rose's hustling style showed them up. But Rose embraced the nickname, and now calling him Charlie Hustle is a badge of honor. If Rose ever goes into the Hall of Fame as a player—which he should—you can rest assured that the words Charlie Hustle will be on his plaque.

"Peter is the only man I know who never—and I mean never—left home with any other intention but to win," said Rose's former manager, the late Sparky Anderson. "To know Peter, you must understand that he is not an 'A' but a 'double-A' type personality—not unlike General George Patton or Douglas MacArthur. Peter was absolutely driven. He didn't type those numbers into the record books, he earned them. I have never in my life seen a man who was tougher physically or mentally than Peter Edward Rose."[30]

Dedicated people are people who never give up. F. Scott Fitzgerald had an extreme desire to be a published writer, and he dedicated 16 hours a day to his craft. He also received 120 rejection letters before *This Side of Paradise* was published in 1920. In fact, Fitzgerald wrote that novel while in the army during World War I, calling it *The Romantic Egotist*. After a publisher told him he had weak plot development, he rewrote the novel twice and added a new story line and title. The rest, of course, is history, with Fitzgerald's later novel, *The Great Gatsby*, hailed by many scholars as the greatest of all American works of fiction.

I like to read a daily devotional called *Our Daily Bread* and found myself copying a story from its December 17, 2014, daily thought. It pointed out that "Pablo Casals was considered to be the preeminent cellist of the first half of the 20th century. When he was still playing his cello in the middle of his tenth decade of life, a young reporter asked, 'Mr. Casals, you are 95 years old and the greatest cellist that ever lived. Why do you still practice six hours a day?' Mr. Casals answered, 'Because I think I'm making progress.'"

As you can see, dedicated people never give up, and they never stop trying to get better. Extreme winners are never content. They never rest on past accomplishments.

Earlier, in Chapter 5, I told you about Michael Jordan's extreme work ethic through the eyes of his trainer, Tim Grover. Relating to just how extremely driven Jordan was, Grover said this:

"After every game, I used to ask Michael Jordan one question: 'Five, six, or seven?' As in, what time are we hitting the gym tomorrow morning? He'd snap back a time, and that was it, especially after a loss when there wasn't a whole lot else to say. No discussion, no debate, no lame attempt to convince me he needed the morning off. You good? I'm good. See you in the morning. No matter what had happened the night before . . . good game, bad game, soreness, fatigue . . . he was up working out every morning, while most of the other guys slept. Interesting how the guy with the most talent and success spent more time working out than anyone else.

"Kobe Bryant is the same; he's insatiable in his desire to work. Some days, we'll go back to the gym, twice a day and once more at night, trying different things, working on certain issues, always looking for that extra edge. At his level of excellence, there's no room for error and no one . . . no one . . . in the game today works harder or invests more in his body and surrounding himself with the right people, to keep in peak condition. It's still not easy, and Kobe makes that decision every day to do the work.

"Again, the most talented guy working harder than anyone else. It's a choice."[31]

The same applies to the coaching profession. After he retired with 323 Division I college football coaching victories, a record at the time, Bear Bryant received a lot of accolades and analysis. Combining both, former Arkansas head coach Frank Broyles, who won 149 games over 21 years, said this about Bryant: "Bear was one of those rare individuals who was truly never satisfied with what he achieved. Most coaches have a hard time maintaining that kind of desire, but he always managed to get hungrier even after incredible success. He was the only one who could set that record. He was the only one who wanted it enough to sacrifice all those years."[32]

Similarly, Tiger Woods is another champion who is never satisfied by his past successes. When he was 37 years old, and clearly on the back nine of his golfing career, Tiger Woods told the *New York Times* this: "I don't want to become as good as I once was. No, I don't. I want to become better."[33]

Which leads me to something else Jerry Rice said in his Hall of Fame speech—that he had pride. It's something I guarantee you that Tiger Woods has, that Derek Jeter has, that Robin Yount has, that Kobe Bryant has, that Michael Jordan has—that all the great ones have. Pride is an important log on the fire when you burn with desire. Pride propels extreme winners to practice relentlessly, to prepare thoroughly, to strive for perfection, to welcome pressure. When you have pride in who you are and what you do, you want to live up to your full potential. You don't want to look back with regret and remorse and ask: What if?

I am convinced that what holds folks back from giving it all, from pouring everything they have into a goal, from truly going all-out, is that they are afraid of failure. What if I do everything I possibly can and still come up short? Answer: You came up short. That's all.

In their wonderful book, *The Truth About Leadership: The No-Fads, Heart-of-the-Matter Facts You Need to Know*, authors James M. Kouzes and Barry Z. Posner make this observation:

> "When you have true grit, you learn from your setbacks and are always willing to keep trying. Whenever you're challenging the status quo, whenever you're tackling demanding problems, whenever you're making meaningful changes, whenever you're confronting adversity, you will sometimes fail. Despite how much you see challenge as an opportunity, despite how focused you can be, despite how driven you are to succeed, there will no doubt be setbacks. Think again about leaders throughout history who are remembered for their greatness. Some lost battles, some were imprisoned, some saw their businesses shut down, and most were ridiculed while trying to achieve the extraordinary. Mistakes happen. Defeats occur. Failure is inevitable. None of these are dirty words . . . rather, they are signs that you're doing something tough, exacting, and out of the ordinary. That's why you need grit."[34]

So be gritty, a gamer, a grinder. Give it your all. Approach what you do with zeal and zest, with pluckiness and persistency. Be consistent. Endure. Be determined, dedicated, and driven. Have heart, hustle, and hunger. Approach whatever you do with resoluteness, resolve, and a relentless never-give-up attitude.

In short, have extreme desire.

As Bruce Springsteen sings on one of his popular tunes: "No retreat, no surrender."

Do that and I guarantee you'll have no regrets.

Chapter 12

EXTREME TEAMWORK

*"I am a member of a team,
and I rely on the team. I defer to
it and sacrifice for it, because
the team, not the individual, is
the ultimate champion."*

—Mia Hamm, soccer player [1]

I can hear you now.

Teamwork?

Why teamwork?

And why now? Why after 11 chapters about personal growth—with anecdotes and quotes, advice and admonition, encouragement and exhortation—are we punctuating this book with a chapter on teamwork? And extreme teamwork, no less.

Here is why. Because if you can take these 11 qualities, characteristics, and attributes and apply them in your own life, your own career, your own field of endeavor, you are guaranteed to have good results. However, the results will still fall short if this 12th principle is not followed, and that is the principle of extreme teamwork.

Winners have discovered that they can get to a level that is extremely high, and that they can be very successful, if they follow what is outlined in the first 11 chapters of this book. However, they have also discovered that they won't be an extreme winner and have ultimate success until it's done as a team. Nothing equals team success. Nothing is as fulfilling. Nothing can touch it.

The realization of that doesn't often come easy, especially when you know you are the best at what you do. When you compete, play, and/or perform at a different level than everyone else, it's hard to give some of that up to perform as a team. Phil Jackson's biggest job when he was the Chicago Bulls' head coach was convincing Michael Jordan that he'd have to surrender some of his individuality, some of the very things that made him so great and the best in the NBA, so that the team could function at its maximum level, which would result in winning championships. Jackson had to convince MJ that if he would do that, and only when he would do that, would the Bulls win championships, and thus would Jordan be more fulfilled. It took time—years, actually—but eventually Jackson sold Jordan on it.

If that is casting Michael Jordan in a negative light, it's not meant to. I can understand—and perhaps you can, too—that when you are by far the best, and everybody knows it, including you and your teammates, the instinct is to trust yourself more than anyone else. If you're Michael Jordan in the prime of your career, you really don't want to trust your teammates to make big plays and take the big shots, because obviously the odds are that you're going to do a lot better job than they will. Why risk that? But eventually Michael succumbed and the Bulls began to win, and win big, claiming six NBA titles.

I like to say, somewhat jokingly, that Michael Jordan agreed to do this—to surrender himself for the greater good of the team—for 46 minutes. NBA games, of course, are 48 minutes. That meant that for the last two minutes, when the game was on the line, Jordan was going to put everything back on his shoulders. He was going to want the ball in his hands, and he was going to want that last shot, and that's okay. Why wouldn't you want your best player to have the ball in his hands when it's the biggest moment, when the game is on the line? To be fair to Jordan, though, there were moments in big playoff games when he smartly acquiesced to other players, who did come through in clutch situations.

It reminds me of something I once heard one of the great NBA guards of all-time, Oscar Robertson, say: "The only way to win games that matter is to make the rest of the players better." The man they called "The Big O" got it, and eventually so did Michael Jordan, much to his advantage.

How many people remember, and can readily recite, the accolades Jordan compiled prior to winning his first NBA championship? And make no mistake, he was piling up a lot of individual honors—1985 NBA Rookie of the Year, 1988 NBA Most Valuable Player, 1988 NBA Defensive Player of the Year, 1988 NBA All-Star Game Most Valuable Player, NBA scoring champion from 1987 until 1993, perennial All-Star from 1985 again to 1993 . . . and on and on. But what really took Jordan's stature into a different stratosphere was winning team championships, which didn't begin until 1991.

When Horace Grant, who was one of Jordan's teammates, came to the Orlando Magic as a free agent, I talked with him about Jordan. Horace told me this, "MJ is the ultimate one-on-one player, yet he understands that winning big is determined by involving his teammates."

The sports landscape is littered with great, record-setting athletes who are not only known for their individual accomplishments, but for also never winning a team championship. In fact, one of my all-time heroes, Ted Williams, never won a World Series, although he played 19 spectacular seasons with the Boston Red Sox. During his career, the man they called "The Splendid Splinter" led the American League in batting six times, hitting 521 home runs and batting .344 during his career. He is also the last man to bat over .400, hitting .406 in 1941. A sensational talent—without ever winning a World Series ring. Why? The answer likely lies in a quote attributed to Williams: "Twenty-five guys, 25 cabs." The implication is clear. The Red Sox, although very talented, were 25 guys going in different directions. Not a team.

Not only did the Red Sox never win a championship during Ted Williams' remarkable career, he never even witnessed one during his lifetime. Boston won the World Series in 1918, two months after Williams was born, and had not won again at the time of his death in 2002. Such a dismal history prompted sportswriter Leigh Montville to write this about the Red Sox in a July 2, 1990, *Sports Illustrated* article:

> "For almost as long as baseball has been played inside the antique, green stadium off Kenmore Square, the knock against this team has been that it is loaded with talent and lacking in certain intestinal virtues. Character? The Red Sox's history has been filled with fat wallets and fatter heads. Twenty-five cabs for 25 ballplayers."[2]

Sadly, it was the knock on Dan Marino during all those years when he was the superstar quarterback for the Miami Dolphins—that he never won a Super Bowl. It hounded Peyton Manning, perhaps the greatest quarterback of his era, until he finally won a Super Bowl with the Indianapolis Colts. It hounded Manning's boss with the Denver Broncos, John Elway, the team's Executive Vice President of Football Operations, until Elway won two Super Bowls in the last two years of his quarterbacking career.

Dan Marino achieved a lot of fame. But if you ask him, he'd tell you that he would trade all of his records and individual accomplishments for one Super Bowl title. Marino was never a quarterback who chased fame. He chased championships. That he never won the ultimate championship in his sport is his great professional disappointment. That's why I am here to tell you that if you're chasing fame, it won't just be fleeting, it will be unfulfilling. I am also here to tell you a story about that. It comes from the book *Rumsfeld's Rules: Leadership Lessons in Business, Politics, War, and Life*, written by former Secretary of Defense Donald Rumsfeld. Rumsfeld writes about his early years when he was in the Nixon administration, and he joined President Nixon in San Francisco for a meeting at the Presidio—a former military base on the northern tip of the city's peninsula. When those in that meeting broke for lunch, they walked down a path toward a dock where a boat was waiting for them to take them on a tour of the harbor. Waiting for them was a large number of people who had gathered to catch a glimpse of President Nixon.

As the dignitaries passed by, Rumsfeld heard people applauding and excitedly remarking: "There's the president!" "There's the vice president." "There's secretary of the interior, Wally Hickel." Rumsfeld was the lowest-ranking member of Nixon's cabinet, and at the very end of the line, but sure enough when he passed the crowd he heard someone say, "There's Rumsfeld." It caused him to smile, "amused at the thought that nobody, not a single soul, had said a word about the tall, lanky man I was walking with. His name was Charles Lindbergh."[3]

It was only a few decades earlier that Lindbergh, the first man in history to fly an airplane nonstop across the Atlantic Ocean, was perhaps the most famous man in the world.

Wrote Rumsfeld: "For me, a former naval aviator, visiting with a man once considered the world's most famous pilot was a special moment; yet, as the two of us continued walking toward the dock, well behind President Nixon, not a single person recognized Lindbergh, pointed him out, or whispered his name. That somebody would call out my name and not his as we walked along was instructive. Fame, as it is said, is fleeting."[4]

I would add to that by saying that individual fame is lonely. As humans, we are designed to be interdependent. We derive great pleasure from collective accomplishments. If you've ever been around a championship team when they have a reunion 10, 20, 30, or more years down the timeline, it's magical to see the warmth and appreciation and love those men and women have for each other.

What about individual sports, though? That's a good question. I will tell you that even individual sports have a certain team element. A golfer, for instance, has a caddie, coaches, trainers, advisors, a nutritionist, and so on. And when their careers are over, golfers like to reminisce with former foes and laugh and recount past battles. Again, nothing we can accomplish individually matters much unless we can share it in some way. I firmly believe we are built for teamwork. When we submit and commit ourselves to something greater than our individual parts, we can accomplish great things.

It struck me in the fall of 2014 that as the San Francisco Giants won their third World Series title in five years, the common theme from within and outside the organization was how a team and an entire organization worked together toward a unified goal. It would have been easy to have simply pointed to left-handed pitcher Madison Bumgarner and reasoned that the Giants won the 2014 World Series because Bumgarner had just turned in the greatest pitching performance in World Series history. But that easy assumption also would've been a lazy one, too. Those who know baseball knew better. In fact, when *Sports Illustrated* published a commemorative issue immediately after the World Series, the cover said:

How San Francisco Built a Dynasty by the Bay
(Hint: The Giants Are More Than Madison Bumgarner)

At the Giants' parade and celebration two days after winning the World Series, San Francisco Mayor Ed Lee addressed the team and said, "Time and time again you keep showing us how 25 people can band together to achieve something greater than any one person. You never gave up. You never stopped fighting. You find ways to win together as a team."

After Mayor Lee spoke, Giants President and CEO Larry Baer took the podium and talked about the dynasty tag the organization had just achieved. Said Baer, "What makes all this work, as corny as it might sound, is a sense of all of us truly being in this together—the fans, the players, the coaches, the front office, the ownership, and every usher and vendor in the park. There is a culture with the Giants of genuinely caring for one another and having each other's back. That's the X factor."

Baer went on to relate an anecdote from the National League Division Series, when the Giants were playing the Washington Nationals and Bumgarner made a throwing error. "I remember," Baer began, "hearing from Madison Bumgarner and Buster Posey [the Giants' catcher] after one of the rarest things in the postseason, a small blip in a historically spectacular postseason, when there was a throwing error in the NLDS. Buster stepped up and took the blame by saying he had told Madison to throw to third base. Madison took the blame right back from Buster and said, 'Don't know about that. He didn't tell me to throw it into left field.' They had each other's backs. It's something you don't just see on the field, you see it throughout our organization. I want to acknowledge the selflessness and camaraderie of all the people at the Giants, who like the players live this job day in and day out. It's not by happenstance that the Giants have won three World Championships."

Baer closed his comments by talking about an organization with a shared vision, where people on and off the field "didn't care about anything but each other."

It's telling that in the big three sports in 2014, championships were won by teams that defined that word *team* in every way—the Super Bowl–winning Seattle Seahawks against the Indianapolis Colts, who had the best quarterback in the game in Peyton Manning; the NBA champion San Antonio Spurs over a team with a lot of individual talent in the LeBron James–Dwyane Wade–Chris Bosh Miami Heat; and MLB's Giants. What's interesting about the Giants, though, is that they beat a team in the Kansas City Royals who were very much like them; a group of 25 players all pulling together on the same rope. That's probably why the World Series went down to seven games, and why the Giants won it by the slimmest of margins—3–2.

You truly need a team to attain true greatness.

A few pages earlier, I shared a Donald Rumsfeld anecdote about Charles Lindbergh. While it illustrated that fame is fleeting, it certainly wasn't meant to imply that what Lindbergh accomplished wasn't important because it certainly was. In fact, when I Googled Charles Lindbergh's name, I got 738,000 results in .36 seconds, proof that Lindbergh is definitely not forgotten. His likeness is depicted in statues. His planes reside in museums. Scores of books and millions of words have been written about him. But why are Lindbergh's feats and accomplishments still remembered and revered to this day? Because, despite people of his day calling him "The Lone Eagle," Lindbergh was anything but. Sure he flew alone nonstop from New York to Paris in 1927, a feat that six famous aviators attempted prior to him, with all attempts ending in death. What made Lindbergh successful, where others died trying, is that he assembled an elite team to make his extreme dream a reality.

Lindbergh's first team members were a pair of St. Louis businessmen —Harry H. Knight and Harold M. Bixby. Those two men secured the financing for the special airplane that was needed. Bixby, in fact, was the head of the St. Louis Chamber of Commerce. He helped Lindbergh fund his venture in exchange for promoting St. Louis, which is why that historic airplane was named the *Spirit of St. Louis.*

After securing funding, Lindbergh hired a highly skilled aviation engineer named Donald A. Hall to design a lightweight, single-engine monoplane. A team of workers at the Ryan Aeronautical Company in San Diego then went to work with Lindbergh. It was an around-the-clock team effort to get that airplane built and ensure that Charles Lindbergh would be the first man to traverse the Atlantic Ocean by air. It was a race, similar to the race in the 1960s to land the first man on the moon. Hall worked 90-hour weeks managing a team of 50 people, many of whom worked extra shifts without pay just so they could be a part of history. And Lindbergh was right there with them, overseeing every rib, rod, and rivet. In fact, he lived, ate, and slept at the factory, which was a converted fish cannery that still reeked of dead fish.

The yeoman's effort by that team of dedicated workers took the *Spirit of St. Louis* from blueprint to rollout in 60 days.

When Lindbergh took the plane for its first test flight, he needed help to just get airborne. Back then, planes needed someone to turn the prop to start the engine. A minor chore, but without it, Lindbergh could have never literally gotten off the ground. So it was chief mechanic John van der Linde who spun the prop to start the engine while the mechanic's assistant, Douglas Corrigan, removed the wheel blocks.

The example of Charles Lindbergh is just one of scores of stories that illustrate how it took a team of dedicated people to achieve history. For instance, if I asked you who painted the Sistine Chapel, you'd likely say Michelangelo. And that's true. But Michelangelo actually assembled a team of artists and helpers to accomplish that enormous feat. There is debate as to whether Robert Peary was the first explorer to actually make it to the exact spot where the North Pole is, but what isn't debated is that Peary didn't accomplish the journey alone. Accompanying him was a team—his right-hand man, Matthew Henson, along with four Inuit tribesmen. Peary could not have accomplished what he did alone.

So just how important is teamwork? A friend of mine who founded a company that grew to a billion dollars in annual revenue told me this: "If you could get all the people in an organization rowing in the same direction, you could dominate any industry, in any market, at any time."

That's powerful.

I hope that what you're seeing when we say *team* is that it isn't limited to sports. It's any organization—whether it be a company, a dot-com venture, a military unit, a classroom project, a nonprofit organization. It is, in short, in every aspect of life.

However, it is true that we especially find teamwork in sports, which often provides us a metaphor to life.

Whenever there is a winner and loser in sports, you'll often hear someone say that the better team won. We hear it so many times, in fact, that it can come across as trite, a throwaway line. But it's much truer than we might think.

Swen Nater, a longtime NBA center, was asked years ago, "Why is the United States men's basketball team losing in the Olympics?" Nater told me that his reply was a quote from Coach John Wooden, who said, "We send great players, while they send great teams." Take the 1988 Olympic basketball team, for example. That team had superstar NBA players like David Robinson, Mitch Richmond, Danny Manning, and Dan Majerle, among others. Yet they lost to the Soviet Union, 82–76, which won the gold while Yugoslavia took the silver. The USA finished third, taking home a disappointing bronze medal. But on the flipside, here is a positive USA Olympic team effort: the 1980 "Miracle on Ice" hockey *team* that won the gold medal. That was a squad made up of amateur and college players, yet they beat the mighty Soviet Union juggernaut, which had won the gold medal in six of the previous seven Olympic Games.

In 1992, four years after that disappointing USA Olympic basketball team letdown, a collection of NBA superstars was assembled to form an Olympic basketball team, with the clear emphasis on that word *team*. True, that squad comprised the greatest individual talent America had to offer. But the focus from those players was on consistently offering themselves as a team. In fact, Olympic coach Chuck Daly told me that he wanted Michael Jordan to present himself as the face of the team, but that Jordan refused. Instead, this collection of superstar players was determined to check their egos at the door, all for the common goal of winning a gold medal. And make no mistake, this was an incredible arsenal of individual talent—Michael Jordan, Magic Johnson, Larry Bird, Charles Barkley, Patrick Ewing, Karl Malone, Clyde Drexler, Scottie

Pippen, David Robinson, Chris Mullin, John Stockton, and Christian Laettner.

Their teamwork worked. Team USA won every game by an average of 43.8 points. Today, they are hailed as perhaps the greatest sports *team* ever assembled. They truly lived up to their nickname—Dream Team.

Along those lines, I can't help but think of my old friend Dr. Jack Ramsay, who was a wonderful basketball coach and insightful student of the game. When I was reading his *New York Times* obituary after he died on April 28, 2014, this quote from him struck me: "Teams that play together beat those teams with superior players who play more as individuals."[5]

Sounds so simple, but more often than not it doesn't happen.

I remember when I was the Philadelphia 76ers' general manager and brought the great Julius "Dr. J" Erving into our franchise. Not only was Dr. J at the time the greatest basketball player in the world, he was the most humble and genuine athlete I'd ever been around. You never caught Julius preening or showboating or doing anything that detracted from the game or his teammates. Unfortunately, Julius' teammates didn't follow his lead. Not only did one of our guards, Lloyd Free, change his name to World B. Free, he dubbed himself the "Prince of Mid-Air." Our center, Darryl Dawkins, had a host of nicknames, like "Chocolate Thunder," to call attention to him when he wasn't too busy trying to shatter backboards. A couple of our other players, Steve Mix and Joe "Jellybean" Bryant (Kobe Bryant's father), were constantly concerned about their playing time. The chemistry wasn't good, even if the talent was probably the best in the league.

In 1977 we made the NBA Finals, playing against the Portland Trail Blazers, and took a 2–0 lead in the series before losing four straight. Sportswriters and sportscasters called us a collection of selfish ball hogs who didn't deserve to win the championship, and the painful truth of it was that they were right. So we apologized to the fans, launching a marketing campaign going into the next season, telling them: We Owe You One.

The next year produced more of the same me-first bad team chemistry, and we didn't even make the NBA Finals, prompting fans to mockingly say, "You owe us two!" We kept trying to get the right mix of team players to complement Julius Erving, but it wasn't easy. That 1977 failure fed into another one in 1978, which fed into 1979 (when we didn't make the Finals), 1980 (when we lost to the Los Angeles Lakers in the Finals), 1981 (when we didn't make the Finals), and 1982 (when we lost again to the Lakers in the Finals). That slogan, We Owe You One, came to feel like a piano on our back.

Then, before the 1982–1983 season, we acquired center Moses Malone from Houston. Moses was an unselfish, defensive-minded player who meshed well with Julius Erving. We also had the right mix of players around Julius and Moses. Not so much name players, but good players and great teammates. In fact, if you look at our roster from that season, it was filled with a lot of journeymen guys. Years later, only two players from that roster made it to the Naismith Memorial Basketball Hall of Fame. As you might have guessed, those two players are Julius Erving and Moses Malone. But it worked. We made it to the Finals, where we were again pitted against Pat Riley's Los Angeles Lakers, which had five future Hall of Famers on its roster—Kareem Abdul-Jabbar, Magic Johnson, Jamaal Wilkes, Bob McAdoo, and James Worthy (although Worthy missed the postseason due to injury).

The result? We swept the mighty Lakers, 4–0.

It remains the last NBA championship in the history of the 76ers' franchise. That team was also cited in a 2014 book published by *Sports Illustrated*, called *Basketball's Greatest*, as the fifth-greatest NBA team of all time.

Rather than teach me something, that championship reinforced in me the belief that you need a team, a real team, to achieve your dream. Nobody goes it alone. You can attain a certain level of success by yourself. But to be an extreme winner, you're going to need help, and you're also going to need to be a helper.

I mentioned earlier the former longtime NBA center Swen Nater, who shared a quote from Coach Wooden. Here is Nater again, with a wonderful poem he shared with me that I'll now share with you:

I have awed at a solo performance
and spectacular flashy display,
But I crave for the best
and my eyes are more blessed
when an unselfish team makes a play

A play that's so perfect and simple
with the weaving of role with a role,
Every piece partly seen
like a fine-tuned machine
and you notice not one but the whole

Like an orchestra tuned to perfection
where harmonious beauty is found,
Every note has a quest
to be part of the rest
so the whole is a masterpiece sound

Every wild one once blinded by glory
is now cured and is one of the tame,
He receives his esteem
as part of the team
and is eager to sacrifice fame

It's amazing what teams
have accomplished
It's astounding how
much they have done,
When the ultimate call
is when one is for all
and the credit is reached for by none

I particularly like that last line, about how no one is trying to grab the credit. Why? Because winners don't care about who gets the credit. Extreme winners are interested in one thing—winning.

I started this book in the Introduction with an anecdote about the great Hall of Fame quarterback Johnny Unitas, and the one-word advice he gave to an autograph seeker—win. His son, John C. Unitas Jr., penned an excellent book that I enjoyed, titled *Johnny U and Me: The Man Behind the Golden Arm.* In it, he wrote about his father not caring about who got the credit. "He worried first and foremost about winning," Unitas Jr. said. "He didn't care who you were or who did the heavy lifting, as long as that football got in the end zone on offense and didn't get in the end zone on defense. . . . One thing he never compromised on was winning. That was what drove him, not fame or money or celebrity. Winning was the only priority."

That kind of selflessness sacrificed at the altar of the greater good reminds me of an inspiring story about Edmund Hillary and Tenzing Norgay, who in 1953 went on a seven-week expedition to reach the highest peak on planet Earth—Mount Everest. Upon reaching that summit, Hillary and Norgay didn't have much time to soak in their accomplishment. A limited oxygen supply only allowed them to spend 15 minutes at the top of the world. Do you know what Hillary did? He looked for evidence that George Mallory had reached the summit some 29 years earlier—in 1924. Mallory and his climbing partner, Andrew Irvine, were spotted just a few hundred yards from the summit, but were never seen again. In fact, it wasn't until 1999 that Mallory's frozen body was discovered by climbers just a couple of hundred yards from Mount Everest's peak. To this day, nobody knows if Mallory reached the summit and died on his way down, or if he died on his way up, never attaining that pinnacle.

So there was Edmund Hillary, spending a chunk of his 15 minutes at the peak of Mount Everest—literally his 15 minutes of fame—searching for the body of George Mallory, wanting to give him the proper credit if credit was due. Unable to locate any sign of Mallory, Hillary took a photo of his partner, Norgay, as the Sherpa climber from India held his ice ax aloft with a British flag flapping from its handle. Then Hillary took photos of the scenery, explaining, "I wanted to take photographs of all the leading ridges of the mountain to give absolute proof that we had reached the summit."[6]

One thing remains missing, though, and still remains missing to this day. What's that? An actual photograph of Edmund Hillary at Mount Everest's peak. Norgay, as it turns out, didn't know how to operate the camera. So while Edmund Hillary is credited with being the first man to reach the peak of the highest mountain in the world, the iconic photo of that incredible accomplishment is that of Tenzing Norgay. The photo of his friend was good enough for Hillary, though. It was also proof, he reasoned, that he had also reached the summit. Commenting on the famous photo of Norgay, Hillary said, "There must have been someone there to take it."[7]

The moral of that story, and also the gist of Swen Nater's poem, is succinctly summed up for us from a no-nonsense guy, President Harry S. Truman, who said, "It's amazing what you can accomplish if you do not care who gets the credit."[8]

Here are some other great quotes on being part of a team:

> *"Not everybody can be first team, but you can always put the team first."*
>
> —Lou Holtz, football coach

> *"It's easy to get good players. Getting them to play together, that's the hard part."*
>
> —Casey Stengel, Hall of Fame baseball coach[9]

> *"Commitment to team—there is no such thing as in-between, you are either in or out."*
>
> —Pat Riley, basketball coach and front-office executive[10]

> *"Talent wins games, but teamwork and intelligence win championships."*
>
> —Michael Jordan, basketball player[11]

"Ask not what your teammates can do for you. Ask what you can do for your teammates."

—Earvin "Magic" Johnson, basketball player, paraphrasing from
President John F. Kennedy's inaugural address[12]

"When you come to practice, you cease to exist as an individual, and you're part of a team."

—John Wooden, Hall of Fame basketball coach[13]

"Everyone needs a team. You can't do anything by yourself."

—Michelle Akers, soccer star[14]

"No matter what accomplishments you achieve, somebody helped you."

—Althea Gibson, tennis player[15]

Doc Rivers has become a friend through the years. He told me that when he coached the Boston Celtics, the media liked to focus on what they called the big three—Kevin Garnett, Paul Pierce, and Ray Allen. That's not the way Doc approached it, though. Within the team, they talked about the big 12. "Your opponent may figure out how to contain two or three guys," Doc said, "but no opponent can figure out how to contain 12 guys who function as one, no matter which five are on the court at any one time. Our motto was *strength in numbers.*"

Doc shared with me his ingredients of teamwork—commitment, passion, empowerment, trust, respect, character, and leadership. And what he meant by leadership was not him as a head coach or someone as CEO, but leadership within a team. Interestingly, after a Game 5 victory in the 2014 World Series, San Francisco Giants outfielder Hunter Pence was on the MLB Network postgame set when player-turned-analyst Al Leiter asked him how much he buys into team chemistry.

Said Pence: "I think it's the strongest thing this team has—its unified vision, a unified willingness to do everything for each other, its passion. You can't just create passion. It takes effort. It takes people who care. We have a tremendous amount of leadership in our clubhouse, and it's not an accident that a lot of these guys have several rings. It's people who care. It's people who look at every little thing, who push each other and get the most out of each other. It's not only me helping others, but my teammates helping me as well. We all pick each other up. That's kind of the idea of this team."

With a little bit of wise guy in him, given that the Giants had just won Game 5 on the back of another dominating performance from pitcher Madison Bumgarner, MLB Network's Greg Amsinger followed up with this question: "What's more important—team chemistry or the best pitcher on the planet right now?" As Amsinger, Leiter, and another analyst, Sean Casey, all laughed at what they thought was an inside joke, Pence gave them another passionate and insightful reply.

"You know what," he said of Bumgarner, "he's doing outstanding, but he is one of the most humble guys. He'll get out there and do anything for any one of us. That's the biggest thing. This guy, it's not, 'Oh, me, me, me. This is my game.' It's *our* game. If you talk to Bumgarner, you talk to Buster Posey, you know that they are always going to share credit with everyone else. He's going to talk about his defense. You don't find that. You don't find people who are that good and that humble. He never makes himself bigger than what it is."

True champions are like that. In fact, the biggest figure the game of baseball has ever known was Babe Ruth. He dominated the game like nobody did before him, or since. When he pitched, he was the best left-handed pitcher of his era. And he is unquestionably the greatest hitter of any era. He has long held records for both pitching and hitting. But even though Babe Ruth was the greatest individual baseball player the game has ever known, he had some sublime thoughts on winning. Here are a few:

★ "The best organization wins."[16]
★ "Baseball always has been, and always will be, a game demanding team play."[17]

★ "The way a team plays as a whole determines its success.
You may have the greatest bunch of individual stars in the world,
but if they don't play together, the club won't be worth a dime."[18]

I love this story about Bill Belichick, the head coach of the New England
Patriots, and what he did on February 3, 2002, at Super Bowl XXXVI. It's
been written about by several people, including the late David Halberstam
in his book about Belichick titled *The Education of a Coach*. I particularly
like the way the account is described by writers Kevin Pritchard and John
Eliot in their book about teamwork:

> Prior to Super Bowl XXXVI, head coach Bill Belichick was given a
> choice by league officials regarding the customary pregame introduc-
> tion. One team would come running out of the locker room to the public
> address announcement of their offense; the other to announcement of
> defensive players. As the designated home team, the Patriots got to pick.
> Which did Belichick want? Neither. He asked that no one be singled out.
> He asked for the team to be introduced as one. The NFL rejected his
> request. Belichick didn't acquiesce. Helping his players maintain their
> unified spirit was worth any commissioner reprimand or fine. Game time
> rolled around, and the hoopla and cheering in the post-9/11 Louisiana
> Superdome was as raucous as ever. The St. Louis Rams entry was broad-
> cast first, Pat Summerall calling out the starters on offense. TV cameras
> shifted to the tunnel where the Patriots were huddled, ensconced in a dry
> ice machine cloud.
> Summerall boomed out: "Ladies and gentleman . . ."
> A long pause.
> "The New England PATRIOTS!"
> In a moment that still elicits butterflies to revisit, the Patriots came
> charging out of the smoke together, all holding hands. Out in front was
> not Tom Brady, not Adam Vinatieri, not Bill Belichick. They were in the
> middle of the pack.[19]

With George H. W. Bush becoming the first president to participate in a Super Bowl coin toss in person, those last few pregame moments struck a chord with America just months after the worst terrorist attack on U.S. soil. The introduction also set the precedent for future Super Bowl pregame introductions.

Oh, and by the way, the Patriots won that game, 20–17, when Adam Vinatieri kicked a 48-yard game-winning field goal as time expired. Patriots quarterback Tom Brady was named the Super Bowl MVP. And to think, just a few hours earlier, in a pregame team tunnel, Brady and Vinatieri were just a couple of middle-of-the-pack guys.

One of the things that consistently struck me during future Hall of Famer Derek Jeter's final season as the New York Yankees' shortstop is just how hard Jeter worked at shifting the attention off of himself and back on to his team. He did it at the preseason news conference when he announced that the 2014 season would be his last, when he kept reiterating that there was a season to play and a championship to try and win. Jeter even apologized to his teammates for any practice time and work they might have missed to be at that news conference. And all through the season, he consistently deflected attention away from himself. It wasn't until after his final game, after the season was over, that Jeter opened up with personal thoughts. And even then, he made this comment after one questioner posed this:

> "Derek, you've talked about being a little bit uncomfortable at times with all of this. Is there a part of that that's because you've spent so much time over your career deflecting attention away from yourself and toward the team and not really wanting the individual spotlight as much for your achievements?"

Jeter's answer was the only time during his news conference when he turned from being reflecting and thoughtful to somewhat forceful in his reply. Listen to what he said:

> "Look, I care about only one thing, and that's winning. That's the bottom line. I've said that since day one. That's the only thing I care about. So any time there is particular attention on you it can be uncomfortable."

That's the way it always was with Derek Jeter: he was always uncomfortable with personal attention. What he was comfortable with, however, was winning; and he'll forever be known as not only one of the great Yankee team captains, but as a guy who played on five World Series championship teams—a winner.

One of Jeter's former teammates, Nick Swisher, was in awe of him when he became a Yankee in 2009, and equally so during Jeter's last season in 2014, when Swisher was playing for the Cleveland Indians. Late in that last season, when it seemed fairly clear that the Yankees weren't going to make the postseason, Swisher shared these thoughts about Jeter with *New York Daily News* sportswriter Christian Red:

> "I think the biggest thing I learned from him is that regardless of what the numbers are, you're there to win the game. You're not out there for yourself. Prime example is last night [an August 8th game], runners on first and second, and he lays down a [sacrifice] bunt. Are you kidding me? This guy is playing in his last year, with all those hits, and he's still about the team. This game can beat you down a little bit. But if you go in there with the mind-set of winning the baseball game every single day and doing whatever you can to help that team, it'll really end up working out for you."[20]

It always did for Jeter. Plus he obviously earned a lot of personal accolades and awards, going back to his first full season in the Major Leagues, in 1996, when he was named the American League Rookie of the Year. It was actually late in the 1995 season, however, when Jeter was called up from the minor leagues, appearing in 15 games for the Yankees. That same season was also the last for Don Mattingly, the Yankee captain before Derek Jeter. Mattingly spent time talking to the younger player during those games when their careers overlapped, schooling Jeter on things on and off the field. Years later, Mattingly recalled how impressed he was that Jeter listened to and applied what he told him.

A good thing, too, because one of the main things Mattingly learned during his great career was how to be a teammate.

"Team sports are really difficult things," Mattingly said. "Sometimes your team wins because of you, sometimes in spite of you, and sometimes it's like you're not even there. That's the reality of the team game. Then at one point in my career something wonderful happened. I don't know why or how, but I came to understand what *team* meant. It meant that although I didn't get a hit or make a great defensive play, I could impact the team in an incredible and consistent way. I learned that I could impact my team by caring first and foremost about the team's success and not my own. I don't mean by rooting for us like a typical fan. Fans are fickle. I mean care—really *care*—about the team, about *us*. I became less selfish, less lazy, less sensitive to negative comments. When I gave up *me*, I became more. I became a captain, a leader, a better person, and I came to understand that life is a team game. And you know what? I've found that most people aren't team players. They don't realize that life is the only game in town. Someone should tell them. It has made all the difference in the world to me."[21]

It will make all the difference in the world to you, too.

You were made to dream, and to see those dreams become a reality. To accomplish that, take that dream and apply preparation to it, focusing on the big picture while also paying attention to the smallest of details. Pursue that dream with passion, which will naturally feed into a relentless work ethic. Be responsible, never shifting the blame when times get tough. Instead, maintain a positive attitude, always believing that whatever goals you set—and you must be goal-oriented—you will achieve. That, of course, takes perseverance. It takes a competitive drive, too, because if life is anything, it is competitive, even if that competition is only against yourself and your burning desire to get better. Finally, you'll need help along the way, and you'll need to be a helper, too. It takes a team to complete your extreme dream.

But once it is complete, once you've done all those things, you'll know what it means to be an extreme winner.

Epilogue

It wasn't until I was 70 that I learned firsthand what an oncologist was. I discovered its meaning the hard way. After getting results from a physical, my family doctor sent me to a medical office near my home in Winter Park, Florida. As I wheeled into the address he'd given me, I saw a sign that said: Cancer Institute of Florida. *Cancer!? What am I doing here?* I soon found out.

"You've got an illness," Dr. Robert Reynolds told me on that truly fateful day.

"What is it?" I asked.

"It's multiple myeloma."

Even then, I didn't get it.

"What's that?"

"It's cancer."

My mind spun into a dizzying vortex of emotions and questions. It's amazing that I remember anything Dr. Reynolds told me after that. What I do remember vividly, though, is that he handed me a box of Kleenex, and boy did I need it.

Was I feeling sorry for myself? You betcha.

Although I was 70, I had so much to live for. I had 19 children, 14 of them adopted, and at the time I had eight grandchildren. I was motoring toward my goal of 100 books written and 100 marathons run. I had my next 10 years planned, and I was even contemplating what I'd do into my 80s—already knowing which books I wanted to write, speeches I wanted to work on, and how old I needed to be to set the age records for running both the New York City and Boston marathons, the former of which I'd completed 10 times, and the latter 13.

Yeah, I needed every bit of that box of Kleenex.

Shortly thereafter, I got a phone call from my longtime friend and co-author on this book—Peter Kerasotis. He reminded me of something. He told me that I had made a career out of motivation, self-help, and positive thinking. In fact, my website is PatWilliamsMotivate.com. Peter reminded me that I was a man of many slogans and scriptures, quotes and quips, anecdotes and aphorisms. Did they really mean anything? Or were they merely wonderful words and fancy phrases? A studious Bible reader, Peter reminded me of a verse at Luke 4:23. That's where Jesus read the minds of his cynical critics and said to them, "No doubt you will apply this saying to me, 'Physician, cure yourself.'"[1] What did Peter mean when he reminded me of that verse? He wanted me to know that people were watching me, and they were *especially* watching me now.

Okay, Mr. Motivational Speaker and self-help guru, who has made a nice living with all your books and speeches, let's see you apply what you've been preaching all these decades.

I'd like to tell you that I did so right away, but I didn't.

It took awhile, but eventually I realized that anybody can live life when things are going well. The real test comes when adversity strikes and setbacks nail you. When that happens, how are you going to deal with it? How are you going to respond? How are you going to turn it into something positive? So I had to stay up. I had to stay positive. I had to stay enthusiastic. I had to believe what I'd been preaching all these years. I had to prove that I bought into my own message.

Did I do that?

I think this book, which arrives four-and-a-half years after my cancer diagnosis, answers that question.

Extreme dream? I want to live. This cancer has no known cure, but you can put it in remission. So that became my mantra: the mission is remission.

Extreme preparation? You have to prepare your mind, heart, and body for the road ahead, for the chemo and radiation and drugs and the gnawing uncertainty.

Extreme focus? Trust me, nothing will narrow your focus more than that one word—cancer. You hear that and you hear a death sentence. I focused on my mission—remission. And I've stayed focused on it.

Extreme passion? Fighting cancer has helped me appreciate even more this time in my life, and the joy I get from writing books, giving motivational speeches, and helping others achieve their dreams. I have not only pursued this battle to beat down cancer with great passion, but also the life I'm living in the process.

Extreme work? My doctors told me that I could no longer run marathons, so my dream of running in 100 of them is over, or perhaps on hold. But as for my extreme dream of writing 100 books . . . well, this book you're holding in your hands is my 100th! And I'm not done. My life's work is, as always, a work in progress.

Extreme responsibility? As you can imagine, I lead a busy life. Adding an ongoing cancer fight to the equation places an extra layer of responsibility to stay strictly on schedule. I have to be extremely responsible to do what my doctors tell me to do, and I have been.

Extreme positive attitude? Along this journey, Peter Kerasotis wrote about my cancer battle for an *Orlando* magazine piece. In it, he quoted Alex Martins, our CEO for the Orlando Magic. Said Martins, "His attitude has really helped him get through this. I don't think it's insignificant to say, considering the types of treatments he's had to go through, that not everybody could've done it. If not for the type of approach and attitude Pat has, who knows where he'd be today?"

Extreme goals? I'm still writing, still speaking, still helping the Orlando Magic run a franchise. And, oh yeah, I still have my next decade, my 80s, mapped out.

Extreme perseverance? Fighting cancer is no fun. I can see why people give up, why they just don't want to go through it. Late in 2011, just months after my diagnosis, I endured a 96-hour chemotherapy session in preparation for a grueling blood and marrow stem cell transplant in February of 2012. It's hard for me to imagine anything requiring more extreme perseverance than that.

Extreme competition? I'm fighting a cancer with no known cure, and there is no quit in me. None.

Extreme desire? I still have children to marry off and grandchildren to put through college. I have a lot of life to live and I have such an extreme desire to live it.

Extreme teamwork? If you're still wondering why I ended this book with teamwork, then let me tell you this: there is no way I'd still be here if not for my wonderful wife, Ruth, my family, my team of doctors, my nurses, and my fellow chemotherapy patients. If you ever want to see the power of teamwork, watch someone fight cancer.

By the time you receive this book I'll be 75 and five years down the road since that day when I learned what an oncologist was, and there hasn't been a day when I haven't implemented one—if not all—of the 12 qualities that constitute this book. And, believe me, I do so to an extreme degree with one goal in mind. It's that one, three-letter word with an exclamation point that in the Introduction to this book, the great quarterback Johnny Unitas said was the best piece of advice he ever received.

Win!

—Pat Williams
September 4, 2015

Notes

Introduction

1 *www.youtube.com/watch?v=VSZgawlbYRI.*

2 By Donald T. Phillips, *Run to Win: Vince Lombardi on Coaching and Leadership* (St. Martin's Press, 2001).

3 By James C. Humes, *The Wit and Wisdom of Ronald Reagan* (Regnery Publishing, Inc., 2007).

4 By Peter Laporta, *A Quote for Every Day* (AuthorHouse, 2011).

5 *www.bayhill.com/His_Attitude-1819.html.*

6 *www.thewinstonsalemstealers.com/founders-philosophy.html.*

7 By Greg Cote, *Miami Herald,* June 6, 2013.

8 *www.brainyquote.com/quotes/quotes/s/stevenash544787.html.*

9 By Pete Rose with Rick Hill, *My Prison Without Bars* (Rodale Books, 2004).

Chapter 1

1 ImagineeringDisney.com, November 1, 2012. *www.imagineeringdisney.com/blog/2012/11/1/thats-what-walt-said .html.*

2 On Leadership, *The Washington Post,* May 13, 2010. *views.washingtonpost.com/leadership/panelists/2010/05 /beauty-of-dreams.html.*

3 NASA.gov. *www.nasa.gov/centers/goddard/about/history/dr_goddard.html#.U1sIavldWSo.*

4 ImagineeringDisney.com, November 1, 2012. *www.imagineeringdisney.com/blog/2012/11/1/thats-what-walt -said.html.*

5 Derek Jeter and Paul Mantell, *The Contract* (New York: Jeter Publishing, 2014).

6 Laura Schlessinger, *10 Stupid Things Women Do to Mess Up Their Lives* (New York: Harper Perennial, 2002), 10.

7 Cal Ripken Jr. with Donald T. Phillips, *Get in the Game: 8 Elements of Perseverance That Make the Difference* (New York: Gotham, 2007), 33.

8 Zig Ziglar, *See You at the Top* (Gretna, LA: Pelican Publishing Company, Inc., 1999), 164.

9 Brian Williams, Guideposts.org, *www.guideposts.org/celebrities/inspiring-story-brian-williams-works-hard -have-broadcasting-career;* Facebook, *www.facebook.com/photo.php?fbid=442192693779&set=a.442192628779 .237551.299210958779&type=3&theater.*

10 Q-and-A.org, *www.q-and-a.org/Transcript/?ProgramID=1002.*

11 Theodore Roosevelt, *In the Words of Theodore Roosevelt: Quotations from the Man in the Arena* (Ithaca, NY: Cornell University Press, 2012), 119.

12 Pearl S. Buck, *The Goddess Abides: A Novel* (New York: Pocket Books, 1973).

13 Scott Griffiths and Eric Elfman, *Beyond Genius: The 12 Essential Traits of Today's Renaissance Men* (Bloomington, IN: AuthorHouse, 2013), 215.

14 *www.SiliconValleyHistoricalAssociation.com.*

15 Monroe Mann and Lou Bortone, *Battle Cries for the Hollywood Underdog: Motivation & Inspiration for Your Journey to the Top* (Bloomington, IN: AuthorHouse, 2013), Chapter 60.

16 Jessamyn West, *The Life I Really Lived: A Novel* (San Diego, CA: Harcourt Brace Jovanovich, 1979), 338.

17 David Young, *Rebound Strong: Daily Inspirational Quotes* (Round Rock, TX: Wind Runner Press, 2012), 17.

18 Karen Weekes, *Women Know Everything!* (Philadelphia, PA: Quirk Books, 2007).

19 Tony Robbins, *Notes from a Friend: A Quick and Simple Guide to Taking Control of Your Life* (New York: Simon and Schuster, 1995), 52.

20 Brian Tracy's Blog, *www.briantracy.com/blog/personal-success/fight-or-flight-overcoming-your-fears/.*

21 BrainyQuote.com, *www.brainyquote.com/quotes/topics/topic_fear.html.*

22 Leif Becker, *Breaking Barriers: Your Guide to Personal Mastery* (Bloomington, IN: AuthorHouse), 142.

23 2InspireDaily.com, *www.2inspiredaily.com/Daily_Motivational_Quotes_Detail.asp?uid=1347&cat=Courage.*

24 BrainyQuote.com, *www.brainyquote.com/quotes/quotes/b/billiejean383677.html.*

25 Goodreads.com, *www.goodreads.com/author/quotes/8246999.George_Addair.*

26 Azhar Saleem Virk, *Inspiration from Lives of Famous People* (Lincoln, NE: Writers, 2003), 134.

27 Carolyn Warner, *The Last Word: A Treasure of Women's Quotes* (Upper Saddle River, NJ: Prentice Hall, 1992), 47.

28 Ben Corbett, About.com Folk Music, *folkmusic.about.com/od/bobdylan/a/Bob-Dylan-Goes-Electric.htm.*

29 Rock & Roll Hall of Fame, *rockhall.com/inductees/bob-dylan/transcript/bruce-springsteen-on-dylan/.*

30 Michael Bradley, *Derek Jeter* (Tarrytown, NY: Benchmark Books, 2004), 19.

31 Ian O'Connor, *The Captain: The Journey of Derek Jeter* (New York: Houghton Mifflin Harcourt, 2011), 52–53.

32 Derek Jeter, *The Life You Imagine: Life Lessons for Achieving Your Dreams* (New York: Random House, 2010), 33–34.

33 Tom Robinson, *Derek Jeter: Captain On and Off the Field* (Berkeley Heights, NJ: Enslow Publishers, Inc.), 50.

34 *American Cowboy*, July–August 2007.

35 Arnaud Romeo Noume, *The Key to Success: A Select Collection of Famous Quotes from Successful People* (UK: Xlibris Corporation), 83.

36 Bruce Chadwick, *George Washington's War: The Forging of a Revolutionary Leader and the American Presidency* (Naperville, IL: Sourcebooks, Inc., 2004), 497–498.

37 Mike Bianchi, "Jimmy Hewitt Believed in Magic When Nobody Else Would," *Orlando Sentinel*, October 26, 2013.

Chapter 2

1 BrainyQuote.com, *www.brainyquote.com/quotes/authors/j/joe_gibbs.html.*

2 Seth Davis, "Before He Was Coach K," *Sports Illustrated*, February 2, 2015, 80.

3 Kara Leverte Farley and Sheila M. Curry, *Get Motivated! Daily Psyche Ups* (New York: Fireside, 1994).

4 William Tecumseh Sherman, *Memoirs of General William T. Sherman: Volume 1* (Bedford, MS: Applewood Books, 1875), 399–400.

5 Enrique Ruiz, *Wisher, Washer, Wishy-Washy* (Lothian, MD: PositivePsyche.Biz, 2010), 114.

6 Kathryn Petras and Ross Petras, *"It Always Seems Impossible Until It's Done": Motivation for Dreamers & Doers* (New York: Warwick Publishing Company, 2014), 278.

7 ASAP Sports, October 16, 2009, *www.asapsports.com.*

8 Tom James, TribStar.com, January 19, 2006.

9 Mike Shalin, *Donnie Baseball: The Definitive Biography of Don Mattingly* (Chicago: Triumph Books, 2011), 66.

10 Sam Amick, *USA Today*, October 31, 2012.

11 Pat Williams with Tommy Ford, *Bear Bryant on Leadership: Life Lessons from a Six-Time National Championship Coach* (Charleston, SC: Advantage, 2010), 116.

12 Hunkar Ozyasar, *When Time Management Fails: How Efficient Managers Create More Value with Less Work* (New Delhi: Peacock Books, 2008), 110.

13 Terry Reese Downing, *Martyrs in Paradise* (Bloomington, IN: AuthorHouse, 2009), 262.

14 Thomas J. Peters and Robert H. Waterman Jr., *In Search of Excellence: Lessons from America's Best-Run Companies* (New York: HarperCollins Publishers, 2004).

15 Curt Schleier, *Investor's Business Daily*, July 30, 2001.

16 David Cataneo, *I Remember Ted Williams: Anecdotes and Memories of Baseball's Splendid Splinter by the Players and People Who Knew Him* (Nashville, TN: Cumberland House Publishing, Inc.), 36, 37.

17 Don Peri, *Working with Walt: Interviews with Disney Artists* (Jackson: University Press of Mississippi, 2008), 143.

18 Michael Barrier, *The Animated Man: A Life of Walt Disney* (Berkeley: University of California Press, 2007).

19 Charles Ridgway, *Spinning Disney's World: Memories of a Magic Kingdom Press Agent* (The Intrepid Traveler, 2007), 43.

20 Pat Williams with Ken Hussar, *The Ultimate Handbook of Motivational Quotes for Coaches and Leaders* (Monterey, CA: Coaches Choice, 2011).

21 Tracy Ellis and Joy White, *Learning from Religions* (Oxford: Heinemann Educational Publishers, 2002), 45.

22 Mark Phillips, *Letters to a Recruit* (Lulu.com, 2008), 15.

23 Bob Knight with Bob Hammel, *The Power of Negative Thinking: An Unconventional Approach to Achieving Positive Results* (New York: Houghton Mifflin Harcourt, 2013), 220–221.

24 Brian Tracy and Dr. Peter Chee, *12 Disciplines of Leadership Excellence: How Leaders Achieve Sustainable High Performance* (New York: McGraw-Hill, 2013), 46.

25 Cal Ripken Jr. with Donald T. Phillips, *8 Elements of Perseverance That Make the Difference* (New York: Gotham Books, 2007), 96, 97.

26 Whitey Herzog with Jonathan Pitts, *You're Missing a Great Game: From Casey to Ozzie, the Magic of Baseball and How to Get It Back* (New York: Simon & Schuster, 2007).

27 Jim Calhoun with Richard Ernsberger Jr., *A Passion to Lead: Seven Leadership Secrets for Success in Business, Sports, and Life* (New York: St. Martin's Press, 2007), 27.

28 William Safire and Leonard Safir, *Words of Wisdom: More Good Advice* (New York: Simon & Schuster, 2005), 66.

29 Cal Ripken Jr. with Donald T. Phillips, *8 Elements of Perseverance That Make the Difference* (New York: Gotham Books, 2007), 120.

30 Bob Verger, *Newsweek*, July 11, 2011.

31 Pete Carroll with Yogi Roth, *Win Forever: Win, Work and Play Like a Champion* (New York: Portfolio, 2010), Chapter 22.

32 *Say Hello to Your Very Own Book of Quotes* (QuotationsBook, n.d.), 9. *books.google.com/books/about/Say_Hello_to_your_very_own_book_of_Quotes.html?id=ECkMkwgeuvcC*.

33 Pat Summitt with Sally Jenkins, *Sum It Up: 1,098 Victories, a Couple of Irrelevant Losses, and a Life in Perspective* (New York: Three Rivers Press, 2014).

34 Joe Calloway, *The Best at What Matters Most: The Only Strategy You Will Ever Need* (Hoboken, NJ: John Wiley & Sons, Inc., 2013).

35 Clay Latimer, *Investor's Business Daily*, August 9, 2012.

Chapter 3

1 Richard Onebamoi, *Success Power Points: Proven Strategies for Success* (Sceptre Publications, 2007).

2 Phil Jackson and Hugh Delehanty, *Sacred Hoops: Spiritual Lessons of a Hardwood Warrior* (New York: Hyperion, 1995), 4.

3 Dan Schlossberg and Wayne Hagin, *The 300 Club: Have We Seen the Last of Baseball's 300-Game Winners?* (Olathe, KS: Ascend Books, 2010).

4 Nolan Ryan and Tom House, *Nolan Ryan's Pitcher's Bible: The Ultimate Guide to Power, Precision, and Long-Term Performance* (New York: Simon & Schuster/Fireside, 1991), 40.

5 Mike Bryan, *Cal Ripken Jr.: My Story* (New York: Dial Books for Young Readers, 1999).

6 Bruce Jenner with Mark Seal, *Finding the Champion Within: A Step-by-Step Plan for Reaching Your Full Potential* (New York: Simon & Schuster, 1996), 247.

7 Kate Meyers, *Parade*, August 29, 2010.

8 Franklin Graham, *The Name* (Nashville, TN: Thomas Nelson, Inc., 2004), 116.

9 Lynn Zinser, *The New York Times,* January 8, 2004.

10 Thomas R. Raber, *Michael Jordan: Returning Champion* (Minneapolis: Lerner Publications Company), 14.

11 Jim Clemmer, *The Leader's Digest: Timeless Principles for Team and Organization Success* (Canada: TCG Press, 2003), 30.

12 Walker Percy, *Lancelot* (New York: Picador, 1999).

13 Bukkyo Dendo Kyokai, *The Teachings of Buddha* (New Delhi: Sterling Publishers, 2004), 122–123.

14 Al Browning, *I Remember Paul "Bear" Bryant: Personal Memories of College Football's Most Legendary Coach as Told by the People Who Knew Him Best* (Nashville: Cumberland House, 2001).

15 Robert Orben, *Speaker's Handbook of Humor* (Springfield, MA: Merriam-Webster, 2000).

16 Joe Montana with Richard Weiner, *Joe Montana's Art and Magic of Quarterbacking: The Secrets of the Game from One of the All-Time Best* (New York: Henry Holt & Co., 1997), 130.

17 Michael Murphy and Rhea A. White, *In the Zone: Transcendent Experience in Sports* (New York: Open Road Media, 2011).

18 Brian Billick and James A. Peterson, *Competitive Leadership: Twelve Principles for Success* (Chicago: Triumph Books, 2001), 51–52.

19 Clay Latimer, *Investor's Business Daily*, June 4, 2012.

20 Pete Carroll with Yogi Roth and Kristoffer A. Garin, *Win Forever: Live, Work, and Play Like a Champion* (Portfolio Trade, 2011).

21 Bob St. John, *Landry: The Legend and the Legacy* (Nashville: Word Publishing, 2000).

22 Michael Murphy and Rhea A. White, *In the Zone: Transcendent Experience in Sports* (New York: Open Road Media, 2011).

23 Pete Sampras with Peter Bodo, *A Champion's Mind: Lessons from a Life in Tennis* (New York: Random House, 2008).

24 Tommy Heinsohn and Joe Fitzgerald, *Give 'Em the Hook* (Upper Saddle River, NJ: Prentice Hall Press, 1988), 232.

25 Jerry Potter, *USA TODAY*, September 5, 1996.

26 Phil Olley, *Result: Think Decisively, Take Action and Get Results* (FT Press, 2012).

27 Tom Swift, *Chief Bender's Burden: The Silent Struggle of a Baseball Star* (Lincoln, NE: Bison Books, 2008), 215.

28 Robert Palestini, *A Game Plan for Effective Leadership: Lessons from 10 Successful Coaches in Moving from Theory to Practice* (Lanham, MD: Rowman & Littlefield Education, 2008), 77.

29 Donna Lopiano, Sports Management Resources, *www.sportsmanagementresources.com/library/doctrine-of-completed-staff-work*.

30 Mike Shalin, *Donnie Baseball: The Definitive Biography of Don Mattingly* (Chicago: Triumph Books, 2011).

Chapter 4

1 Esmonde Holowaty, *Unleash the Billionaire Within: Learn the Mastermind Principles for Acquiring Wealth Beyond Imagination* (Ontario: AuthorHouse, 2011).

2 Elaine Sciolino, *The New York Times*, March 25, 2006.

3 John Leonard, *The New York Times*, August 31, 1981.

4 Gregory K. Ericksen, *Women Entrepreneurs Only: 12 Women Entrepreneurs Tell the Stories of Their Success* (New York: Wiley, 2007).

5 Peter Ames Carlin, *Bruce* (New York: Touchstone, 2012).

6 Bly.com Newsletter Archives, *www.bly.com/archive/?m=200807*.

7 Addicted2Success, *addicted2success.com/quotes/50-inspirational-john-maxwell-quotes/*.

8 Tuck News Blog, *www.tuckclinic.com/coach-bennetts-five-pillars-of-success*.

9 Johnny M. Hunt, *Building Your Leadership Résumé: Developing the Legacy That Will Outlast You* (Nashville: B&H Publishing Group, 2009).

10 The Clemmer Group, *www.clemmergroup.com/articles/building-passion-commitment-wal-mart-way/*.

11 Hoop Boost blog, *hoopboost.blogspot.com/2010/09/excitement-of-game-day.html*.

12 Jim and Julie S. Bettinger, *The Book of Bowden* (Lanham, MD: Taylor Trade Publishing, 2001).

13 Gerald Klickstein, *The Musician's Way* (Oxford, UK: Oxford University Press, 2009).

14 Laura Rich, *The Accidental Zillionaire: Demystifying Paul Allen* (Hoboken, NJ: John Wiley & Sons, 2003).

15 Brainy Quote.com, *www.brainyquote.com/quotes/quotes/g/georgehala106214.html*.

16 David Whitley, *Orlando Sentinel*, July 20, 2000.

17 Mike Bianchi, *Orlando Sentinel*, June 21, 2003.

18 Lawrence Baldassaro, editor, *Reflections on a Splendid Life* (Boston: Northeastern University Press, 2003).

19 Kurt W. Mortensen, *Laws of Charisma: How to Captivate, Inspire, and Influence for Maximum Success* (New York: AMACOM, 2010).

20 Jim Calhoun with Richard Ernsberger Jr., *Passion to Lead: Seven Leadership Secrets for Success in Business, Sports, and Life* (New York: St. Martin's Press, 2007).

21 Donald J. Trump, @realDonald Trump, twitter.com/realDonaldTrump/status/491478458732515328.

22 Goodreads.com, *www.goodreads.com/quotes/108968-we-may-affirm-absolutely-that-nothing-great-in-the-world*.

23 Marjorie Quimpo-Espino, *Philippine Daily Inquirer*, April 12, 2008.

24 Maya Angelou, *www.facebook.com/MayaAngelou/posts/82825840895*.

25 Mike Symes, *Light Your Firebrand* (Hertfordshire, UK: Ecademy Press, 2011).

26 Goodreads.com, *www.goodreads.com/quotes/62238-a-man-is-only-as-good-as-what-he-loves*.

27 Peter Castro, *People*, March 27, 1995.

28 Jim Bryant, *Life: Tips for the Journey* (Rockwall, TX: CrossHouse Publishing, 2007).

29 Steve May, *The Story File: 1,001 Contemporary Illustrations for Speakers, Writers & Preachers* (Peabody, MA: Hendrickson Publishing, 2000).

30 Gerald R. Kramer, *Instant Replay: The Green Bay Diary of Jerry Kramer* (New York: Anchor, 2011).

31 Arnie Stapleton, Associated Press, December 27, 2004.

32 RepeatAfterUs.com, *www.repeatafterus.com/title.php?i=5475*.

33 Ross Bernstein, *World Series Winners: What It Takes to Claim Baseball's Ultimate Prize* (Chicago: Triumph Books, 2012).

34 Ibid.

35 Kevin Cashman, *Leadership from the Inside Out: Becoming a Leader for Life* (Oakland, CA: Berrett-Koehler Publishers, 2008).

36 David Claerbaut, *Bart Starr: When Leadership Mattered* (Lanham, MD: Taylor Trade Publishing, 2004).

37 John C. Maxwell, *Good Leaders Ask Great Questions: Your Foundation for Successful Leadership* (New York: Center Street, 2014).

38 *davidcottrell.com/*.

39 Roger Ellerton, *Live Your Dreams: Let Reality Catch Up* (Ontario: Renewal Technologies, 2007).

40 Anna Muoio, *Fast Company*, June/July 1997.

41 Thomas A. Edison, Edison Innovation Foundation, *www.thomasedison.org/index.php/education/edison-quotes/*.

42 Derek Jeter with Jack Curry, *The Life You Imagine: Life Lessons for Achieving Your Dreams* (New York: Broadway Books, 2001).

43 Tom Verducci, *Sports Illustrated*, "Derek Jeter: In His Own Words," *www.si.com/sports-man/2009/11/30/jeter-interview*.

44 Alex A. Lluch, *How God Can Save Your Marriage in 40 Days* (San Diego, CA: WS Publishing Co., 2010).

45 Golf Digest, *www.golfdigest.com/magazine/2006-09/0009britishopenreport?currentPage=3*.

46 EPSN, *espn.go.com/classic/000725williemaysquote.html*.

47 BrainyQuote. com, *www.brainyquote.com/quotes/quotes/j/joenamath163808.html*.

48 Ed Sherman, *Chicago Tribune*, June 19, 2005.

49 Murray Chass, *New York Times*, April 10, 2002.

50 Dave Kindred, *Sports Illustrated,* July 6, 2002.

51 QuoteGarden.com, *www.quotegarden.com/baseball.html*.

52 William Kristol, *New York Times*, October 5, 2008.

Chapter 5

1 QuoteGarden.com, *www.quotegarden.com/effort.html*.

2 Joyce Chapman, *Live Your Dream: Discover and Achieve Your Life Purpose* (Franklin Lakes, NJ: Career Press, 2002).

3 *twitter.com/ESPNNFL/status/331759549478473728*.

4 Brian Tracy, *Goals! How to Get Everything You Want—Faster Than You Ever Thought Possible* (Oakland, CA: Berrett-Koehler Publishers, 2010).

5 Malcolm Gladwell, *Outlier: The Story of Success* (New York: Penguin Books, 2008).

6 Alain de Botton, @alaindebotton, *twitter.com/alaindebotton/status/437095872175017984*.

7 Geoff Colvin, *Talent Is Overrated: What Separates World-Class Performers from Everybody Else* (New York: Penguin, 2010).

8 Freeman Hrabowski, TED.com, *www.ted.com/speakers/freeman_hrabowski*.

9 Geoff Colvin, *Talent Is Overrated: What Separates World-Class Performers from Everybody Else* (New York: Penguin, 2010).

10 "Jobs: 'Find What You Love,'" *Wall Street Journal*, October 6, 2011.

11 Deanne Durrett, *Jim Henson (Importance of)* (Independence, KY: Lucent Books, 1994).

12 John C. Maxwell, *Talent Is Never Enough: Discover the Choices That Will Take You Beyond Your Talent* (Nashville: Thomas Nelson, 2007).

13 Pat Williams with Ken Hussar, *The Ultimate Handbook of Motivational Quotes for Coaches and Leaders* (Monterey, CA: Coaches Choice, 2011).

14 William S. Pretzer, ed., *Working at Inventing: Thomas A. Edison & the Menlo Park Experience* (Baltimore, MD: Johns Hopkins University Press, 2001).

15 Wayne W. Dyer, *It's Never Crowded Along the Extra Mile* (Carlsbad, CA: Hay House, 2002).

16 Pat Williams with Jim Denney, *Extreme Focus: Harnessing the Life-Changing Power to Achieve Your Dreams* (Deerfield Beach, FL: Health Communications, Inc., 2011).

17 HRZone.com, *www.hrzone.com/topic/strategies/hr-headmistress-asks-overtime-it-bad-business/111585*.

18 Brainy Quote.com, *www.brainyquote.com/quotes/quotes/t/thomasaed109928.html*.

19 BarryPopik.com, *www.barrypopik.com/index.php/new_york_city/entry/no_one_ever_drowned_in_sweat/*.

20 Tony Gwynn and Roger Vaughan, *The Art of Hitting* (Vancouver, BC: GT Publishing Company, 2000).

21 Tony Gwynn with Jim Rosenthal, *Tony Gwynn's Total Baseball Player: Winning Techniques for Hitting, Fielding, and Baserunning* (New York: St. Martin's Griffin, 1992).

22 Tyler Kepner, "In a .338 Lifetime Average, Every Day Counted," *New York Times,* June 17, 2014.

23 Goodreads.com, *www.goodreads.com/quotes/24889-the-three-great-essentials-to-achieve-anything-worthwhile-are-first*.

24 David Young, *Breakthrough Power for Athletes: A Daily Guide to an Extraordinary Life* (Round Rock, TX: Wind Runner Press, 2011).

25 Michael Mink, *Investor's Business Daily*, February 1, 2013.

26 ManifestingMe.com, *www.manifestingme.com/blog/2010/february/%E2%80%9Cif-people-only-knew-how-hard-i-work-gain-mastery-it-wouldn%E2%80%99t-seem-so-wonderful-a*.

27 Jack Nicklaus with Ken Bowden, *Jack Nicklaus: My Story* (New York: Simon & Schuster, 2007).

28 BrainyQuote.com, *www.brainyquote.com/quotes/quotes/a/abrahamlin132309.html*.

29 Paul "Bear" Bryant with John Underwood, *Bear: The Hard Life & Good Times of Alabama's Coach Bryant* (Chicago: Triumph Books, 2012).

30 Tyler Kepner, *New York Times*, April 30, 2002.

31 David King, *San Antonio at Bat: Professional Baseball in the Alamo City* (College Station: Texas A&M University Press, 2004).

32 *theleadershipcenter.org/tag/action/*.

33 Henry David Thoreau, Bradley P. Dean, Harrison Gray Blake, *Letters to a Spiritual Seeker* (New York: W. W. Norton & Company, 2005).

34 Barry Johnston, comp., *The Wit of Golf* (UK: Hodder & Stoughton, 2010).

35 "Hard Work and Sacrifice" (handout), Newport Harbor Girls Soccer, *www.nhgirlssoccer.com/forms/hardwork.pdf*.

36 Bola Essien-Nelson, *The Diary of a Desperate Naija Woman in the Year 20-Ten* (Bloomington, IN: Xlibris Corporation, 2011).

37 Ron Moses, *The 15 Secrets of Millionaires* (Colorado Springs, CO: CreateSpace Independent Publishing Platform, 2012).

38 John Maxwell, *Success 101: What Every Leader Needs to Know* (Nashville: Thomas Nelson, 2008).

39 Demi Lovato, *Staying Strong: 365 Days a Year* (New York: Feiwel & Friends, 2013).

40 Sue Hadfield, *Change One Thing! Make One Change and Embrace a Happier, More Successful You* (New York: John Wiley and Sons, 2014).

41 Quotations Book (QB), *quotationsbook.com/quote/34311/*.

42 Brian Tracy, Brian Tracy International, *www.briantracy.com*.

43 Pat Williams with David Wimbish, *How to Be Like Coach Wooden: Life Lessons from Basketball's Greatest Leader* (Deerfield Beach, FL: Health Communications, Inc., 2006).

44 Bryan Tracy, *Million-Dollar Habits: Proven Power Principles to Double and Triple Your Income* (Irvine, CA: Entrepreneur Media, 2006).

45 Julia Vitullo-Martin and J. Robert Moskin, *The Executive's Book of Quotations: A Guide to the Right Quote for Every Occasion* (Oxford, UK: Oxford University Press, 1994).

46 Eddie Payton with Paul T. Brown and Craig Wiley, *Walter & Me: Standing in the Shadow of Sweetness* (Chicago: Triumph Books, 2012).

47 Brad Brewer, *Mentored by the King: Arnold Palmer's Success Lessons for Golf, Business, and Life* (Grand Rapids, MI: Zondervan, 2010).

48 Kerry Jackson, *Investor's Business Daily*, September 21, 1998.

49 Scott S. Smith, *Investor's Business Daily*, January 29, 2015.

Chapter 6

1 BrainyQuote.com, *www.brainyquote.com/quotes/quotes/n/nancypelos410715.html*.

2 Dr. Jacqueline Peters and Dr. Catherine Carr, *50 Tips for Terrific Teams: Proven Strategies for Building High-Performance Teams* (Victoria, BC: FriesenPress, 2013).

3 Michael Mink, *Investor's Business Daily*, June 6, 2006.

4 Churchill Centre, *www.winstonchurchill.org/resources/speeches/1941-1945-war-leader/420-the-price-of-greatness-is-responsibility*.

5 Cal Ripken Jr. and Mike Bryan, *Cal Ripken Jr.: My Story* (New York: Dial, 1999).

6 *www.brainyquote.com/quotes/quotes/d/donshula155890.html*.

7 Brian Tracy, *No Excuses! The Power of Self-Discipline* (New York: Vanguard Press, 2010).

8 Bobby Unser, *Winners Are Driven: A Champion's Guide to Success in Business and Life* (New York: John Wiley & Sons, 2003).

9 Ibid.

10 Ibid.

11 Ibid.

12 Bob Phillips, *Controlling Your Emotions Before They Control You* (Eugene, OR: Harvest House Publishers, 1995).

13 Genesis 3:12–13, *New World Translation of the Holy Scriptures* (New York: Watch Tower Bible and Tract Society of Pennsylvania, 1961).

14 LeadershipNow.com, *www.leadershipnow.com/responsibilityquotes.html*.

15 MoneyClass.com, *www.moneyclass.com/quotes2.aspx*.

16 Peter Allman, *Little Me Can Live a Big Life: Integrating Paradoxes for Change* (Bloomington, IN: iUniverse, 2009).

17 Wade D. Sadlier, *Unlocking Your Potential: The Keys to Discovering Your Hidden Treasure* (Mustang, OK: Tate Publishing, 2010).

18 CoachDeck.com, *blog.coachdeck.com/2010/08/11/more-baseball-wisdom/*.

19 Richard A. Couto, *Political and Civic Leadership: A Reference Handbook* (Thousand Oaks, CA: SAGE Publications, 2010).

20 LeadershipNow.com, *www.leadershipnow.com/responsibilityquotes.html*.

21 BrainyQuote.com, *www.brainyquote.com/quotes/quotes/g/georgewash158549.html*.

22 John C. Maxwell, *Your Road Map for Success* (Nashville: Thomas Nelson Publishers, 2010).

23 Ibid.

24 Ibid.

25 Monroe Mann and Lou Bortone, *Battle Cries for the Hollywood Underdog: Motivation & Inspiration for Your Journey to the Top* (Bloomington, IN: AuthorHouse, 2013).

26 Bill Parcells and Nunyo Demasio, *Parcells: A Football Life* (New York: Crown Archetype, 2014).

27 QuotesEverlasting.com, *quoteseverlasting.com/quotations/2013/03/04/4716/snowflake/no-snowflake-in-an-avalanche-ever-feels-responsible/*.

28 Laura Livsey, *The Steve Young Story* (Roseville, CA: Prima Lifestyles, 1995).

29 Tom Limbert, *Dad's Playbook: Wisdom for Fathers from the Greatest Coaches of All Time* (San Francisco: Chronicle Books, 2012).

30 Sam Silverstein, *No More Excuses: The Five Accountabilities for Personal and Organizational Growth* (New York: Wiley, 2009).

31 *psycho4jesus.wordpress.com/tag/jim-collins/.*

32 Robert D. Ramsey, *What Matters Most for School Leaders: 25 Reminders of What Really Is Important* (Thousand Oaks, CA: SAGE Publications, 2005).

33 BrainyQuote.com, *www.brainyquote.com/quotes/quotes/r/robertloui163019.html.*

34 Goodreads.com, *www.goodreads.com/quotes/405686-life-is-a-sum-of-all-your-choices-so-what.*

35 BrainyQuote.com, *www.brainyquote.com/quotes/quotes/b/benjaminfr383794.html.*

Chapter 7

1 SellingPower.com, *www.sellingpower.com/content/article/index.php?a=3528/the-pat-riley-formula-for-a-winning-team&page=2.*

2 Goodreads.com, *www.goodreads.com/quotes/585536-a-man-who-acquires-the-ability-to-take-full-possession.*

3 QuotationsBook.com (QB), *quotationsbook.com/quote/38988/.*

4 Goodreads.com, *www.goodreads.com/quotes/4324-shoot-for-the-moon-even-if-you-miss-you-ll-land.*

5 LeadershipNow.com, *www.leadershipnow.com/attitudequotes.html.*

6 Goodreads.com, *www.goodreads.com/quotes/132678-what-the-mind-can-conceive-and-believe-and-the-heart.*

7 Goodreads.com, *www.goodreads.com/author/quotes/8435.Norman_Vincent_Peale.*

8 James Allen, *As a Man Thinketh* (US: A James Allen Book, 2012).

9 John C. Maxwell, *Make Today Count* (New York: Center Street, 2008).

10 Mark Joseph Macalino, @MJosephM, *twitter.com/MJosephM_/status/269239783719575552.*

11 A-Bittersweet-Life, *a-bittersweet-life.tumblr.com/post/52151062616/im-often-asked-by-younger-filmmakers-why-do-i.*

12 Goodreads.com, *www.goodreads.com/quotes/121066-i-not-only-use-all-the-brains that i have.*

13 Earl Nightingale, *Earl Nightingale's Greatest Discovery: Six Words That Changed the Author's Life Can Ensure Success to Anyone Who Uses Them* (New York: Dodd Mead, 1987).

14 Larry Chang, comp. and ed., *Wisdom for the Soul: Five Millennia of Prescriptions for Spiritual Healing* (Washington, DC: Gnosophia Publishers, 2006).

15 BrainyQuote.com, *www.brainyquote.com/quotes/quotes/e/earlnighti402602.html.*

16 BrainyQuote.com, *www.brainyquote.com/quotes/quotes/e/earlnighti119375.html.*

17 BrainyQuote.com, *www.brainyquote.com/quotes/quotes/e/earlnighti379417.html.*

18 BrainyQuote.com, *www.brainyquote.com/quotes/quotes/w/willienels184361.html.*

19 Pat Williams, *The Magic of Team Work: Proven Principles for Building a Winning Team* (Nashville: Thomas Nelson Publishers, 1997).

20 Pete Carroll with Yogi Roth, *Win Forever: Live, Work, and Play Like a Champion* (New York: Portfolio Books, 2010).

21 Brian Tracy, *Time Power: A Proven System for Getting More Done in Less Time Than You Ever Thought Possible* (New York: AMACOM, 2007).

22 Ibid.

23 BrianTracy.com (blog), *www.briantracy.com/blog/personal-success/good-habits-worth-developing-3-things-hard-working-and-successful-people-do-differently/.*

24 Del Jones, "Race Driver Unser's Secret to Success: Go Fast," *USA TODAY*, May 17, 2004, *usatoday30.usatoday.com/educate/college/careers/Advice/advice5-17-04.htm.*

25 Ibid.

26 Lee Jenkins, "Kobe Bryant: Reflections on a Cold-Blooded Career," *Sports Illustrated*, October 21, 2013.

27 *www.biography.com/people/william-randolph-hearst-9332973#synopsis*.

28 Sport Business Journal, *www.sportsbusinessdaily.com/Journal/Issues/2011/06/27/People-and-Pop-Culture /Graduation-speakers.aspx*.

29 John Heisler, *"Then Ara Said to Joe . . .": The Best Notre Dame Football Stories Ever Told* (Chicago: Triumph Books, 2007).

30 BrainyQuote.com, *www.brainyquote.com/quotes/quotes/d/dalecarneg140990.html*.

31 Alan Axelrod and Peter Georgescu, *Eisenhower on Leadership: Ike's Enduring Lessons in Total Victory Management* (Hoboken, NJ: Jossey-Bass, 2006).

32 Ibid.

33 BrainyQuote.com, *www.brainyquote.com/quotes/quotes/d/dwightdei149110.html*.

34 Stephen E. Ambrose, *Eisenhower: Soldier and President* (New York: Simon & Schuster, 1990).

35 BrainyQuote.com, *www.brainyquote.com/quotes/quotes/w/winstonchu103739.html*.

36 Pat Williams and Tommy Ford, *Bear Bryant on Leadership: Life Lessons from a Six-Time National Championship Coach* (Charleston, SC: Advantage Media Group, 2010).

37 Jim Calhoun with Richard Ernsberger Jr., *Passion to Lead: Seven Leadership Secrets for Success in Business, Sports & Life* (New York: St. Martin's Press, 2007).

38 Alan Axelrod, *Profiles in Audacity: Great Decisions and How They Were Made* (New York: Sterling Publishing Co., Inc., 2006).

39 Ibid.

Chapter 8

1 BrainyQuote.com, *www.brainyquote.com/quotes/quotes/m/muhammadal148630.html*.

2 Goodreads.com, *www.goodreads.com/quotes/497480-arriving-at-one-goal-is-the-starting-point-to-another*.

3 Our Daily Bread, *odb.org/2010/11/08/aim-high/*.

4 BrainyQuote.com, *www.brainyquote.com/quotes/quotes/z/zigziglar617761.html*.

5 George Harrison, *Brainwashed*, Track 1: "Any Road" (Dark Horse/EMI, 2002).

6 Neil A. Rock, *How to Catch a Roadrunner: Three Simple Principles That Can Transform Your Life* (Anderson, CA: Red Tail Publishing, 2004).

7 John Edmund Haggai, *The Influential Leader: 12 Steps to Igniting Visionary Decision Making* (Eugene, OR: Harvest House Publishers, 2009).

8 Don M. Green, *Everything I Know About Success I Learned from Napoleon Hill: Essential Lessons for Using the Power of Positive Thinking* (New York: McGraw-Hill, 2013).

9 Baseball Almanac, *www.baseball-almanac.com/quotes/quowilt.shtml*.

10 Goodreads.com, *www.goodreads.com/quotes/141245-if-you-want-to-live-a-happy-life-tie-it*.

11 Dr. John N. Chacha, *Total Life Management* (Martinsville, VA: Teamwork Publishing, 1987).

12 Gary Spirer, *Quick Steps to Direct Selling Success: Turn Your Relationships into Money* (New York: Morgan James Publishing, 2010).

13 Zig Ziglar, *See You at the Top* (New York: Pelican Publishing Company, 1975).

14 Quotations Page, *www.quotationspage.com/quote/2595.html*.

15 Richard Scott, *I Don't Have Time* (Croydon, UK: Filament Publishing Ltd., 2010).

16 BrainyQuote.com, *www.brainyquote.com/quotes/quotes/n/nelsonmand178785.html*.

17 Beverly K. Bachel, *What Do You Really Want* (Minneapolis, MN: Free Spirit Publishing, 2001).

18 Dr. Jim Afremow, *The Champion's Mind: How Great Athletes Think, Train and Thrive* (Emmaus, PA: Rodale Books, 2014).

19 Ron Higgins, *Tales from the Memphis Grizzlies Hardwood* (New York: Sports Publishing, 2006).

20 Lee Jenkins, "Kobe Bryant: Reflections on a Cold-Blooded Career," *Sports Illustrated,* October 21, 2013.

21 Ibid.

22 Laura Davis, *lauradavis.net/when-you-can-only-see-as-far-as-your-headlights/.*

23 Anne Lamott, *Bird by Bird: Some Instructions on Writing and Life* (New York: Anchor, 1995).

24 Mark H. McCormack, *Never Wrestle with a Pig and Ninety Other Ideas to Build Your Business and Career* (New York: Penguin, 2000).

25 Ibid.

26 Isiah Thomas and Wes Smith, *The Fundamentals: 8 Plays for Winning the Games of Business and Life* (New York: Collins, 2001).

27 Allen Richardson, *Personal Discipline: Tools for Consistent Success* (Raleigh, NC: lulu.com, 2012).

28 Art Chansky, *Blue Blood: Duke-Carolina, Inside the Most Storied Rivalry in College Hoops* (New York: Thomas Dunne Books, 2005).

29 Strength in God, Inspirational Quotes, *www.freewebs.com/strengthingod/inspirationalquotes.htm.*

30 Goodreads.com, *www.goodreads.com/quotes/595976-the-first-and-best-victory-is-to-conquer-self-to.*

31 Brian Tracy, *The 21 Success Secrets of Self-Made Millionaires* (Oakland, CA: Berrett-Koehler Publishers, 2001).

32 Creed and Heidi Tyline King, *Don't Play for the Tie: Bear Bryant on Life* (Nashville: Rutledge Hill Press, 2006).

33 BrainyQuote.com, *www.brainyquote.com/quotes/quotes/z/zigziglar381973.html.*

34 BrainyQuote.com, *www.brainyquote.com/quotes/quotes/j/jimrohn121202.html.*

35 Motivational Quotes for Athletes (MQFA), *motivational-quotes-for-athletes.com/7-motivational-american -football-quotes/quote06/.*

36 BrainyQuote.com, *www.brainyquote.com/quotes/quotes/j/julieandre129112.html.*

37 BrainyQuote.com, *www.brainyquote.com/quotes/quotes/j/johnwooden446992.html.*

38 *New World Translation of the Holy Scriptures* (New York: Watch Tower Bible and Tract Society of Pennsylvania, 1961).

39 Quoteland.com, *www.quoteland.com/author/J-Paul-Getty-Quotes/366/.*

40 Brian Tracy, *The 100 Absolutely Unbreakable Laws of Business Success* (Oakland, CA: Berrett-Koehler Publishers, 2002).

41 BrainyQuote.com, *www.brainyquote.com/quotes/quotes/j/johndryden101523.html.*

42 BrainyQuote.com, *www.brainyquote.com/quotes/quotes/a/aristotle145967.html.*

43 Michael D. Pollock (blog), *www.michaeldpollock.com/habits/.*

44 Dennis Merritt Jones, *The Huffington Post,* April 2, 2012.

45 QuotationsPage, *www.quotationspage.com/quote/34160.html.*

46 Mike Murdock, *One-Minute Pocket Bible for Men* (Colorado Springs, CO: Honor Books, 1994).

Chapter 9

1 BrainyQuote.com, *www.brainyquote.com/quotes/quotes/j/junotdiaz516030.html.*

2 DisneyParks (blog), *disneyparks.disney.go.com/blog/2013/07/windows-on-main-street-u-s-a-at-disneyland-park -chuck-boyajian/.*

3 Pat Williams and Jim Denney, *How to Be Like Walt: Capturing the Disney Magic Every Day of Your Life* (Health Communications, Inc., 2004).

4 Ibid.

5 Ibid.

6 Ibid.

7 Ibid.

8 Ibid.

9 Ibid.

10 Ibid.

11 Ibid.

12 Curt Schleier, *Investor's Business Daily*, May 19, 1999.

13 Ibid.

14 Harrison Ford, "10 Questions for Harrison Ford," *Time*, January 25, 2010; Inspiring Quotes and Stories, *www.motivationtoday.com/motivational_quotes/inspiring_quotes_and_stories.php*.

15 BrainyQuote.com, *www.brainyquote.com/quotes/quotes/r/rossperot101658.html*.

16 Wikiquote.org, *en.wikiquote.org/wiki/Thomas_Edison*.

17 Goodreads.com, *www.goodreads.com/quotes/24065-you-may-have-to-fight-a-battle-more-than-once*.

18 BrainyQuote.com, *www.brainyquote.com/quotes/quotes/w/winstonchu103788.html*.

19 Churchill Centre, *www.winstonchurchill.org/learn/speeches/speeches-of-winston-churchill/103-never-give-in*.

20 Quotations Page, *www.quotationspage.com/quote/40115.html*.

21 CBS Money Watch, CBS News, *www.cbsnews.com/pictures/celebs-who-went-from-failures-to-success-stories/5/*.

22 The Positivity Blog, *www.positivityblog.com/index.php/2009/10/02/elvis-presleys-top-3-pearls-of-wisdom/*.

23 BrainyQuote.com, *www.brainyquote.com/quotes/quotes/c/confucius140908.html*.

24 Goodreads.com, *www.goodreads.com/author/quotes/126903.Marie_Curie*.

25 BrainyQuote.com, *www.brainyquote.com/quotes/quotes/w/walterelli190719.html*.

26 ThinkExist.com, *thinkexist.com/quotation/by_perseverance_the_snail_reached_the_ark/147376.html*.

27 BrainyQuote.com, *www.brainyquote.com/quotes/quotes/s/samueljohn121919.html*.

28 Quotes.net, *www.quotes.net/quote/5981*.

29 Values.com, *www.values.com/inspirational-quotes/3601-Perseverance-Secret-Of-All-*.

30 *Frontline*, PBS, *www.pbs.org/wgbh/pages/frontline/newt/newtquotes.html*.

31 J. Timothy King, *Walking in the Moment Between Tick and Tock: From Passover to Pentecost* (Boston: J. Timothy King, 2013).

32 Martin Meredith, *Mandela: A Biography* (New York: Penguin Group, 1997).

33 University of Kentucky, But They Did Not Give Up (Quotes), *www.uky.edu/~eushe2/Pajares/OnFailing.html*.

34 BrainyQuote.com, *www.brainyquote.com/quotes/quotes/e/elisabethk119810.html*.

35 Wikiquote.org, *en.wikiquote.org/wiki/Thomas_Edison*.

36 John Marks Templeton, *Discovering the Laws of Life* (New York: Continuum, 1995).

37 Joanne Lannin, *Billie Jean King: Tennis Trailblazer* (Minneapolis, MN: Lerner Biographies, 1999).

38 Robert Wuthnow, *Boundless Faith: The Global Outreach of American Churches* (Berkeley: University of California Press, 2009).

39 Demitri C. Kornegay, *MAN UP! No Excuses—Do the Work! Life Lessons for Men Under Construction* (Camarillo, CA: Xulon Press, Salem Communications, 2007).

40 John C. Maxwell, *The 15 Invaluable Laws of Growth: Live Them and Reach Your Potential* (New York: Center Street, 2014).

41 Creed King, *Don't Play for the Tie: Bear Bryant on Life* (Nashville: Rutledge Hill Press, 2006).

42 Monte Drenner, @MTC_Counseling, *www.mtccounseling.com/719*.

43 BrainyQuote.com, *www.brainyquote.com/quotes/quotes/t/trumancapo103858.html*.

44 Gary Richmond, *A View From the Zoo* (Nashville: W Publishing Group, 1987).

45 *New World Translation of the Holy Scriptures.*

46 Bill Glass, *How to Win When the Roof Caves In* (New York: F. H. Revell Co., 1988).

47 izquotes.com, *izquotes.com/quote/327993.*

48 Goodreads.com, *www.goodreads.com/quotes/241056-hardships-make-or-break-people.*

49 BrainyQuote.com, *www.brainyquote.com/quotes/quotes/m/michaeljor165967.html.*

50 BrainyQuote.com, *www.brainyquote.com/quotes/quotes/a/abrahamlin121354.html.*

51 Quotations Page, *www.quotationspage.com/quote/2337.html.*

52 BrainyQuote.com, *www.brainyquote.com/quotes/quotes/h/henryford121339.html.*

53 BrainyQuote.com, *www.brainyquote.com/quotes/authors/a/alexander_graham_bell.html.*

54 Goodreads.com, *www.goodreads.com/quotes/96713-never-confuse-a-single-defeat-with-a-final-defeat.*

55 ThinkExist.com, *thinkexist.com/quotation/if_you-re_not_failing_every_now_and_again-it-s_a/15282.html.*

56 Joe Torre with Harry Dreher, *Joe Torre's Ground Rules for Winners: 12 Keys to Managing Team Players, Tough Bosses, Setbacks, and Success* (New York: Hyperion, 2000).

57 BrainyQuote.com, *www.brainyquote.com/quotes/authors/h/h_g_wells.html.*

58 Ron Moses, *The 15 Secrets of Millionaires* (Colorado Springs, CO: CreateSpace Independent Publishing Platform, 2012).

59 Richard Langworth, ed., *Churchill by Himself: The Definitive Collection of Quotations* (New York: PublicAffairs, 2008).

60 Goodreads.com, *www.goodreads.com/quotes/19742-success-is-stumbling-from-failure-to-failure-with-no-loss.*

61 Wikiquote.org, *en.wikiquote.org/wiki/Paulo_Coelho.*

62 Essential Life Skills.net, *www.essentiallifeskills.net/persistence-quotes.html.*

Chapter 10

1 Jan Hubbard, Michael Jordan interview, *Hoop* magazine, April 1997.

2 Jimmy Connors (website), *jimmyconnors.net/about/.*

3 Girl from the Hills (blog), *girlfromthehills.wordpress.com/2010/11/12/that-friday-feeling-shopping/.*

4 Vince Lombardi Jr., *What It Takes to Be #1: Vince Lombardi on Leadership* (New York: McGraw-Hill, 2001).

5 Harvey MacKay, *Swim with the Sharks Without Being Eaten Alive* (New York: HarperBusiness, 2005).

6 Tom Verducci, "2009 Sportsman of the Year: Derek Jeter," *Sports Illustrated*, December 7, 2009.

7 BrainyQuote.com, *www.brainyquote.com/quotes/quotes/l/leoduroche139427.html.*

8 BrainyQuote.com, *www.brainyquote.com/quotes/authors/g/gene_mauch.html.*

9 James Charlton, ed., *The Military Quotation Book: More Than 1,100 of the Best Quotations About War, Leadership, Courage, and Victory* (New York: Thomas Dunne Books, 2013).

10 Jeremy Schaap, *Triumph: The Untold Story of Jesse Owens and Hitler's Olympics* (Boston: Houghton Mifflin Company, 2007).

11 Rod Beaton, *USA TODAY*, March 6, 2002.

12 Pat Riley, *The Winner Within: A Life Plan for Team Players* (New York: Berkley Trade, 1994).

13 Frank Litsky, "Bill Musselman, 59, Intense Basketball Coach," *The New York Times*, May 6, 2000.

14 Quotes Daddy, *www.quotesdaddy.com/quote/234253/wayne-calloway/nothing-focuses-the-mind-better-than-the-constant.*

15 Sports Management Resources (SMR), *www.sportsmanagementresources.com/our-consultants/donna-lopiano.*

16 Proverbs 27, *New World Translation of the Holy Scriptures.*

17 Pat Williams with David Wimbish, *How to Be Like Coach Wooden: Life Lessons from Basketball's Greatest Leader* (Deerfield Beach, FL: HCI, 2006).

18 Damon Hack, *The New York Times*, September 5, 2006.

19 Nate Ryan, "Gordon Fits the Soul of a Champion," *USA TODAY*, November 13, 2006.

20 Arnold Palmer (website), *www.arnoldpalmer.com/experience/whatsnew/archive/whats_new/homepage_headlines/*.

21 BrainyQuote.com, *www.brainyquote.com/quotes/quotes/k/katarinawi460031.html*.

22 Vince Lombardi Jr., *What It Takes to Be #1: Vince Lombardi on Leadership* (New York: McGraw-Hill, 2001).

23 Ragan's Health Care Communication News, *healthcarecommunication.com/Main/Articles/Idea_Files_Quotes_2616.aspx*.

24 SellingPower.com, *www.sellingpower.com/content/article/?a=4261/mary-lou-retton*.

25 Wikiquote.org, *en.wikiquote.org/wiki/Competition*.

26 Kurt Warner, ed., *Friday Night Light: Inspiration for the Game of Life* (Grand Rapids, MI: Zondervan, 2009).

27 Bobby Bowden and Mark Schlabach, *Called to Coach: Reflections on Life, Faith, and Football* (Brentwood, TN: Howard Books, 2010).

28 *www.biography.com/people/franklin-d-roosevelt-9463381*.

29 Paula Broadwell, "General David Petraeus's Rules for Living," *Newsweek*, November 5, 2012.

30 Michael Mink, *Investor's Business Daily*, January 29, 2001.

31 The Associated Press, October 29, 1987.

32 Dale Carnegie, *How to Win Friends and Influence People* (New York: Pocket Books, 1998).

33 Fran Blinebury, NBA.com, September 11, 2009.

34 Nino Frostino, *Right on the Numbers: The Debate of the Greatest Players in Sports to Wear the Numbers 0 to 99* (Manchester, UK: Trafford, 2004).

35 Pat Summitt Foundation, "Pat's Definite Dozen," *www.patsummitt.org/our_role/pats_story/pats_definite_dozen.aspx*.

36 BrainyQuote.com, *www.brainyquote.com/quotes/quotes/m/mikhailbar416118.html*.

37 Terry Bradshaw with David Fisher, *It's Only a Game* (New York: Pocket Books, 2001).

38 SearchQuotes.com, *www.searchquotes.com/search/Richard_Halverson/*.

39 Ultrapreneur Sayings, *www.ultrapreneursayings.com*.

40 iz quotes.com, *izquotes.com/quote/355573*.

41 Dan Spainhour, *Coach Yourself: A Motivation Guide for Coaches and Leaders* (Educational Coaching & Business Communications, 2007).

42 ThinkExist.com, *thinkexist.com/quotation/our_business_in_life_is_not_to_get_ahead_of/12071.html*.

43 Ship Sticks, *news.shipsticks.com/greatest-golf-quotes-of-all-time/*.

44 About.com, Running & Jogging, *running.about.com/od/runninghumor/a/georgesheehanrunningquotes.htm*.

45 Goodreads.com, *www.goodreads.com/quotes/269295-don-t-bother-just-to-be-better-than-your-contemporaries-or*.

46 BrainyQuote.com, *www.brainyquote.com/quotes/quotes/a/alannajameso169908.html*.

47 Phil Jackson with Hugh Delehanty, *Eleven Rings: The Soul of Success* (New York: Penguin Books, 2014).

Chapter 11

1 Napoleon Hill, *Think and Grow Rich* (New York: Tarcher, 2005).

2 Lee Jenkins, "Reflections on a Cold-Blooded Career," *Sports Illustrated*, October 21, 2013.

3 Daniel Coenn, *Kahlil Gibran: His Words* (BookRix, 2014).

4 Adam Fluck, NBA.com, "Bulls Chairman Jerry Reinsdorf: Michael Jordan's Will to Win Made Him the Best," *www.nba.com/bulls/news/jordanhof_reinsdorf_090902.html.*

5 Rick Weinberg, *ESPN.com*, "79: Jordan Battles Flu, Makes Jazz Sick," *sports.espn.go.com/espn/espn25/story? page=moments/79.*

6 *www.sportingnews.com/nba/story/2014-06-11/michael-jordan-flu-game-june-11-1997-video-photos.*

7 Ibid.

8 YesNetwork.com, *web.yesnetwork.com/news/article.jsp?ymd=20130425&content_id=45807172.*

9 Peter Golenbock, *George: The Poor Little Rich Boy Who Built the Yankee Empire* (New York: Wiley, 2010).

10 Mike Towle, *I Remember Jim Valvano: Personal Memories of and Anecdotes to Basketball's Most Exuberant Final Four Coach, as Told by the People and Players Who Knew Him* (Nashville: Cumberland House Publishing, 2001).

11 Napoleon Hill, *Think and Grow Rich* (New York: Tarcher, 2005).

12 Kathryn Petras and Ross Petras, *Don't Forget to Sing in the Lifeboats* (New York: Workman Publishing Company, 2009).

13 Louis Montgomery Jr., *A Year's Worth of Inspiration* (Pittsburgh, PA: Dorrance Publishing Company, 2011).

14 *www.profitsonwallstreet.com/.*

15 Aasef Shafik, *Global Peace Lovers* (Bloomington, IN: AuthorHouse, 2011).

16 Brian Tracy, *GOALS! How to Get Everything You Want—Faster Than You Ever Thought Possible* (San Francisco: Berrett-Koehler Publishers, 2010).

17 Ann Hood, *Creating Character Emotions* (Burbank, CA: Story Press Books, 1998).

18 Bobby Unser, *Winners Are Driven: A Champion's Guide to Success in Business & Life* (New York: Wiley, 2008).

19 Boomer Esiason, *Sports Illustrated*, The Vault, "A Fan's Notes," *www.si.com/vault/2013/12/23/106410359/a-fans-notes.*

20 Johnathon Schaech, *Rick Dempsey's Caught Stealing: Unbelievable Stories from a Lifetime of Baseball* (Forest Hill, MD: Cemetery Dance Publications, 2014).

21 Gary Mihoces, *USA TODAY*, "On Paper, They're OK, Yet Somehow Jets Win," December 28, 2006, *usatoday30 .usatoday.com/sports/football/nfl/jets/2006-12-28-contenders-cover_x.htm.*

22 African American Quotes, Michael Jordan, *www.africanamericanquotes.org/michael-jordan.html.*

23 Gammons Daily, "Just Like His Idol, Mike Trout Always Plays the Game Hard," *www.gammonsdaily.com/peter -gammons-just-like-his-idol-mike-trout-always-plays-the-game-hard/.*

24 Tim Kurkjian, *Is This a Great Game, or What?* (New York: St. Martin's Press, 2007).

25 Allinspiration.com, *www.allinspiration.com/a/more-sports-motivational-quotes-and-sayings/2/.*

26 Cal Ripken Jr. with Donald T. Phillips, *Get in the Game: 8 Elements of Perseverance That Make the Difference* (New York: Gotham Books, 2008).

27 Arnold Palmer, "That Burning Desire," *AppleSeeds.org, www.appleseeds.org/burn_desire.htm.*

28 Inspirational Quotes for May 2009 (Sanderson), *webcache.googleusercontent.com/search?q=cache:ZIjLWwy 5yBIJ:apstatsmonkey.com/StatsMonkey/Quotes_files/INSPIRATIONALquotes%28MAY2009%29 .doc+&cd=2&hl=en&ct=clnk&gl=us.*

29 Joe Sillett and Karl Morris, *Mentality* (eBook, 2011).

30 Pete Rose with Rick Hill, *My Prison Without Bars* (Emmaus, PA: Rodale, 2004).

31 Tim S. Grover, *Relentless: From Good to Great to Unstoppable* (New York: Scribner, 2014).

32 Keith Dunnavant, *Coach: The Life of Paul "Bear" Bryant* (New York: St. Martin's Press, 2005).

33 Karen Crouse, *New York Times*, "Woods Is Smiling Now, and He Has Reasons," March 20, 2013.

34 James M. Kouzes and Barry Z. Posner, *The Truth About Leadership: The No-Fads, Heart-of-the-Matter Facts You Need to Know* (New York: Jossey-Bass, 2010).

Chapter 12

1 John C. Maxwell, *Ultimate Leadership: Maximize Your Potential and Empower Your Team* (Nashville: Thomas Nelson, 2007).

2 Leigh Montville, *Sports Illustrated*, July 2, 1990.

3 Donald Rumsfeld, *Rumsfeld's Rules: Leadership Lessons in Business, Politics, War, and Life* (New York: Broadside Books, 2013).

4 Ibid.

5 Richard Goldstein, *New York Times*, April 28, 2014.

6 Sir Edmund Hillary, *People*, June 14, 1999.

7 Ibid.

8 *www.goodreads.com/author/quotes/203941.Harry_S_Truman.*

9 Jeff Davenport, *Chatter Up!—Helping Your Child Succeed in Little League* (Minneapolis, MN: Mill City Press, 2007).

10 Dan Spainhour, *A Season in Words: A Coach's Guide to Motivation from the Preseason to the Postseason* (Educational Coaching and Business Communications, 2007).

11 Nancy Lieberman and Earvin "Magic" Johnson, *Playbook for Success: A Hall of Famer's Business Tactics for Teamwork and Leadership* (New York: Wiley, 2010).

12 John C. Maxwell, *Team: The 17 Indisputable Laws of Teamwork* (Nashville: Thomas Nelson, 2001).

13 Pat Williams with Ken Hussar, *The Ultimate Handbook of Motivational Quotes for Coaches and Leaders* (Monterey, CA: Coaches Choice, 2011).

14 Ibid.

15 M. J. Ryan, *Attitudes of Gratitude: How to Give and Receive Joy Every Day of Your Life* (Newburyport, MA: Conari Press, 1995).

16 George Herman Ruth, *Babe Ruth's Own Book of Baseball* (Lincoln: University of Nebraska Press, 1992).

17 Ibid.

18 Larry Chang, comp. and ed., *Wisdom for the Soul: Five Millennia of Prescriptions for Spiritual Healing* (Washington, DC: Gnosophia Publishers, 2006).

19 Ken Pritchard and John Eliot, *Help the Helper: Building a Culture of Extreme Teamwork* (New York: Penguin Group, 2012).

20 Christian Red, *New York Daily News*, September 7, 2014.

21 John C. Maxwell, *Teamwork Makes the Dream Work* (Lawrenceville, GA: Maxwell Motivation, 2002).

Epilogue

1 *New World Translation of the Holy Scriptures.*

About the Authors

PAT WILLIAMS

Pat Williams is Senior Vice President of the NBA's Orlando Magic. He has more than a half century of professional sports experience. This is his 100th book; others include the popular *Coach Wooden's Greatest Secret* and *The Difference You Make*. He is one of America's most sought-after motivational and inspirational speakers. He and his wife, Ruth, live in Winter Park, Florida. Learn more at www.PatWilliams.com.

You can contact Pat Williams at:

Pat Williams
c/o Orlando Magic
8701 Maitland Summit Boulevard
Orlando, FL 32810
(407) 916-2404
pwilliams@orlandomagic.com

Visit Pat Williams' website at:

www.PatWilliams.com

Follow Pat on Twitter at:

www.twitter.com/OrlandoMagicPat

Stay in touch with Pat on Facebook at:

www.Facebook.com/PatWilliams.OrlandoMagic

If you would like to set up a speaking engagement for Pat Williams, please call Andrew Herdliska at 407-916-2401 or e-mail him at aherdliska@orlandomagic.com.

PETER KERASOTIS

Peter Kerasotis is an award-winning journalist and author. He has won 10 prestigious APSE awards for his newspaper columns and feature stories. The Florida Magazine Association twice named him its best feature writer. The Football Writers Association of America named him the 2011 top columnist. He and his wife, Shelley, live in Merritt Island, Florida. Learn more at *www.HeyPeterK.com*. If you would like to book Peter as a speaker, contact him at *HeyPeterK@aol.com*.